exploring

3D ANIMATION WITH 3DS MAX 8

Steven Till

THOMSON

DELMAR LEARNING

Australia Canada Mexico Singapore Spain United Kingdom United States

Exploring 3D Animation with 3ds Max 8

Steven Till

Vice President, Technology and Trades ABU:
Dave Garza

Director of Learning Solutions:
Sandy Clark

Managing Editor:
Larry Main

Senior Acquisitions Editor:
James Gish

Product Manager:
Nicole Bruno

Marketing Director:
Deborah Yarnell

Director of Production:
Patty Stephan

Marketing Manager:
Penelope Crosby

Production Manager:
Andrew Crouth

Content Project Manager:
Nicole Stagg

Technology Project Manager:
Kevin Smith

Editorial Assistant:
Niamh Matthews

Cover Design:
Steven Brower

Cover Image:
Just Passing By
Oil on canvas
© David Arsenault

ISBN 1-4283-0408-8

Library of Congress Cataloging-in-Publication Data

Till, Steven.
Exploring 3D animation with 3ds max 8 / Steven Till.
p. cm.
Includes index.
ISBN 1-4283-0408-8
1. Computer animation. 2. 3ds max (Computer file) 3. Computer graphics. 4. Three-dimensional display systems. I. Title.
TR897.7.T5953 2006b
006.6'96--dc22
                2006039033

NOTICE TO THE READER

This book is dedicated to those individuals who wish to better themselves and to my loyal readers to whom I owe a great deal. Thanks and keep learning!

—Steve

contents

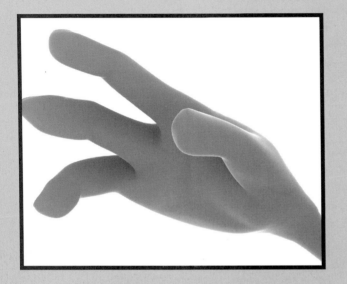

contents

| preface |

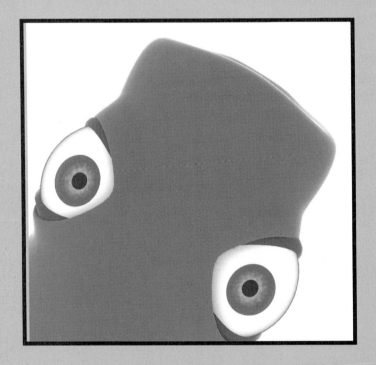

preface

AUDIENCE

If you have an interest in computer animation, or you are a graphic designer who is curious about 3D design and who wants to learn more, this is the book for you. This text is geared toward those who have little or no prior experience with 3D modeling and animation tools. It is unfortunate that many texts and manuals for 3D software programs tend to be written with terminology and techniques that can sometimes confuse, perplex, and intimidate the reader. Because of this, many newbies get discouraged and give up without giving the learning process a chance. This book presents the information in a clear and concise manner, using plain English instead of all the techno-speak that permeates many of the books published these days. I decided to put this book together for those of you who want to dig into the core fundamentals of 3D animation with 3ds (3D Studio) Max 8 to gain the foundational knowledge necessary to continue on to bigger and better things. It is recommended that you have at least a basic understanding of the 3ds Max 8 interface, as this book is an extension of *Exploring 3D Modeling with 3ds Max 8*.

EMERGING TRENDS

With the seemingly unsure and unstable nature of our economy these days, more and more companies are foregoing the "in-house artist" and opting for freelancers to fulfill their design needs. Because of this, many artists and graphic designers are being forced to work in more and more capacities. One project might require them to be a graphic designer, whereas another project might make them a web or multimedia developer. To compete with the ever-growing population of artists who are vying for those same jobs, designers are constantly trying to acquire new skills that they can market to potential clients. Three-dimensional artwork is becoming more and more prevalent in a variety of industries, which gives freelancers a tremendous opportunity to break into this emerging field. With a little bit of practice and patience, artists who are willing to learn how to use a 3D software application can open doors to employment involving 3D visualizations, 3D illustrations, and forensic simulations and re-creations, as well as film, broadcast, or video games.

BACKGROUND OF THIS TEXT

As a former educator, I know how daunting it can be to learn such an in-depth program as 3ds Max 8, and after sifting through countless books and resources, I realized that there are very few books out there that cater to the novice. Unfortunately, the nature of 3D design requires learning a lot of terminology, tools, techniques, and concepts that can at times be intimidating. I wrote this text to distill the techno-lingo to simple, easy-to-understand concepts that allow you to digest and process the information a lot easier.

Schools and other educational institutions that provide training in 3D production software have been sending a steady stream of 3D artists into an industry that until fairly recently has been rather stagnant. The good news is that the sector of the job market that offers opportunities that require 3D skills has been growing, and the trend now seems to be heading to a new boom in 3D-related jobs. This is a very competitive field, and an artist needs to have a solid understanding of the core fundamentals of this unique art form in order to compete. This book responds to these trends by presenting these core concepts clearly and simply, and by incorporating real-world industry scenarios that expose you to potential situations that might be encountered on the job.

This text will provide you with the basic building blocks of knowledge that you will need to get started. I strongly encourage you to continue your education by subscribing to industry publications, visiting online message boards and 3D-related web sites, purchasing more advanced books on the subject, and doing as many tutorials as you can get your hands on. If you are seriously considering becoming a creative force within this industry, you might even want to continue your education at an institution that will allow you to specialize in this area. The more you practice, the better off you will be.

When I began to develop this text, I wanted to ensure the material was presented in the best way possible. To achieve that goal, I surveyed a number of students extensively. They were able to give me valuable insight into their different learning styles, as well as the areas that they really wanted to focus on. All exercises and projects found in this book have been tested within a real classroom environment, making this a great text for introductory courses or for individuals who wish to learn on their own. In addition to picking students' brains, I also turned to the vast amount of information online, to industry professionals, and to literature in the industry, such as *3D World magazine*.

I also had some basic assumptions in mind in regard to the base of knowledge readers should have when going through this information. Because this book really targets graphic design professionals and design students, I am assuming you have at least a basic understanding of computer functionality such as opening, saving, and managing files. It is also recommended that you have some familiarity with some sort of image-editing application, such as Photoshop or Paint Shop Pro, as well as with page-layout software such as Adobe InDesign or QuarkXPress. Even though the bulk of the exercises deal directly with 3ds Max, some projects will require you to utilize some of the aforementioned software to create textures and materials, as well as final layouts for projects. If you do not have any prior design background, do not worry; I have included all of the necessary files needed to complete all of the projects. The files are located on the companion CD-ROM at the back of the book.

ORGANIZATION

Chapter 1: Life Is Motion: Introduction to Animation Fundamentals

This chapter presents basic animation principles—including squash and stretch, exaggeration, and anticipation—while stressing the importance of using these principles. Relationships are made between 2D cel animation and 3D computer-generated animation.

Chapter 2: Breathing Life into Objects: Basic Keyframing

This chapter focuses on the process of basic keyframing as it relates to the 3ds Max animation timeline. Track View is also introduced in this chapter, as it will be utilized throughout most of the book. Students learn how to manipulate animation keys and animation curves within the Track View editor.

Chapter 3: The Digital Marionette: Basic Character Rigging

Animating biped characters correctly can be one of the trickier things to accomplish in 3D animation software. This chapter demonstrates the best way to rig a basic 3D character for motion and discusses the difference between forward and inverse kinematics.

Chapter 4: Digital Puppeteering: Introduction to Character Studio

This section is dedicated to the Character Studio character animation plug-in (now included in the core build of the software). This demonstrates how to use footstep-driven animation for characters.

Chapter 5: Animating It All: Moving Lights, Cameras, and Materials

This chapter covers animating light and camera objects in a scene and introduces video post effects. Animating special effects elements is discussed and outputting methods for a finished animation are demonstrated.

Chapter 6: Go with the Flow: Particle Systems and Dynamics

This portion of the text explores the creation and manipulation of particle effects, which can be used to produce amazing effects such as fire, water, smoke, sparks, and lava. Dynamic forces, such as wind and gravity, are applied to the finished particle object.

Chapter 7: Moving Your World: Projects

This chapter features several complete, step-by-step tutorial projects that use techniques discussed throughout the text. These can be done independently of the book exercises, which should be an asset for instructors who wish to mix up the project assignments.

FEATURES

The following list provides some of the salient features of the text:

● Learning goals are clearly stated at the beginning of each chapter.

● The text is written to meet the needs of design students and professionals for a visually oriented introduction to the basic principles and the functions and tools of 3ds Max.

● Client projects involve tools and techniques that a designer might encounter on the job to complete a project.

● Exploring on Your Own sections offer suggestions for further study of content covered in each chapter.

● In Review sections are provided at the end of each chapter to test the reader's understanding and retention of the material covered.

COMPANION CD-ROM

The companion CD-ROM is where you will find some great resources that will help you as you work through the book. Here you will find companion files for the exercises found in each chapter, including project files for the larger-scale projects found in Chapter 7. In addition to exercise files, there are also numerous audio clips that you may use in your projects.

E-RESOURCE

The CD instructor's guide developed in conjunction with this book is intended to assist instructors in planning and implementing instructional programs. It includes sample syllabi for using this book in either an eleven- or fifteen-week semester. It also provides chapter review questions and answers, exercises, PowerPoint slides highlighting the main topics, and additional instructor resources.

ISBN: 1428304096

HOW TO USE THIS TEXT

The following features can be found throughout the book:

◢ Charting Your Course

Each chapter begins with the section Charting Your Course (a brief summary of the intent of the chapter). These sections describe the competencies the readers should achieve upon working through and understanding the chapter.

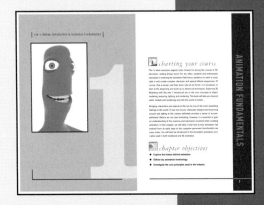

◢ Don't Go There

Material with the heading Don't Go There appears throughout the text, highlighting common pitfalls and explaining ways to avoid them.

! DON'T GO THERE In the prior process, you will note that I had you create two swatches of the same color with varying alphas. This was purposeful. If you blend two different colors with two different alphas some pretty strange things can happen. Typically you end up with some haloing effects—where there are hints of one or the other color in the transparency. To avoid haloing, anytime you are creating a gradient that gradates Alpha, use the exact same RGB values in the two chips.

◢ Sidebar Tips

Boxed sections present tips with useful information. These will give the readers an advantage in working with 3ds Max 8.

▶ Measuring Flicker Rate

A simple way to determine the flicker rate is to merely double the frame rate and convert it to hertz. For instance, the flicker threshold is said to be about 16 Hz, though ideally 48 Hz is preferred for a smooth playback. Coincidentally, a modern-day film projector runs at a 24 fps frame rate and has a flicker rate of 48 Hz (24 fps x 2 = 48 Hz). The frame rate for the PAL video standard is 25 fps and the flicker rate is 50 Hz (25 fps x 2 = 50 Hz). Can you guess what the flicker rate for NTSC video is?

In Review and Exploring on Your Own

In Review and Exploring on Your Own are sections found at the end of each chapter. These allow the reader to assess his or her understanding of the chapter. The Exploring on Your Own sections contain exercises that reinforce chapter material through practical application.

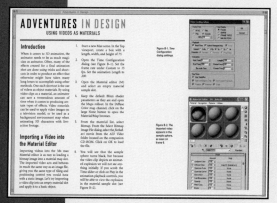

Adventures in Design

These spreads contain assignments showing readers how to approach a design project using the tools and design concepts taught in the book.

ABOUT THE AUTHOR

Steven Till studied Film Scoring and Composition at Berklee College of Music in Boston before undertaking Animation and Multimedia Design at The Art Institute of Pittsburgh. After attaining his associate's degree in Animation, Steve acquired his BFA in Visual Communications from American Intercontinental University. While working as a multimedia animator at Sightsound.com, he helped create the groundbreaking made-for-Internet Hollywood film *Quantum Project* and the highly interactive 3D planetarium show "Gray Matters: The Brain Project" for the National Science Foundation and Carnegie Mellon University. Steve has designed corporate identity and multimedia application packages for companies worldwide.

ACKNOWLEDGMENTS

I would like to take this opportunity to express my thanks to a few individuals without whom this book would not have been possible. Many thanks go to my past students for inspiring me to share my knowledge with others. Gratitude also goes to Wendy DiLeonardo for planting the writing bug in me—thank you so very much!

A huge hooray goes to my wonderful staff at Thomson Delmar Learning for their unwavering support and understanding throughout production of this project. Among the many people who made this experience possible are Senior Acquisitions Editor Jim Gish, Senior Production Editor Tom Stover, Production Manager Larry Main, Marketing Coordinator Mark Pierro, and my Product Manager, Jaimie Weiss, who has helped me through every step of this process. I can't thank all of you enough!

Last, but certainly not least, I would like to extend my overwhelming gratitude to all of the students and professionals who have graciously contributed their amazing artwork for this book. A special thanks goes out to animator Patrick Beaulieu for his contribution of the Mr. Blue character that appears throughout this text.

Thomson Delmar Learning and the author also extend special thanks to the following individuals who contributed content to the book and helped ensure the technical accuracy of this text:

David Dawson
Jon McFarland
Stephen Steinbach
Fred Zlock

QUESTIONS AND FEEDBACK

Thomson Delmar Learning and the author welcome your questions and feedback. If you have suggestions you think others would benefit from, please let us know and we will try to include them in the next edition.

To send us your questions and/or feedback, you can contact the publisher at:

Thomson Delmar Learning
Executive Woods
5 Maxwell Drive
Clifton Park, NY 12065
Attn: Media Arts and Design Team
800-998-7498

Or the author at: *steventill@verizon.net*

1

charting your course

This is what everyone eagerly looks forward to during the course of 3D education: making things move! Far too often, students and enthusiasts interested in entering the animation field have a tendency to want to jump right in and create complex character and special effects sequences. Of course, that is easier said than done. Like all art forms, it is necessary to start at the beginning and build up to advanced techniques. *Exploring 3D Modeling with 3ds Max 8* introduced the core concepts of object modeling, texturing, lighting, and rendering. This book will take you beyond static models and renderings and into the world of motion.

Bringing characters and objects to life can be one of the most rewarding feelings in the world. To see one of your character designs start bouncing around and talking to the camera definitely provides a sense of accomplishment. Before we can start animating, however, it is essential to gain an understanding of the nuances and mechanics involved when creating animation. In this chapter, we will take a brief look at how animation has evolved from its early days to the computer-generated blockbusters we enjoy today. You will also be introduced to the foundational animation principles used in both traditional and 3D animation.

 chapter objectives

- **Explore the history behind animation**
- **Define key animation terminology**
- **Investigate the core principles used in the industry**

A BRIEF HISTORY

Since the dawn of humankind, we have tried to preserve our culture and way of life through the telling of stories. Initially, these stories were passed down orally from generation to generation, until alphabets and writing allowed us to document history on stone, wood, and animal skins. But what did early humans do before spoken language was developed? It would be rather difficult to talk about a great hunt with grunts, hoots, and wild hand gestures. An effective way they had to tell their tales was through the use of pictures (see Figure 1-1). Cave paintings became the medium through which the human saga was told.

If you think about it, modern animation is not that much different from those ancient cave paintings made ages ago. The point of both concepts is to tell a story. A good animation is one that is able to effectively tell a story, convey emotion, and evoke some sort of emotion from the audience. If the artist is able to completely immerse the viewer in the story, the characters, and the imagery, the artist has done a tremendous job. These are just some of the things an animator has to consider when producing an animated piece.

figure |1-1|

Here is a great example of ancient "animation"; the telling of stories through pictures.

The actual concept of animation has been evolving since 1824, when Peter Roget introduced the idea of "persistence of vision." This theory states that the brain and eye (more specifically, the retina in the eye) will look at a broken image and the retina and brain will attempt to fill the gaps in the broken image. Once the gaps have been filled, the brain can then recognize what the image is. This may be why we see a sequence of images from a filmstrip or video as one continuous motion. There has been debate on this theory among psychologists/psychiatrists and animation/film instructors for quite some time.

Those in the educational field who teach animation, film, and video believe that persistence of vision is the reason we see film and video as one fluid motion. Professionals in the psychology arena tend to disagree, claiming that the illusion of movement created by the rapid display of still images is actually caused by what is called the flicker fusion threshold, often referred to as the flicker fusion rate. This concept can be defined as the frequency at which all flicker of an intermittent light stimulus disappears.

This idea can be applied to film, video, animation, or any other medium in which images are projected at a rapid rate via light. Basically, what this means is that the rate at which frames are displayed depends on the threshold at which the human brain can distinguish a flicker in the playback of those images. This can get tricky, in that the flicker rate is not an absolute number but is more like a range, depending on the person. How does this relate to animation? Well, if we take the example of a film projector, it has been found that motion can be perceived at 10 frames per second (fps) and lower (e.g., a flip-book animation), though the "flicker" would be quite noticeable. During the evolution of film-projector technology, it was found that 16 fps was the threshold at which the "flicker effect" was not distracting.

Today, modern projectors run at a rate of 24 fps. You should note though that there is a difference between frame rate and flicker rate. The flicker rate is gauged in hertz (Hz). There certainly seems to be a relationship between persistence of vision and the flicker fusion threshold. Both theories present interesting and convincing reasoning behind each phenomenon. We will leave it up to you as to which theory to subscribe to. Anyway, enough about all of this psychological stuff; let's get back to a little history.

Measuring Flicker Rate

A simple way to determine the flicker rate is to merely double the frame rate and convert it to hertz. For instance, the flicker threshold is said to be about 16 Hz, though ideally 48 Hz is preferred for a smooth playboack. Coincidentally, a modern-day film projector runs at a 24 fps frame rate and has a flicker rate of 48 Hz (24 fps × 2 = 48 Hz). The frame rate for the PAL video standard is 25 fps and the flicker rate is 50 Hz (25 fps × 2 = 50 Hz). Can you guess what the flicker rate for NTSC video is?

Thomas Edison took a crack at animation in 1889 when he invented the kinetoscope, which was a contraption that projected 50 feet of film in approximately 13 seconds. J. Stuart Blackton made the first animated film in 1906, which he called "Humorous Phases of Funny Faces." It is interesting to note that Blackton created this animation by drawing a face on a blackboard and then filming it. He would then stop the film, erase the picture, and draw another face in its place. This new drawing would then be filmed. He would repeat this process until the desired resulting animation was achieved. Talk about time consuming!

In 1914, Winsor McCay, often considered by many to be one of the founding fathers of animation, created a cartoon titled *Gertie the Trained Dinosaur*. This is a rather significant piece because not only was it released in theaters, but it was also used on a live stage, where McCay actually interacted with the animated Gertie. This animation, from start to finish, consisted of approximately 10,000 individual drawings. Just one year later, Max Fleisher developed the technique of rotoscoping, which is the process of using live-action footage as a template for animation frames. The frames are traced directly from the live footage, which gives the animation a smoother appearance compared to animation done without this method. Rotoscoping is still used today, especially in traditional cel animation, although motion capture is the preferred way to achieve realistic motion in computer-generated films because the animators can gather precise motion information from the moving subject.

Felix the Cat made his debut in 1920 and quickly became one of the most popular cartoon characters of the time. Felix also had the distinction of being one of the very first cartoon characters to be heavily merchandised, with Felix items ranging from wristwatches to dolls. This marketing angle blazed a trail for other cartoon merchandising.

In 1923, Walt and Roy Disney started Disney Brothers Cartoon Studio. In 1928, they released *Steamboat Willie*, which was the first animation to be produced with sound. This film made Mickey Mouse an overnight international star and helped launch Disney Studios into the entertainment powerhouse it is today. Just two short years after the release of *Steamboat Willie*, Warner Brothers Cartoons was formed in 1930. That same year, Warner Brothers released its first animated short, *Sinking in the Bathtub*. In 1935, Porky Pig made his debut in *I Haven't Got a Hat*.

A big event occurred in 1937 with the release of *Snow White and the Seven Dwarfs* by Disney Studios. This was a huge undertaking for Disney, and during the course of production the foundational animation principles began to emerge. Another significant year was 1940, in which Disney released *Pinocchio* and *Fantasia*. Warner Brothers released Tex Avery's *A Wild Hare*, in which the affable Bugs Bunny was introduced to the world. That same year, the first *Tom and Jerry* cartoon was made, which was also the first time Bill Hanna and Joe Barbera collaborated. Throughout the 1940s, cartoon characters from all of the major studios continued to be born and evolve. Among new faces were Droopy Dog, Yosemite Sam, Foghorn Leghorn, Pepe Le Pew, and the Road Runner.

Let's fast forward to 1950, when animation began to be included in television commercials. This quickly became an integral part of the animation industry and provided studios an additional source of revenue, rather than having to rely on studio moneys or box office ticket sales. The year 1953 saw the appearance of Gumby and the emergence of stop-motion animation into mainstream animation programming. In 1957, Hanna-Barbera was formed. In 1960, Hanna-Barbera released *The Flintstones*—a huge milestone for animation, as it was the very first prime-time cartoon.

If we speed up the timeline a little bit more, we begin to see more technological advancements in animation, with the integration and use of computers. In 1982, TRON was released, and boasted more than 20 minutes of computer-generated imagery (CGI). This was a significant milestone, as it was the first live-action film to incorporate such a large volume of CGI. That same year, the "Genesis Effect" for *Star Trek II: The Wrath of Khan* was produced by Industrial Light & Magic, and was the first visual effects shot that was entirely computer generated. Disney's *The Black Cauldron*, released in 1985, was Disney's first animated feature to incorporate computer-generated animation.

Director James Cameron brought the first convincing 3D character animation to the big screen in 1989 with his sci-fi film *The Abyss*. Disney continued to make technological advances in animation by utilizing fully 3D computer-generated characters and organic surfaces in the 1992 release of *Aladdin*. In 1994, Disney let loose with *The Lion King* by creating the breathtaking wildebeest stampede sequence. Disney and Pixar Animation Studios teamed up with the release of *Toy Story* in 1995. This was the first full-length 3D animated motion picture.

With the growing popularity in 3D CGI motion pictures, in 2001, the Academy of Motion Picture Arts and Sciences (AMPAS) created the new category Best Animated Feature for its Academy Awards show. Today, studios are pushing the limits of technology and are always seeking out new ways of integrating advances in animation technology with traditional, time-tested animation methods in order to produce amazing and immersive animated worlds. Next we will take a look at some of these methods and see how animators are able to bring such life into their work.

THE FOUNDATIONS OF ANIMATION

Creating believable motion within an animated sequence can be quite challenging. After all, next to telling a story, the whole point is to make the audience believe that what they are seeing is real—even if what they are watching is a cartoon. To help make things look believable, animators often look at real life for inspiration. This method can be quite helpful by making everything look realistic, but does it make the motion itself look natural? For this problem we must turn to the foundations of animation.

Modern animation is built on core concepts that are applied to characters and even objects, to make the motion in the sequence seem smooth, natural, and realistic. These concepts are known as the "principles of animation." There is debate as to exactly how many core principles there are. Some people say there are eight core principles, some say ten, and others say twelve. The majority of the industry agrees that there are twelve principles of animation, so we will go with the majority on this one. It is important to keep in mind that these concepts are applied to all animation, whether it is stop-motion, 2D cel, or even 3D CGI animation. While you progress through this book and begin making things move on your own, keep these concepts in mind. You will produce much better animation with them than without them.

The Origins: The Walt Disney Contribution

Okay, we know you just endured a history lesson with dates and everything, but it is important to get some facts about these animation principles before we dive in. Do you know who the think tank was behind these principles? If you guessed Walt Disney, you are right! During the 1930s, Disney wanted to bring new life to the films he made, and also wanted to push the envelope of animation capabilities and effects. At the same time, he wanted to find ways to more effectively convey both story and emotion within the animation.

Luckily, Walt was a big advocate of education, and believed that the key to making great films is having a great education to pull from. To help accomplish this seemingly insurmountable task, Disney sent his animators to the Chouinard School of Art in Los Angeles, California, for night classes, where they took life drawing. Eventually, as production on *Snow White* and then later *Bambi* became more intense, the night classes did not seem as feasible, in that Walt was not only paying for the tuition but driving his animators to and from class. This began to interfere with the schedules of films in production, so Disney decided to hold the classes on-site at the studio by hiring Don Graham of Chouinard to continue educating and refining his animators' skills.

In addition to the traditional fine-art approach to these class sessions, Graham held a keen interest in athletics and how the human body moved. The mechanics of the human body are essential in animation, so both Graham and Disney believed that this aspect of life drawing could be beneficial. The Disney animators enthusiastically jumped on the bandwagon and began studying how aspects of the human body moved and interacted with one another.

At this time, the intensive classes shifted from how to draw the subject to how to draw the subject moving. In the course of honing their life drawing and traditional art skills, the artists were breaking new ground and developing skills that never existed to the extent Walt Disney envisioned how animation should be. In addition to their life studies, animators would create action studies in which the subject would both pose and perform simple movements, which the artists would analyze and attempt to convey in their sketches.

Soon, the Disney artists began to think more about the motion of the subject and how that motion could help convey emotion and support the story. Disney had Graham analyze some of the studio's previous work, and after reviewing these comments, Disney went through the critiques with the studio directors, pointing out areas that needed work in terms of how the characters moved. The directors then sat down with the "in-betweeners" (considered the "junior animators" responsible for drawing all frames between the key pose drawings, which are the key positions within an action) and helped them develop ways to make the motions more believable.

By the early 1940s, Disney and his team of animators had a system in place that added beauty and grace to their productions and redefined how animation was to be approached. The techniques developed were passed down to new animators as they joined the Disney ranks. As other studios saw these methods being used, they began to pay closer attention to how Disney was approaching its character and object motions and began adopting these techniques. Before long, the concepts that began as mere night classes at a local art school became an industry standard being employed at breakneck speed.

The Twelve Golden Rules (More or Less)

Now comes the moment you have been waiting for: the concepts you will live by as an animator. As we stated before, without these principles your animation will look jerky, unrealistic, and mediocre. Believe it or not, even animation produced to intentionally look "rough around the edges" (such as *South Park*) uses at least some of these principles. As you begin to step out of your shell and start producing your own motion sequences, keep these techniques in mind and be sure to use them whenever possible. You may be tired of hearing that, as we have been constantly pounding that thought into your head so far, but the following information is so important it is imperative that you have a solid understanding of these animation principles before you begin to tackle animation projects.

As stated before, there is some debate as to what the core principles exactly are. These "animation laws" can be compared to one view of the U.S. Constitution. This is true in the way that it is meant to be a guideline for laws and governance and is open to interpretation. With this in mind, some of these principles may differ from those you find in other texts. Just remember that our interpretation is just one interpretation of the animation principles, and others can still be considered sound and correct.

Squash and Stretch

You will quickly find that this is probably the absolute best concept to use to keep your animations from appearing too rigid. This principle can be defined simply as the distortion of an object as it is being acted upon by an external force. That force can be gravity, wind, another object, or even the object itself. For instance, when a tennis ball is thrown at a solid wall at a relatively high speed, the ball will become squashed upon impact (see Figure 1-2). The wall stops the motion of the ball so suddenly that the momentum of the ball keeps the back of the ball moving, even after the front of the ball has been planted onto the bricks. Because of this, the ball will deform until the back of the ball also comes to a stop.

This technique is quite essential in character animation as well, especially if it is a cartoon animation. Do you remember Wile E. Coyote from the Road Runner cartoons? Every time he walked off a cliff, gravity would stretch his neck out until his body finally pulled his head down. After he hit the ground, the camera would then cut to a shot of the coyote squashed flat as a pancake. Even realistic characters have some squashing and stretching occurring during a motion. It might not be as obvious as in a Road Runner cartoon, but you should try to show a little squash and stretch in your character motions if possible. Otherwise, your characters will look stiff, rigid, and generally inflexible. It should be noted that with this technique, the object maintains a constant volume through its deformations.

Anticipation

Another of the core principles is the concept of anticipation, in which the animated character or object anticipates the main action

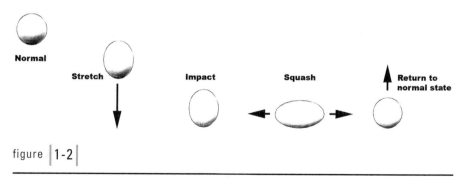

figure | 1-2 |

In this example, we can see the ball deform as it falls and hits the ground.

with a preparatory motion. If a character wanted to jump from point A to point B, he could not do it from a standing position. He would first have to crouch down before springing up and traveling any amount of distance. The motion of crouching is considered the anticipation for the actual action of the jump itself.

Another example of a good anticipation movement is a golf swing. Even if you have not played golf before, you should at least know that you cannot hit a ball 150 to 200 yards with the head of the golf club down at the ball. You must first start your swing in a higher position by raising the club back over your head. That is your anticipation to the swing. Once the club is over your head, you can swing it down, which will give you the power needed to drive the ball down the fairway. You will find that there are almost endless anticipations in any given animation sequence, which makes this principle a big one! Another such anticipatory "movement" is illustrated in Figure 1-3.

Follow-Through

Okay, this is an easy one. Think of the principle of follow-through as the opposite of anticipation. If your character does in fact jump successfully from point A to point B, does he land with his legs straight, and that is it? No, of course not. He would sustain some fairly painful injuries that way. To help cushion the blow of the landing, the character will bend the knees and crouch down a little bit, using the legs as natural shock absorbers (see Figure 1-4).

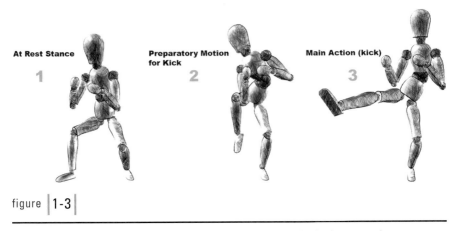

At Rest Stance

1

Preparatory Motion for Kick

2

Main Action (kick)

3

figure | 1-3 |

Step 2 shows the character's anticipation pose for the karate kick he is about to perform.

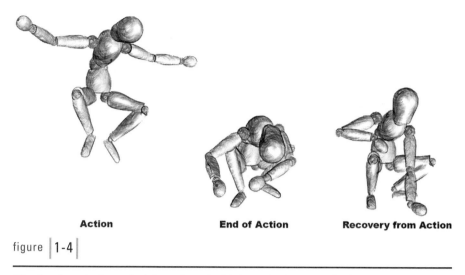

| Action | End of Action | Recovery from Action |

figure | 1-4 |

After the character jumps, he follows through with the motion by recovering from the landing and moving into a resting position.

Using the golf swing example again, once the golf ball is hit with the club, you would not stop the swing down at the tee would you? Of course not. The momentum of the downward swing requires you to continue the swing past the tee and laterally upward, allowing you time to slow the club down. The follow-through also helps in directing the ball to the aim point, so in this particular instance the follow-through is essential. Just as a movement needs some preparation to achieve the motion, it also requires some recovery, which is why most actions have a follow-through.

Overlapping and Secondary Action

Here is where we get into some confusion. The concepts "overlapping" and "secondary action" are extremely similar and easily can be confused. In fact, there are even some animators out there who use the two terms interchangeably, although they are incorrect. Actually, there is a difference between the two.

Overlapping action can be defined as motions that occur at the same time the primary action is taking place but that are unrelated to the primary action. Let's say your character is riding a bike. The primary action of that sequence would be the character's legs churning up and down on the pedals, and possibly the arms moving the handlebars to steer the bike. A possible overlapping action could be the character lifting up her arm to take a drink from a water bottle.

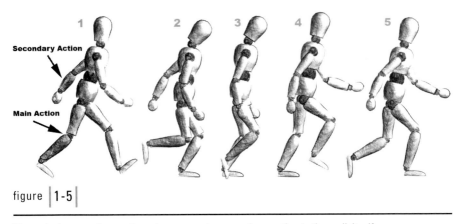

The swinging arms in a walk cycle represent a secondary motion to the walk itself.

Secondary action can almost be thought of as a "cause-and-effect" motion. The primary action is the cause, and the secondary action is the resulting movement. For instance, the arms of a character walking naturally want to swing during the walk (see Figure 1-5). Another way of thinking of secondary action is this: not all parts of an object or character move at the same speed. Thus, if a dog with big floppy ears is running and then suddenly stops, the ears would keep moving a bit, and then would swing back to a resting position. Both overlapping and secondary actions are extremely important when it comes to believable animation. You will want to be sure to include these types of motion whenever possible to add realism to your work.

Slow In and Slow Out

Whenever you begin a motion, do you perform the entire motion at the same speed? It would be a neat trick if that were the case. Just about every movement happens at different speeds throughout the action. More specifically, the beginning and end of the motion show the most obvious change. This phenomenon is known as the slow-in/slow-out principle.

When a character begins to move, the action starts a little slower than the speed at which the action should be. For instance, if you wanted to do jumping jacks you could not do them at a constant speed. Doing so would place entirely too much stress on your muscles, tendons, and bones and would most certainly cause an injury. If you were to perform the jumping jacks by starting and ending the jumps slightly slower than the middle of the jump, you would give your body a chance to compensate for the sudden change in arm/leg direction. This would definitely be a safer and more natural approach.

Essentially, slow in and slow out means that you start a motion, accelerate that motion to full speed, and then decelerate the motion toward the end. This technique is also known as easing or ease-in/ease-out. The character eases into the motion, and after the motion reaches its fastest point the character begins to ease out of the motion (see Figure 1-6). This is a crucial principle to implement in your animations, as it will provide a more natural look and feel to your work and ultimately more believable movement. In the next chapter, you will learn how to perform some basic animation and explore how to control the easing in and out of each motion with what are known as function curves.

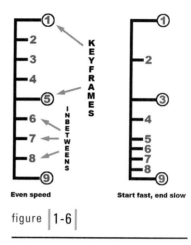

figure | 1-6 |

Two timing charts often used in traditional cel animation to help determine the timing of an action. The chart on the left depicts a nine-frame motion that progresses at an even rate. The chart on the right shows how using fewer frames will cause the beginning of the action to move fast, and how using more frames at the end will cause the action to end more slowly.

Weight and Timing

Another sign of a good animator is the ability to convey an object or character's mass within an animated sequence. This is done by being able to effectively demonstrate weight within a scene. Remember the dancing hippos and alligators (or crocodiles) in Disney's *Fantasia*? The hippo ballerinas gracefully (as gracefully as a hippo can) dance their ballet. The humor, of course, is in seeing very rotund hippos tip-toe around the screen. Even though they are able to move around fairly quickly, it is still obvious that the hippos are extremely heavy. This is due to the way in which the Disney animators depicted the physical attributes of the hippo, by intentionally making aspects of their bodies sag from their weight. This was then emphasized as the ballerinas moved by making those sagging areas move a little more slowly than the body as a whole, causing a lag in the motion (another example of secondary action).

Another thing that helps depict the hippos' weight is the reaction of the alligators dancing with them. At one point during the ballet, an alligator hoists one of the hippo ballerinas over his head. However, he does not simply lift her over his head, but instead struggles to get her in the air. You can actually see the alligator's exertion just to get that hippo airborne. So, you can see that the way a character interacts with other objects and characters has a lot to do with how weight and mass are conveyed.

Let's look at it another way. Take the Olympic sport of the shot put. If someone were to look at the steel or brass ball the Olympians hurl, how would they know whether it were heavy or light? The only way they could know, aside from picking it up themselves, is by how much effort the athlete exerts during a throw. If the athlete kicked up the ball with a heel and flicked it with a finger, we would have to come to the conclusion that the ball was in fact light as a feather and not made of heavy metal. If, however, our athlete winced and slowly heaved the ball up and perhaps gave a loud grunt as she propelled the ball forward, we would be more inclined to think the ball was really heavy.

This brings us to the concept of timing, which is just as important as showing the degree of exertion. If we use the example of the shot put, the athlete who "kicked 'n' flicked" the "light shot" would have to do it relatively quickly in order to reinforce the notion that the shot was light. On the flip side, in order for us to think that the shot was heavy, the athlete would have to move much more slowly, in addition to the winces, grunts, and sweat associated with throwing the shot put. By paying close attention to how slow or fast a character or object is moving, in conjunction with how external forces are acting upon those objects, a very believable and natural animation can be achieved (see Figure 1-7).

figure | 1-7 |

Dancer A would most likely move more slowly and less gracefully than dancer B. Being able to accurately depict mass will help you determine the appropriate timing for animation.

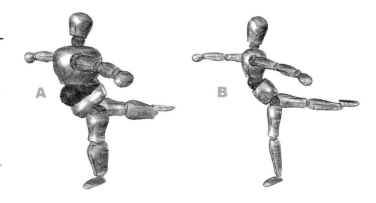

Exaggeration

Exaggeration is one of those principles that can be used in both small and large doses, depending on the style and effect you are trying to achieve. We like to call this the "go beyond" principle because that is essentially all it is. You take a key pose or position and "go beyond" it a little to add more emphasis to it. This concept is exploited quite heavily in cartoon animation, in which characters perform a simple action and make it humorous by being overly zealous with it. If you recall the discussion of anticipation and Wile E. Coyote, we mentioned how the coyote always ended up falling off a cliff. Well, the act of his neck stretching right before he fell and the end result of him turning into a coyote accordion or pancake are both exaggerations of the act of him falling off the cliff. It is this exaggeration that gives that moment its humor.

In more realistic animation, exaggeration can be used to help accentuate a motion. In this instance, the exaggeration does not need to be as profound as it would need to be in a Bugs Bunny cartoon; it just needs to be enough to make the motion clearer and more defined. This is especially helpful and often essential in 3D animation, because 3D movement is inherently stiff and difficult to follow. 3D animation software cannot generate the subtle nuances of an action, which results in the stiff appearance. Because of this, the animator must manipulate the animation to include these subtleties in the action. Exaggeration can make movement look more natural and can better differentiate among motions that might otherwise appear similar when presented in rapid sequence (see Figure 1-8).

Normal   **Exaggerated**   figure | 1-8 |

Exaggeration can enhance various other animation principles. Here we see an anticipation for a jump being exaggerated. Even a little exaggeration can have a tremendous effect.

Is "Far" Far Enough?

In the process of animating a character it is often difficult to determine exactly when a pose should be exaggerated or not, especially if you are creating a realistic motion. The following is a good rule of thumb when trying to exaggerate a pose: Position the character in the position that looks right to you and that seems natural. Most of the time, the position you end up with is not actually correct. To fix it, simply move the character a bit more than you think it should be moved, and more often than not you will end up with a better result. The more you animate and the longer you do it the easier it will be to distinguish an appropriate amount of exaggeration.

Arcs

For the most part, the principle of "arcs" is applied to character animation. This concept states that nothing moves in a straight line. When a character walks, the arms and legs move in an arc-like motion. When a character turns his head, the head should dip down slightly halfway through the turn. This creates another arc. Any character movement that is located at a joint will produce an arc. Why is that, you ask? The answer is simple: joints operate on the same premise as a drafting compass (i.e., they all involve pivot points). A character's arm pivots at the shoulder and elbow, and thus if he raises the entire arm from a resting position to an outstretched position pointing away from the body, the hand will create a sweeping arc (see Figure 1-9). The same goes for legs, fingers, and even eyelids. Every aspect of a character's motion operates on the principle of arcs. Without them, we can pretty much guarantee that you will get the most incredibly incomprehensible mish-mash of moving parts; it would be absolutely awful!

figure | 1-9 |

You cannot move without creating an arc. Here we see a bowler moving his arm forward to roll the ball down the alley.

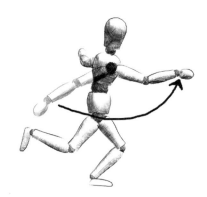

Straight-Ahead and Pose-to-Pose

The following concepts are not really principles but are more like animation approaches. When creating an animated sequence, there are two main ways an animator can produce it. The first method, known as straight-ahead animation, has the animator starting at frame 1 and continuing sequentially with frames 2, 3, 4, 5, and so on until the animation is finished. This can be a dangerous way to animate because it provides no real sense of timing to the animator.

Let's say the artist needs to make a character perform a two-second movement for a film. Film uses a 24-fps frame rate, which means that the animator would need to generate forty-eight frames for that character. Using the straight-ahead approach, the animator risks getting to the end of the motion either too late, with the end of the motion occurring after frame 48, or too early, with the last frame of the motion occurring before frame 48. Unless you have been animating for a really long time, we recommend that you steer clear of this approach. That said, that there are some occasions for which this method works well.

This approach tends to produce erratic motion, which for some styles works well, and if that is the effect you are going for then animating in a straight-ahead fashion would be appropriate. If you want a "jittery" feel to the animation, go with this method. A good example of this effect is Comedy Central's *Dr. Katz: Professional Therapist*. The style of this cartoon looks like the animators drank way too much coffee when they made it. The characters' outlines appear very squiggly. Because this was an animated series, the producers decided to use limited animation, meaning that the only things that really moved were the eyes and mouth, and occasionally an arm. This saves on production time and cost and allows a lot of animation to be produced in a short amount of time. This is very reminiscent of Hanna-Barbera cartoons.

Getting back to the point, the *Dr. Katz* animators would draw the character in the same position for three to five frames, giving each frame a very slight variation in the outline, which then causes the "jitter" effect when these frames are looped throughout the course of the animation. So, if it is a stylized look you are trying to achieve, then the straight-ahead method will work great for you. However, if realism is needed, we recommend using the pose-to-pose approach.

The pose-to-pose animation method is the preferred way to go about animating because it provides precise control over the timing of the actions taking place. In traditional animation, the key artist analyzes, times, and breaks the action down into key poses known as keyframes. The key artist draws the key poses and then breaks down the speed and timing of the animation and creates a timing chart. The timing chart depicts the number of frames in the sequence, which of those frames are keyframes, and where the middle positions should occur. After that is done, the key artist sends the key-frame drawings and the timing chart to artists known as in-betweeners, who, as we previously mentioned, draw the animation frames between the keyframes. Using the timing chart as a guide, the in-betweener can accurately finish the movement by drawing all of the character's poses that occur within the keyframes provided by the key artist.

This same technique can be used in computer animation. 3ds Max allows us to set keyframes for characters and objects in the scene. The best part is that the software acts as our in-betweener, which takes a lot of the tediousness out of animating, although we still need to worry about the timing of keyframes. We will be using pose-to-pose animation throughout the text, so you will have ample opportunity to become familiar with this technique.

Staging

Staging is an extremely important aspect of animation and of film-making in general. Staging deals with how each camera shot is composed. The more interesting the shot's composition, the more interesting the scene will appear. An intriguing shot can certainly add drama to an otherwise hum-drum scene or sequence. You could have a character performing a rather mundane task, but if you give it some dynamic staging, that mundane task will appear to be more interesting than it really is.

Staging actually involves more than just the composition of a shot. The actual positioning and posing of the character can enhance a shot as well. This holds especially true when it comes to cartoon animation. When posing your characters you will want to consider using silhouettes to help guide you. Basically, if you look at your character as a silhouette after you set the pose and you can clearly see what the character is doing, then the pose is good. If the character's silhouette is muddled and you are unclear as to its action, you might want to think about changing the pose to a more dynamic one that will better illustrate the intended action. This is a technique that has been used in traditional cel animation for many years, and it carries over to 3D animation quite well.

The big thing to keep in mind when planning the composition of your shots is that you are attempting to create drama and to focus the viewer's attention to a specific area of the frame. If you like, think of it as a traditional fine-arts piece or photograph. When composing a photo or painting, you should always be directing the viewer's eye to a specific point within the piece (see Figure 1-10). Whether the point of interest is in the center of the image or not is up to you, as long as you are able to effectively convey the focus of the image.

Appeal

This principle of appeal is exactly what it sounds like. Your animation should appeal to the audience for which you are creating it. Granted, everyone has different taste, so this can be a little tricky. After all, you cannot please everyone, but you should try your hardest to make your animations appeal to those whom you want to see it.

The closest thing we can associate this with is the advertising industry. If you have worked as a designer, you might already know where we are going with this. In advertising, the single most important thing (even more important than the product itself) is the target audience. Who is this product geared toward? Who will be using it? Who should be buying it? These questions are asked on a constant basis during an ad campaign. From concept to completion, the target audience is always kept in mind. The same applies to film, television, and even the Web.

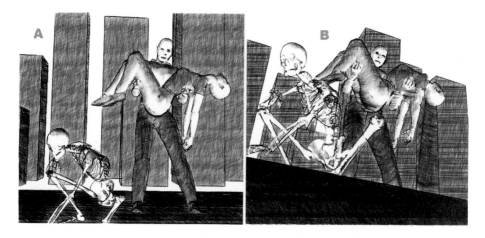

figure | 1-10 |

Frame A shows a particular shot from a standard front view. A more interesting choice in staging and frame composition can be found in frame B. This angle creates much more drama and interest in the shot.

figure | 1-11 |

Our character is throwing quite a big punch here, so it is important that his center of gravity is correct. Otherwise, he will not be able to keep his balance during the punch. By using line of action, you can get an idea of where the center of gravity should be during the action.

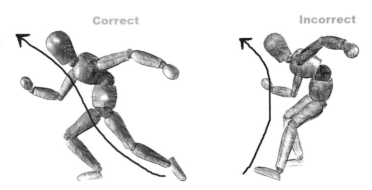

Correct   Incorrect

An animation always starts with an idea. Once you have the basic concept you want to convey, the next step (and the biggest) is to determine who you want to see your animation. Is it for kids? Or perhaps it will contain more adult humor and innuendo, making it more suitable for mature audiences. Maybe it will be used in a corporate or educational environment. If you market an animated movie to kids and the film contains explicit language, you did not effectively target the audience you originally intended. You will most likely have a lot of parents in an uproar for that, so this aspect needs to be crystal clear to everyone involved in the animation process.

After you have determined your target audience, you will be better equipped to write your script and storyboards. If you can produce your animated masterpieces with the audience in mind, they will most certainly appeal to the right people. This is why studios such as Pixar and DreamWorks Animation have so much success with their films. They spend so much time keeping in mind the intended audience that it plays a big role in how the story is shaped and told. A lot of the time, entire sequences are cut from films at the last minute because the producers and directors feel that they do not support the story enough and therefore would not be as appealing to the audience.

Line of Action

This is an extremely useful animation principle to utilize, especially with exaggerated cartoon animation. Line of action can be thought of as an imaginary line that passes through the primary motion the character is performing. This technique is often used to enhance the dramatic effect of the action. When animating, it is a good habit to plan your character poses with the line of action in mind. When you fail to utilize the line of action, you run the risk of producing motions and postures that appear awkward and ineffective.

The line of action principle runs in parallel with the concept of balance. Just as you need to remember the line of action when planning poses, you need to think about whether or not the character can physically exist in that pose (see Figure 1-11). Even "cartoony" pieces need to have a hint of realism to them, so be sure to make the positioning believable.

SUMMARY

In this chapter, you gained some insight into a little history of animation and its origins. You have also been exposed to the most important core principles of animation, which have been employed by animators and effects artists for many decades and are still used today. As you progress through this book and begin to learn how to use 3ds Max as an animation tool, keep these principles in mind. They will certainly make you a better animator, and you will have much more fun making things move if you are putting these principles to work.

in review

1. What is the main idea animation attempts to convey?

2. Who introduced the idea of "persistence of vision" in 1824?

3. Explain the persistence of vision theory.

4. At what projector frame rate does the "flicker effect" cease being a distraction?

5. Explain how to find the flicker rate of an animation, video, or film.

6. How many individual drawings did it take to animate the 1914 animation *Gertie the Trained Dinosaur* ?

7. In what year did Felix the Cat make his debut?

8. Who did Walt Disney hire to teach his animators life drawing?

9. List the twelve animation principles.

10. Name the first prime-time cartoon.

↗ EXPLORING ON YOUR OWN

1. Research early computer animation and compare and contrast the differences among the technologies used then and now and describe the animation process.

2. Watch examples of animations and analyze the motion. Can you see the fundamental animation principles at work? Examine how the animators applied those principles in each of the examples you view.

charting your course

In Chapter 1, you learned about a number of different concepts, techniques, and approaches to animation, including how to effectively stage your shots to increase the mood and drama of your work. This chapter introduces you to the process of animating objects within 3ds Max, as well as how to control and modify your animations with the various Track View utilities.

You will learn how to set up keyframes for your objects, adjust the trajectories of the objects' motion, and manipulate the behavior of the animation using what are known as function curves and key frame tangents. These concepts are an essential foundation in animating with 3ds Max and will benefit you tremendously when moving to more complex techniques such as character and effects animation.

 chapter objectives

- **Get familiar with the TrackBar and animation controls**
- **Understand the Set Key and Auto Key methods**
- **Edit an object's trajectory using the Motion panel**
- **Move, copy, and modify keyframes using the Track View Dope Sheet function**
- **Modify keyframe behaviors by manipulating keyframe tangents**
- **Make adjustments to an animation by manipulating function curves in the Track View Curve editor**
- **Create animation beyond the animation range by using the Parameter Curve Out-of-Range Types function**
- **Import audio files into the Track View editor**

TOOLS OF THE TRADE

In traditional cel animation, animators use pencils, paper, cels, paint, brushes, ink, and other tools. In 3ds Max, the animator has different tools at his disposal. Some of these tools can be found within the main interface, whereas others can be accessed through the menu and toolbar systems. Here we will take a look at some of the tools you will be using to produce some simple movements.

The most obvious animation tools can be found right within the 3ds Max interface. At the bottom of the interface, right below the viewports, you will notice what seems to be a ruler containing numbers and ticks along its length. However, this ruler isn't used to measure distance; it is used to measure time. This is known as the trackbar, which depicts the total number of frames within the animation range.

The trackbar can be configured to display time in increments other than frames. For instance, you can set up the trackbar to display Society of Motion Picture and Television Engineers (SMPTE) time code, which displays minutes, seconds, and frames. This is useful when animating to audio or other prerecorded material because this time code is somewhat standard (NTSC, PAL, and Film time code will use different frame counts within the time code due to their different frame rates). The time display can be changed within the Time Configuration window, discussed later. Figure 2-1 shows the trackbar and Time slider, which is used to scrub (manually navigate) through the frames manually.

▶ Video Formats

You should be aware that there are different video formats used in different parts of the world. The NTSC (National Television System Committee) video format is used in the United States and has a frame rate of 30 fps. The PAL (Phase Alternating Line) format is one of the dominant formats utilized throughout Europe and other regions of the world and has a frame rate of 25 fps. SECAM (Sequential Couleur Avec Memoire) is the other dominant video format used aside from PAL.

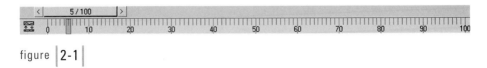

figure | 2-1 |

Trackbar and Time slider.

Next we come to the animation playback controls. These should look somewhat similar because they mimic most audio/video playback equipment. The animation controls allow you to navigate through your timeline quickly and provide you with playback control over your animation. Located at the bottom right of the interface, directly to the left of the viewport navigation tools, the playback controls include Play/Stop Animation, Next/Previous Frame, Go to Start, Go to End, Key Mode Toggle (to jump from one keyframe to another), Current Frame (Go to Frame), and Time Configuration. Figure 2-2 depicts the playback controls.

figure |2-2|

Animation playback controls.

Found to the left of the playback controls are the keyframe tools. These tools allow you to determine what keyframe mode you want to animate in, as well as set up keyframe filters that allow you to dictate which aspects of the scene receive a keyframe. To the left of the filters are In/Out tangent behaviors that you can assign as a default value for newly created keyframes. You will be exposed to both keyframing approaches in upcoming exercises. Figure 2-3 shows the keyframe tools.

figure |2-3|

Keyframe tools.

More animation features can be found within the Motion panel (Figure 2-4) on the right-hand side of the interface. The Motion panel allows you to assign various controllers to animated objects, as well as manipulate an object's trajectory. This can be extremely useful when setting up controllers such as a path constraint to animate objects along a given path, or a LookAt constraint, which will cause an object to rotate in relation to the position of another object.

figure |2-4|

Motion panel.

The final set of animation tools we will be looking at are the different Track View modes. There are two Track Views included within 3ds Max: the Dope Sheet and the Curve editor. The Dope Sheet provides you with a view of all keyframes created during the animation process. You also have access to all of the animation tracks associated with each object in your scene. In this view, you have the ability to move, add, delete, copy, and tweak each keyframe in order to make adjustments to the animation.

The Curve editor allows you to see a graphical representation of your animation on a track-by-track basis. Each animation track describes a specific aspect of an object, such as the X position of an object or the Z rotation of an object. Animation in each track is depicted as a *function curve*, with keyframes acting as control points in the curve. Just as with a spline shape, you are able to manipulate the shape of the curve by adjusting control handles connected to each keyframe. By manipulating the shape of the curve, you modify the overall behavior of the animation for that track. This is an extremely useful and intuitive method for making adjustments to the motion of your characters and objects. Figure 2-5 shows the Dope Sheet view. The Curve editor can be seen in Figure 2-6.

These will be the main tools discussed in this chapter. Other animation tools pertaining to character and effects animation will be addressed later in the text. Once you have a firm grasp of these fundamentals, you will be able to work with the more advanced animation features more effectively (not to mention have a lot of fun doing it).

BASIC KEYFRAMING

In traditional cel animation, motion is created by first timing out an action, determining what the key poses are for that action, and

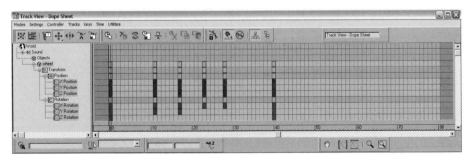

figure │ 2-5 │

The Dope Sheet editor allows you to manipulate the keyframes themselves.

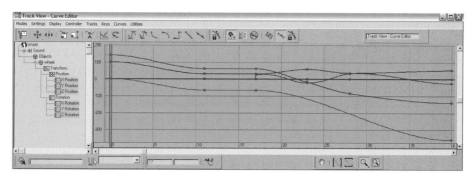

figure | 2-6 |

The Curve editor allows you to manipulate the shape of a track's function curve to alter the behavior of an animation.

then filling in the rest of the motion by drawing each of the in-between poses. The animation process within 3ds Max works much the same way. Key poses (or keyframes) are set up within the trackbar, except instead of having to manually create the in-between poses, 3ds Max will perform the "tweens" for you, allowing you to focus on the keyframes and timing of the animation.

There are two main methods that can be used when setting keyframes: Auto Key and Set Key. The Auto Key animation mode, when activated, acts in much the same way as a record button on a VCR or tape deck. When this mode is active, all position, rotation, and scale changes performed will be recorded and set as a keyframe within the trackbar. With the Auto Key button active, drag the Time slider to the frame you wish to create a keyframe on and make any necessary changes to the position, rotation, or scale of the object you wish to animate (parameter changes to the object's properties and modifiers can also be animated in this way).

As soon as a change has been made, a keyframe will register within the trackbar. You can continue setting keyframes in this manner by moving the Time slider to each frame you would like a keyframe to appear and modifying objects in the scene. When using the Set Key animation mode, 3ds Max will allow you to manually set your keyframes by using the Set Key button. This mode provides more flexibility and control over the keyframes by allowing the animator to selectively set keys for particular tracks. This can be done by setting up key filters, which will prevent unwanted tracks or object parameters from receiving a keyframe. The Set Key approach is ideal when it comes to character animation, because it allows you to try out different poses before committing a pose to a keyframe. If you do not like the pose, simply drag the Time slider to a different point in time and the pose (and/or parameter changes) will be discarded. Now that you are more familiar with these two main animation methods, let's begin to make some motion!

DON'T GO THERE   When using the Auto Key method, you will need to be extremely careful. Because the Auto Key feature behaves like a record button, *everything* you do will be set as keyframes, which means that it is extremely easy to inadvertently create unwanted animation. If you wish to make changes to your scene and do not want to have those changes animated, be sure to deactivate the Auto Key button.

Using Auto Key

The technique we will take a look at in this chapter is the Auto Key approach. This is a really good method to start with, because 3ds Max sets keyframes automatically every time an object is altered, moved, rotated, or scaled.

1. Open the *wheel_start.max* file found in the *Chapter 2* folder of the companion CD-ROM. You will see a wheel sitting at rest on a road.

2. Let's begin by animating the wheel along the length of the road. Using the Move transform tool, select the wheel object in the Top viewport. Activate the Auto Key button located below the trackbar. When active, you will notice that the button, trackbar, and active viewport border will turn red to indicate that you are recording (see Figure 2-7).

3. Move the Time slider all the way to the right so that it is on frame 100.

4. In the X axis coordinate field at the bottom of the interface, enter a value of *–140.0* and press Enter (or you may use the Move Transform Type-In dialog box). This will place the wheel on the opposite end of the road.

5. Click the Auto Key button again to deactivate it. Note that you now have two keyframes in the trackbar: one on frame 0, which describes the starting position (and properties) of the wheel, and one on frame 100, which describes the ending position of the wheel on the road.

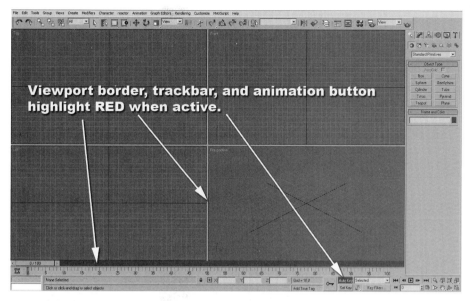

Viewport border, trackbar, and animation button highlight RED when active.

figure |2-7|

Some elements of the interface will turn red when the Auto Key button is active, indicating that you are in animation mode.

6. Click the Go to Start button in the animation playback controls to rewind the animation to the beginning.

7. Activate the Perspective viewport and click the Play Animation button.

You will see that the wheel now moves from one end of the road to the other. You might also notice that the animation starts a bit slowly, then accelerates a little, and then slows down as it approaches the end keyframe. 3ds Max is automatically "easing in and out" those two keyframes in an attempt to give the motion a more natural look. In a moment, we will look at how we can change the behavior of those keyframes within the different Track Views. Now let's give the wheel some bounce, as well as some rotation.

1. Click the Stop Animation button to stop the animation. Save your work at this point. If you opened the file from the companion CD-ROM, be sure to save the file locally to your hard drive.

2. Select the wheel if it is not already selected and activate the Front viewport.

3. Move the Time slider back to frame 0.

4. With your Move transform tool active, enter a value of *100.0* in the Z axis coordinate field to move the wheel above the road surface. If you were to preview the animation now, you would see the wheel float laterally over the road. Because we changed the Z coordinate with the Auto Key button disabled, the new location merely reorients the animation and applies the change in position globally to the wheel. If we wanted to affect the Z position of only one of the keyframes, we would have had to either activate the Auto Key or manually change the coordinate value in the Track View.

5. Activate the Auto Key button and drag the Time slider to frame 50. Keeping the Move tool active, enter a value of *29.5* in the Z axis coordinate field. This will position the wheel back onto the road.

6. Move the Time slider to frame 100. Right-click the Rotate transform tool to open the Rotate Transform Type-In dialog box (Figure 2-8). On the right-hand side, enter a value of *–360.0* in the Y Offset field.

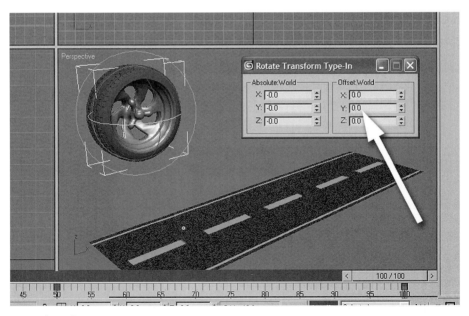

figure | 2-8 |

Adding rotation to the wheel using the Rotate Transform Type-In dialog box.

7. Turn off the Auto Key button and click Play Animation to see the results. You should now see the wheel bouncing once as it moves along the road, spinning as it does so.

8. Save your work.

Trajectories

A trajectory is the path or direction in which an object moves. 3ds Max provides you with the ability to easily modify and manipulate the trajectories of your animated objects. This can be done through the Motion panel, within the Trajectories settings. When the trajectory path is displayed for the selected object, a series of dots can be seen along the path of motion. These dots represent the frames of the animation. Larger boxes indicate that there is a keyframe on a particular frame. These boxes can be moved in 3D space, which will affect the trajectory of the object. You also have the option of adding keyframes along the trajectory path, which will give you more control over the shape of the trajectory. Figure 2-9 shows the trajectory settings within the Motion panel, as well as the trajectory of an object.

As you can see from the figure, the trajectory will display both empty frames and keyframes along the trajectory path. To manipulate the keys, you must be in the Keys sub-object mode. Let's go ahead and play with the trajectory of the wheel you just animated.

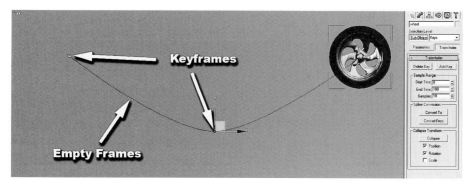

figure | 2-9 |

The animated object's trajectory can be seen and manipulated within the viewport.

1. Open the *wheel_trajectory.max* file from the *Chapter 2* folder of the companion CD-ROM, or use your saved file from the previous exercise.

2. Select the wheel. In the trackbar, you will see the keyframes you set up when we made the wheel bounce, spin, and move. Click the keyframe on frame 50 to select it. Move the keyframe to frame 25.

3. Activate the Front viewport, keeping the wheel selected. Select the Motion panel tab in Control Panels. Select the Trajectories button beneath the Motion tab to activate it. Turn on the Sub-Object button to be able to manipulate the keys (see Figure 2-10).

4. Activate the Move transform tool and select the keyframe in the middle of the trajectory path. On the X axis, slide the keyframe control point to the right about half the distance toward the wheel.

5. Click the Add Key button to insert keyframes along the trajectory. Insert two keyframes between the last key and the second key you just moved. Try to space them out evenly. Once you have added the new keys, turn off the Add Key button.

6. With the Move tool, move the first and last keys on the Y axis until the trajectory appears like a "wave" shape (see Figure 2-11). Note that by moving the keys in the trajectory, the keys in the trackbar will also move.

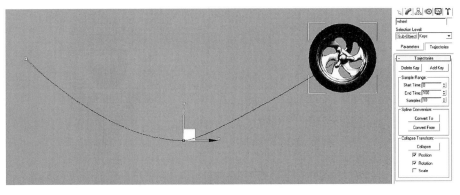

figure | 2-10 |

The wheel selected and sub-object mode enabled within the Trajectories parameters.

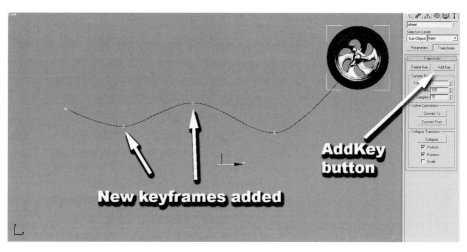

figure | 2-11 |

The newly modified trajectory with the two new keyframes added.

7. Now all we have left to do is to position the keys that appear in the "valleys" of the trajectory path at exact coordinates that will keep the wheel from passing through the road. Select the third keyframe in the trackbar and move it to frame 55. Right-click that key to bring up a fly-out menu. At the top of the menu, select *wheel: Z Position* to open the keyframe properties (Figure 2-12).

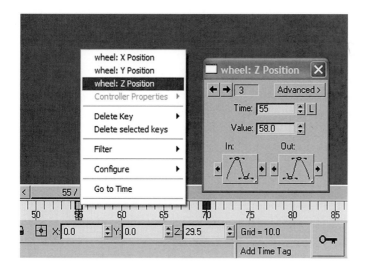

figure | 2-12 |

Keyframe properties window.

In this dialog box, enter *58* in the Value field. This will set the position of the wheel's pivot point to 58 in the World Space.

8. With the keyframe properties window still open, click the right arrow in the upper left of the window to select the next keyframe in the trackbar. In the Time field, enter a value of *70* to move the key to that frame. In the Value field, enter *29.5* to position the wheel on the road surface.

9. Following the same procedure as the previous step, move to the next key and set the Value field to *51*.

10. Close the keyframe properties window and play your animation. As you can see, you have now made your wheel bounce as it travels down the road. Save your work.

Congratulations, you have successfully created your first animation! In addition to making the wheel move, you have manipulated the wheel's trajectory. Next we will take a look at the 3ds Max Track Views, which will allow us to further manipulate your animation.

THE 3DS MAX TRACK VIEWS

When creating animation within 3ds Max, you will find that it is necessary to further modify the animation beyond the basic manipulations that can be achieved through the trackbar and Motion panel. These more advanced modifications can be achieved through the use of 3ds Max's two Track Views: the Dope Sheet and Curve editor. The Dope Sheet allows you to move, copy, and add keys, as well as to modify the animation range (the length of time in which a particular motion occurs) of a particular animation track.

You can also modify how 3ds Max addresses each key in the animation as it approaches and leaves each keyframe, enabling you to manipulate the easing in/easing out effects that good animation usually displays. The Curve editor allows you to further alter the behavior of your animations by allowing you to modify the motion through the use of graphical representations of each animated track. These graphs resemble the trajectories you worked with in the previous exercise. Each key is represented as a control point on the graph. The shape of each curve can be modified through the use of Bezier handles, much the same way you would modify a spline shape.

The Track View Toolbars

Just like the main 3ds Max interface and Material editor, the different Track Views offer a variety of tools to aid you in your animating. Knowing these various tools will make you a more efficient animator, so be sure to study and work with them as much as possible. We will now take a look at the toolbars for both the Dope Sheet and Curve editors. The following outlines the main Dope Sheet tools. Refer to Figure 2-13 for icon references.

Dope Sheet Tools

1 —		12 —	
2 —		13 —	
3 —		14 —	
4 —		15 —	
5 —		16 —	
6 —		17 —	
7 —		18 —	
8 —		19 —	
9 —		20 —	
10 —		21 —	
11 —		22 —	

figure |2-13|

Dope Sheet tools.

1. *Edit Keys:* This provides you with a Dope Sheet editing mode that displays the keys as boxes on a graph. This mode is used to cut, paste, and insert time within your animation.

2. *Edit Ranges:* This displays the keyed tracks as range bars that allow you to edit the length of animation in each track.

3. *Filters:* Use this to control what tracks are displayed in the Controller window (to the left of the Track View) and the Dope Sheet-Key window. For instance, you can opt to display only tracks that contain animation.

4. *Move Keys:* This enables you to move keys both horizontally and vertically on the graph.

5. *Move Keys Horizontal:* This restricts the movement of keys horizontally along the graph.

6. *Move Keys Vertical:* This restricts the movement of keys vertically along the graph.

7. *Slide Keys:* Use this to slide a key or groups of keys along the timeline. You can only slide keys in the same controller track.

8. *Add Keys:* This allows you to create additional keys on existing controller tracks.

9. *Scale Keys:* When this tool is used, the amount of time between keys can be increased or decreased. This works in both the Dope Sheet and Curve editors.

10. *Select Time:* This allows you to select a range of time. Any keys that fall within the time selection will be included.

11. *Delete Time:* This removes time from selected controller tracks. Note that this does not globally remove time from the active time segment. This can be used to delete keys within the "delete time selection," but empty frames will be left behind.

12. *Reverse Time:* This reverses the keyframes on a selected track within a given time selection.

13. *Scale Time:* This scales the keys that exist within selected tracks in a given time selection.

14. *Insert Time:* This allows you to insert a range of frames within the track. Existing keyframes will slide to allow for the newly inserted time.

15. *Cut Time:* This deletes time selections from selected controller tracks. Cut time will remain in memory and can be pasted if needed.

16. *Copy Time:* This will duplicate time selections from selected tracks in memory.

17. *Paste Time:* This adds into selected tracks time that has been cut or copied.

18. *Lock Selection:* This prevents you from inadvertently modifying selected keys.

19. *Snap Frames:* Active by default, this enables you to move keys so that they always snap to a frame. When this is turned off, you can position keys between frames so that they act as sub-frame keys.

20. *Show Keyable Icons:* Used in conjunction with the Set Key animation mode, this tool displays an icon next to each controller track that defines whether a track can receive keyframes or not. A red icon indicates a track that can be keyed, and a black icon indicates a track that cannot receive keys.

21. *Modify Subtree:* When active, modifications made to keys of parent objects affect children objects as well. This is active by default.

22. *Modify Child Keys:* If you modify a parent with Modify Subtree turned off, this tool will enable you to apply those changes to child keys.

Now let's take a look at the main Curve editor tools. Refer to Figure 2-14 for icon references.

1. *Filters:* As in the Dope Sheet, use this to control what tracks are displayed in the Controller window.

2. *Move Keys: This* enables you to move keys both horizontally and vertically on the function curve graph.

3. *Move Keys Horizontal:* This restricts the movement of keys horizontally along the graph.

4. *Move Keys Vertical:* this restricts the movement of keys vertically along the graph.

5. *Slide Keys:* This is used to slide a key or groups of keys along the timeline; it repositions adjacent keys away as you move.

6. *Scale Keys:* As in the Dope Sheet, the amount of time between keys can be increased or decreased.

Curve Editor Tools

1	13
2	14
3	15
4	16
5	17
6	18
7	19
8	20
9	21
10	22
11	23
12	24

figure | 2-14 |

Curve editor tools.

7. *Scale Values:* This increases the values of keys proportionally, instead of scaling the keys in time.

8. *Add Keys:* This creates keys on existing function curves.

9. *Draw Curves:* Use this tool to draw new function curves or to edit existing ones directly on the function curve graph.

10. *Reduce Keys: This is* used to reduce the total number of keys within a given track.

NOTE: Items 11 through 17 have additional options found under their fly-out buttons.

11. *Set Tangents to Auto:* This automatically sets selected key tangents. If a tangent that has been automatically set is moved, the tangents then become custom tangents.

12. *Set Tangents to Custom:* Select a key and activate this button to make the key tangents available for editing.

13. *Set Tangents to Fast:* This sets key tangents to fast-in, fast-out, or both; it also causes the animation to move more quickly entering and leaving keys.

14. *Set Tangents to Slow:* This is the same as Set Tangents to Fast, but it causes the animation to move more slowly entering and leaving keys.

15. *Set Tangents to Step:* This extends the value of a key to the next key. Use this to freeze motion until the next keyframe.

16. *Set Tangents to Linear:* By changing tangents to linear, animation entering and leaving keys becomes even, with no acceleration or deceleration to and from the keys.

17. *Set Tangents to Smooth:* This smooths out erratic motion between keys.

18. *Lock Selection:* Like the Dope Sheet, this prevents you from inadvertently modifying selected keys.

19. *Snap Frames:* Active by default, this enables you to move keys so that they always snap to a frame. When this is turned off, you can position keys between frames so that they act as sub-frame keys.

20. *Parameter Curve Out-of-Range Types:* This enables you to repeat keyed animation beyond the track's animation range; it also allows you to loop, ping-pong, and cycle (among other actions) animation.

21. *Show Keyable Icons:* Used in conjunction with the Set Key animation mode, this tool displays an icon next to each controller track that defines whether a track can receive keyframes or not. A red icon indicates a track that can be keyed, and a black icon indicates a track that cannot receive keys.

22. *Show All Tangents:* This hides or displays tangent handles on all curves.

23. *Show Tangents:* This hides or displays tangent handles on individual curves.

24. *Lock Tangents:* This locks tangent handles, allowing you to manipulate several tangents at once.

Okay, so this might seem like a lot to remember, but, just like anything else in 3ds Max, it just takes working with these tools to get a good handle on them. It may seem intimidating at first, but the more you play within the Track Views the easier it will be to work with and navigate animation tracks.

Track Views

It is possible to save your various Track View layouts for later use. Just like the main user interface, the Track Views can be customized. You can move various toolbars around or make them floating tool windows over the graph window. To save a Track View layout, simply right-click on the Track View menu bar or within the blank area in the toolbars and select Save Layout As. To open a saved layout, simply right-click again and select Load Layout.

The Dope Sheet

Now that you have a handle on the Track View tools, we can manipulate some keyframes within the Track View Dope Sheet. In addition to moving keys around the timeline graph, we will also take a quick look at the Time Configuration window, where we can apply global changes to the animation.

1. Open the *wheel_dopesheet.max* file found in the *Chapter 2* folder of the companion CD-ROM, or open the file you saved in the previous exercise.

2. Click the Time Configuration button found in the playback controls to open the Time Configuration window. Within the Frame Rate section, select Custom and enter a value of *15* to set the frame rate to 15 fps.

3. After setting the frame rate, you will notice that the Length (found in the Animation section of the Time Configuration window) changed from 100 to 50 frames. This is because you set the fps to 15, which is half of the original frame rate. Once the fps is changed, the animation length changes relative to the frame rate. We are going to change the total length of the animation. Change the Length value to *40* (see Figure 2-15). Click OK to close the Time Configuration window, which will save the changes made to the time properties.

4. Select the wheel object and open the Dope Sheet by selecting Graph Editors > Track View - Dope Sheet from the menu system.

5. You will notice that there are a lot of tracks displayed in the Controller window on the left. You can minimize the number of tracks in the Controller window with the use of filters. Click

figure | 2-15 |

Time Configuration
window.

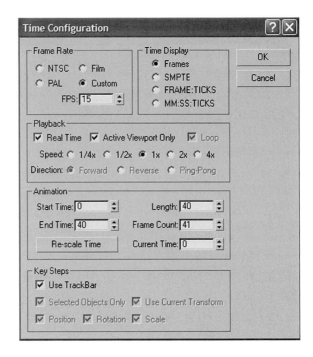

the Filters button in the toolbar. In the Show Only section in the upper-right corner of the Filters window, check the box next to Animated Tracks (Figure 2-16). Click OK. You should now see fewer tracks displayed in the Controller window.

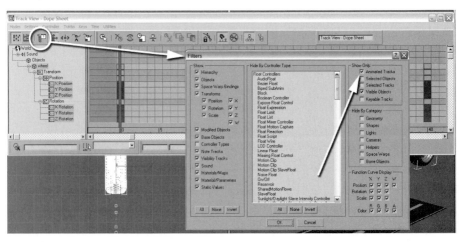

figure | 2-16 |

Animated Tracks option.

6. Using the Track View Zoom tool (found in the lower right of the Track View), zoom out of the graph window until you can see all of the keyframes. Note that the last keyframe extends past frame 40. We will correct this by adjusting the animation range for the wheel object. Select the Move Keys button and then activate the Edit Ranges button from the toolbar to display the animation ranges. Click-drag the right topmost range handle to the left and place it on frame 40.

7. Select the Edit Keys button to view the keyframes. Now you will notice that the last set of keyframes now ends on frame 40. Expand the Transform and Rotation tracks. Activate the Add Keys button and click in frame 11 on the wheel's Y Rotation track (see Figure 2-17).

8. Select all keys in frame 11. Activate the Move Keys tool and Shift + click + drag the column of frames to frame 17. This will make a copy of those frames to create a hold on the wheel's position and rotation, causing the wheel to pause during the animation. Play the animation to see the results. Save your work.

This is just a simple example of what the Track View Dope Sheet can do. You will utilize the Dope Sheet a lot more in later chapters of this book. Just remember that most of your moving and copying will be done within the Dope Sheet.

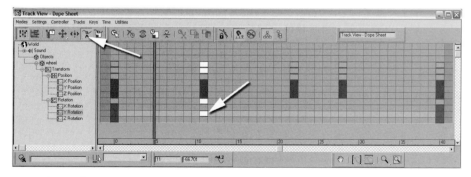

figure | 2-17 |

Adding keyframes to the Y Rotation track of the wheel object.

The Curve Editor

At this point, we are going to take a look at the Curve editor. Within this Track View, you will learn how to manipulate function curves within the Track View graph to change the behavior of the animation, as well as learn how to set Parameter Curve Out-of-Range types. You will quickly find that the Curve editor is an extremely powerful tool that will help you greatly with your animation endeavors.

Curve Editor
(Open) button

There are actually two ways the Curve editor can be opened. The first way is to either select Graph Editors > Track View-Curve Editor from the menu bar, or to click the Curve Editor (Open) button on the main toolbar. This will open the Curve editor in a floating window. The second way to access the Curve editor is through the trackbar. Just click the Open Mini Curve Editor button at the far left of the trackbar, and the trackbar keyframes will be replaced with the animation curves. Figure 2-18 shows the Mini Curve editor.

The Mini Curve editor is a wonderful thing because it allows you to manipulate the animation and still see all viewports (there is no floating window covering the views). This way you do not have to keep toggling between the Curve Editor window and the viewports, although the floating window is good to use if you are dealing with a lot of tracks at once. Now let's go ahead and add some erratic rotation to the wheel as it bounces down the road.

1. Open the *wheel_curves.max* file from the *Chapter 2* folder of the companion CD-ROM, or open the *.max* file you saved from the previous exercise.

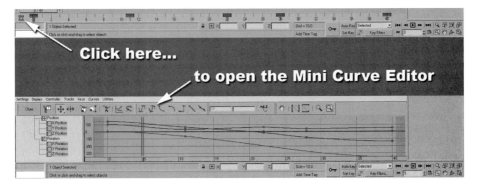

figure 2-18

The Trackbar's Mini Curve editor.

2. Select the wheel object and open the Curve editor by selecting Graph Editors > Track View-Curve Editor.

3. What we are going to do is add keys within the X Rotation track under Rotation Transform. Expand the Transform tracks if needed. Select the X Rotation track, which will hide all other curves and display the X Rotation curve only, though at the moment it is simply a straight line along the dark thick 0 line (that will change as we move forward).

4. Click the Add Keys button and click on the "curve" to add a key on frame 11.

5. Repeat step 4 by adding keys on frames 17, 23, and 28.

6. Now that we have the keys created, it is time to change the rotation values on those newly created keys. This will start to give the wheel some nice erratic rotation. Right-click key 17 to open the key properties. Under Value, enter *25.0* and leave the tangents as they are.

7. Click the right arrow in the upper-left corner of the key properties window to move to the key on frame 23 (or select the key on frame 23). Enter a Value of *–22.25* to make the wheel rotate in the other direction.

8. Move to the key on frame 28 and enter a Value of *33.0*.

9. Finally, move to the last keyframe and enter a value of *–26.25*.

10. Now that all keys have the appropriate parameter values, it is time to make some adjustments to the curve shape. The first thing we are going to do is to tell 3ds Max to keep the rotation of the wheel set to 0 until after the wheel falls and pauses. Once the wheel lifts back off the road during its first bounce, the rotations will begin. To do this, we will assign a specific tangent type to certain keys. Select the key on frame 11. On the Key Tangents toolbar in the Track View, select the Set Tangents to Step button. This will cause the value of key 11 to be carried through the animation until the key on frame 17 is reached.

Step button

11. At this point, select each keyframe and move the tangents around until you achieve a curve that resembles that shown in Figure 2-19.

12. Go ahead and play the animation to see how the changes to the curve have affected the wheel's animation. You can see that the wheel now has some cool funky bounce to its motion.

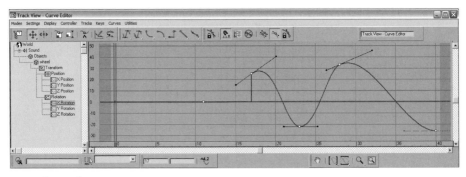

figure |2-19|

The finished animation curve for the X Rotation track.

13. Next, we will increase the animation length (without adjusting any of the keyframes), which will cause the animation to finish halfway through the timeline. The way we can force the movement of the wheel to continue throughout the empty frames at the end is to use Parameter Curve Out-of-Range Type. Open the Time Configuration window, and under the Animation section set the Length to *80* frames (see Figure 2-20). Click OK. This will double the length of the entire animation without adjusting the animation ranges of the animated tracks.

14. Once the timeline has been extended, make sure all the animated tracks are selected. You should see all the function curves displayed at once.

figure |2-20|

Time Configuration window. The animation Length has been set to 80 frames.

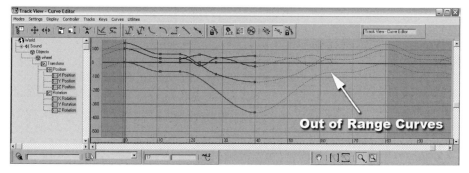

figure | 2-21|

The various Out-of-Range types.

15. Under the Curve Editor menus, Select Controller > Out-of-Range Types to open the Param Curve Out-of-Range Types dialog box (Figure 2-21). Select the Ping-Pong Out-of-Range type. Because the wheel starts at point A and ends at point B, simply looping the animation would cause the wheel to jerk back to the starting position, causing a serious break in the continuity of the animation. By selecting the Ping-Pong controller, the animation will essentially be "mirrored" in the empty frames at the end of the animation range, causing the animation to play backward after reaching the end of the original animation. Although it looks a little funny, it prevents the horrible jump effect that would normally occur if the motion were simply looped.

16. If you look at your Curve Editor graph now, you will see that the function curves are solid until frame 40, where they then turn into dotted lines. These dotted lines indicate that there is animation there and that they represent an Out-of-Range type being used (see Figure 2-22). Now play your animation. Note that it can now be looped without the risk of skipping.

figure | 2-22|

The function curves with Out-of-Range types as seen in the Curve Editor graph.

17. Save your work. If you like, you can render your Perspective view or view the final animation by opening the *Final_Wheel.avi* movie found in the *Chapter 2* folder of the companion CD-ROM. Note that lights have been added to the scene for this rendering to "make it all pretty." Feel free to add some lights to your own scene.

So that is really all there is to it. You have now successfully created your first animation project. During the course of animating the wheel, you managed to set keyframes, manipulate those keys within the Track View Dope Sheet, adjust the timeline through the Time Configuration window, create additional keys on a specific animation track within the Curve editor, manipulate the shape of the animation's function curve by adjusting tangents and assigning tangent types, and set up Parameter Curve Out-of-Range types to continue a motion throughout the specified time frame.

Wow, that is a lot of stuff. You should give yourself a well-deserved pat on the back! If you are wondering why we didn't cover the Set Key approach to keyframing, not to worry. That will be discussed once we start moving into character rigging and animation in later chapters. We do, however, have one more topic to address before we move forward to Chapter 3. You need to learn how to import a soundtrack into the Track View editors.

THE IMPORTANCE OF IMPORTING SOUND

If you do not yet know how animated films, television shows, and commercials are made, you may be wondering how the dialogue, music, and sound effects all match up with the animation. If you already know the answer to this, the following information will be a good review. In motion pictures, all of the sound is usually either added or enhanced after the scenes have been filmed. Foley artists record various sound effects such as footsteps, punches, slamming doors, gunshots, and virtually any other little sound byte that might "appear" in the film footage. They synchronize these sounds in accordance with the precise point in time that these sounds should occur.

Film composers also use key moments and occurrences in the footage to determine how the musical score should be written, in an effort to help support what is seen on the screen. A lot of the time, dialogue that actors say during filming sometimes gets lost in surrounding noise, despite the use of microphones, at which point automated dialogue replacement (ADR) is done to clean up the dialogue so that all lines can be heard. During this process, the actors are placed in a sound studio, where they watch a monitor of themselves and recite the lines the same way as when the scene was filmed. The old dialogue track is then swapped for the newly recorded dialogue and is mixed with the rest of the soundtrack (sound effects, ambient noise, and musical score) to make everything sound well blended.

In the animation world—whether it be computer, traditional, or stop-motion—it is extremely difficult to achieve realistic timing without any sort of audible reference, especially when it comes to dialogue. Because of this, the dialogue for an animated piece is recorded first, before any animation has been done. Once the voice track is finished, it is then given to the animators, who can begin to animate the numerous scenes. A common practice in the industry is to videotape the actors in the studio while they record their lines. Doing this provides the animators with visual reference to facial expressions and body gestures that are made while a character is speaking.

Armed with the voice track and video reference, the animators can then begin animating the characters. Once the animation has been completed and rendered out, and has gone through the editing stages, it is treated much like a live-action film. The sound effects and musical score are incorporated with the dialogue and mixed down into a cohesive soundtrack and synced to the animation. This is how animated films are born. Now let's import an audio file into 3ds Max, so that you, too, can begin animating to sound.

IMPORTING YOUR AUDIO FILE

In this next exercise, we will not be actually animating anything. The purpose of the following exercise is to expose you to importing audio into 3ds Max 8. This will be short and sweet, as it is extremely easy to do. This will probably take you all of 20 seconds to complete.

1. Start with a fresh 3ds Max file. Open the Dope Sheet by selecting Graph Editors > Track View - Dope Sheet.

2. Select and then right-click the Sound track (within the graph area to the right of the track list). This will open the Sound Options dialog box.

3. Under the Audio section, make sure the Active box is checked and then click the Choose Sound button (Figure 2-23).

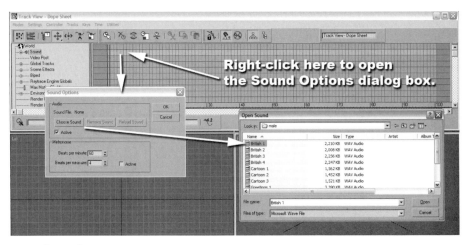

figure | 2-23 |

The Sound Options window allows you to import an audio file into the Track View.

4. In the *Audio* folder on the companion CD-ROM, select any audio file you like. (We used the British*1.wav* found in the *Dialog/Male* directory.)

5. If you expand the Sound track, you will see an audio waveform appear in the Track View graph window (Figure 2-24). If you click the Play Animation button in the animation controls, you will hear the audio file being played. If you scroll through the timeline either in the Track View or the Time slider, you will be able to "scrub" through the audio slowly, which will enable you to precisely place your keyframes.

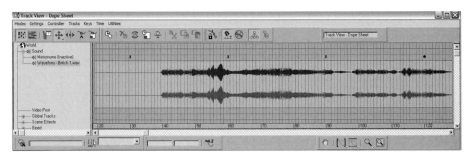

figure | 2-24 |

The sound file can now be seen graphically as an audio waveform.

6. That's it! All that you would have to do is adjust the animation length in the Time Configuration window to extend the animation length to match the length of the audio file and you would be ready to animate!

Piece of cake! Now that you know how to bring audio into 3ds Max, you will be able to animate more effectively using a soundtrack as a guide. You will find it much easier to time your motions when you know where important parts of the dialogue, sound effects, and/or music lie.

SUMMARY

Well, you certainly have come a long way since the beginning of the chapter! You have successfully created your first animated piece using a variety of 3ds Max's powerful animation tools, such as the Motion panel, Dope Sheet and Curve editor Track Views, and trackbar. As you continue through the text, you will utilize these tools often and will quickly become proficient in using them. We also discussed the role of sound in both motion pictures and animated pieces. Understanding how sound can play a role in the creation of animation will enable you to produce better motion in your work.

in review

1. What is SMPTE time code and why is it used?

2. Where do you change the timeline properties (such as animation length, frame rate, and time display)?

3. What are the two keyframing approaches?

4. Which keyframing approach is better suited for character animation?

5. What are trajectories?

6. Where do you go to edit trajectories?

7. Describe what the Track View Dope Sheet is used for.

8. Explain what the Curve editor does.

9. Discuss what Parameter Curve Out-of-Range types enable the animator to do.

10. What are key tangents?

11. Why is it important to use a Sound track during the animation process?

↗ EXPLORING ON YOUR OWN

1. Practice animating various objects using transforms (Move, Rotate, and Scale) and object parameter changes using the Auto Key method. Make adjustments to the animation using the various Track View editors.

2. Find an audio file that has music and sound effects in it and import the sound into one of the Track Views. Attempt to animate an object using the audio file as a guide for keyframing.

charting your course

The goal of a character animator is to display his characters' thoughts and emotions through movement. This is no easy task. The last thing you want to deal with is a rig that does not allow you to focus solely on the movement of your character. A large number of first-time animators spend hours struggling with incorrectly rigged characters and never achieve their animation goals.

After learning the basics of character modeling and rig setup, most novice animators find that character rigging is just as rewarding as animating. In this chapter we discuss some basic topics that are the foundation of good character animation, such as solid character modeling techniques, creating proper bone structures, applying inverse and forward kinematics to a finished bone system, skinning a bone rig to a mesh through the use of envelopes, as well as other character development tools. In addition, we will explore generating facial movement through the use of morph targets.

 chapter objectives

- **Exploring rigging theory**
- **Getting the model ready to animate**
- **Creating a skeleton for a character**
- **Defining forward kinematics and inverted kinematics controllers**
- **Creating iconic controllers**
- **Skinning and manipulating envelopes**
- **Defining and demonstrating constraints**
- **Exploring lip syncing with the Morpher modifier**

DO'S AND DON'TS OF CHARACTER SETUP

To put it simply, an animation rig is a digital version of our muscles, bones, and tendons. A rig enables the animator to control the movements of her character. It is very easy to fall into the trap of overcomplicating the rigging process. The controls for a rig should be clear, unobtrusive, and easy to manipulate. Do not create controls that are difficult to see or pick in your scene, such as those shown in Figure 3-1.

Try using particular shapes or colors for the controllers of your rig so that you can easily distinguish among them and other objects in your scene. Make controls that are intuitive. For example, do not place a control for a foot next to a hand. Do not create controls that obstruct the view of your character. You should be able to clearly see and manipulate the controls, as shown in Figure 3-2. Finally, do not create controls that are so complicated they slow you down when animating.

It is important to create a rig with a specific purpose in mind. Think of what the character is going to do in a particular scene. Is the character going to be talking in your scene? If not, it would be a mistake to create an intricate rig that allows for lip sync. This is one of many reasons it is

figure | 3-1 |

These controls would be tough to select and key.

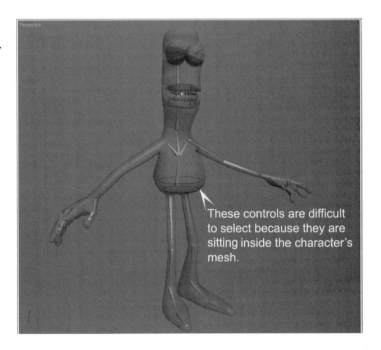

These controls are difficult to select because they are sitting inside the character's mesh.

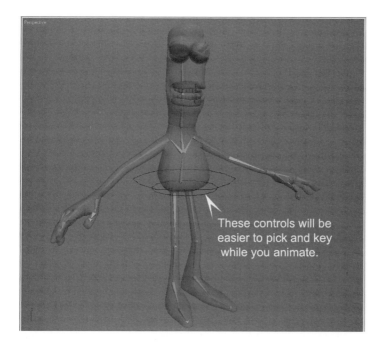

figure | 3-2 |

Controls that are simple and easily distinguished.

important to generate a storyboard or a set of thumbnails that define key poses for your scene. With a clear vision of what your character's movements look like, you can create a more efficient and deliberate rig.

THE SCHEMATIC VIEW

Organization is an important trait to adopt when creating a rig. One of the tools in 3ds Max that can help you better manage files is the Schematic View. The Schematic View is a viewport used to organize a scene file graphically. This viewport has many uses, but in this chapter we focus on its ability to visually represent the objects in our scene and their relationship to one another. The Schematic View displays the objects in a scene as boxes stacked in a hierarchy. The boxes are connected by lines, and these lines indicate the relationships the boxes or the objects in the scene have with one another. The Schematic View button is found at the right side of 3ds Max's main toolbar. You can also access it by going to Graph Editors > New Schematic View.

NOTE: The objects in a 3D scene are often referred to as a node.

GETTING THE MODEL READY FOR ANIMATION

There are a few key concepts to keep in mind when creating the geometry of a character. The first is the bind pose, or the position in which you model your character. This is important because it affects certain aspects of the rigging process, such as skinning. You want to pick a neutral pose, such as having your character stand with feet shoulder-width apart and arms positioned at about 45 degrees. This stance will help you later when skinning the character, as indicated in Figure 3-3.

A term widely used when modeling is *edge looping*. An edge loop is a series of interlocking edges within your character's geometry (see Figure 3-4). By using these edge loops to define the volumes of your character, you create a grid that makes up your character's mesh. The more evenly spaced this grid is, the easier it is to skin to a bone system.

A variety of modeling techniques can be used to generate the mesh of your character. Regardless of which technique you use, there are certain attributes that make a character's geometry easy to rig and animate. During the modeling process you should attempt to use only four-sided faces (quads), as indicated in Figure 3-5.

figure | 3-3 |

This character's mesh will be easier to envelope when it comes time to skin.

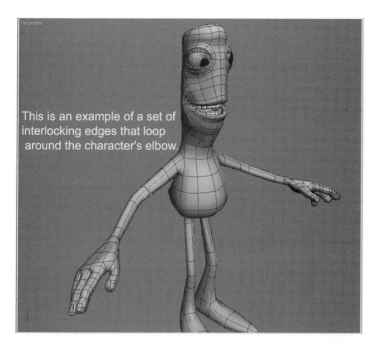

This is an example of a set of interlocking edges that loop around the character's elbow.

figure | 3-4 |

This interlocking set of edges makes a complete loop around the character's elbow.

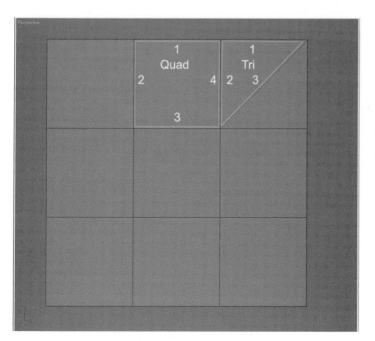

figure | 3-5 |

An occasional three-sided face (tri) is okay, and at times even necessary, but when ever possible you should use four-sided faces.

The quad topology helps keep the grid that makes up your character's geometry (mesh) more uniformly spaced. This uniformity makes skinning your character's geometry a much simpler process and cuts down on unexpected results when your character's mesh is deformed. It is also a good idea to keep a relatively uniform spacing between the edge loops of your model. However, there are certain areas on your character's mesh you should pay particular attention to, such as elbows, knees, and shoulders. These points of articulation tend to require a few more edge loops in order to maintain volume when deformed, as in Figure 3-6.

CREATING A SKELETON WITH THE BONES SYSTEM

The Bones system in 3ds Max is the functionality used to deform a character's mesh during animation. Before we get started we need to do a couple of things to the character's geometry.

1. Open the file *Chapter03/Mr_Blue_Rig_Start.max*.

2. In the Perspective viewport, activate the Select Object tool. Select all geometry of the character by click-dragging a marquee around all of the pieces that make up its mesh, as indicated in Figure 3-7.

3. With the geometry still selected, press Alt+X. This will cause the mesh to become transparent, so that we can easily place bone components inside the character's geometry.

figure | 3-6 |

The extra edge loops around the character's arm keep it from collapsing in on itself when the elbow is rotated.

Points of articulation like these require more edge loops to deform properly.

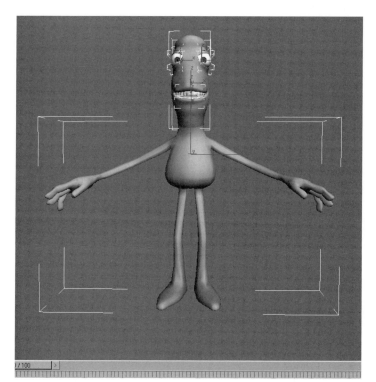

figure | 3-7 |

Bounding boxes will highlight around the objects when they are selected.

4. Click the Layer Manager button. The Layer Manager button is located in the top right-hand side of 3ds Max's user interface. It looks similar to three stacked sheets of paper. The button will turn yellow when active, and the Layer dialog box will open.

5. In the Layer dialog box, click the Create New Layer (Containing Selected Objects) button. It is the first button to the left in the Layer dialog box. This button automatically assigns all selected objects in the scene to a new layer.

6. Rename the layer from *Layer01* to *Mesh*. Once renamed, expand the list of objects by clicking the little plus sign next to the name of the layer.

7. Freeze all geometry of the character so that you do not accidentally select it while creating the bones. To freeze the geometry, click the field under the Freeze column in the Layer dialog box. As you do this, a snowflake indicator will appear next to the frozen geometry (see Figure 3-8).

8. Create another layer and rename it Bones. This will contain the bones after we create them. Close the Layer dialog box.

figure | 3-8 |

Snowflake indicator
next to frozen
geometry.

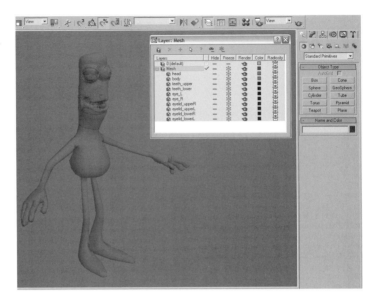

Creating the Skeleton

We are now ready to begin placing bones in our character's mesh.
We will be using orthographic views to create the bone chains.

1. Press the L key to go to the left viewport (Figure 3 9).

figure | 3-9 |

Left viewport.

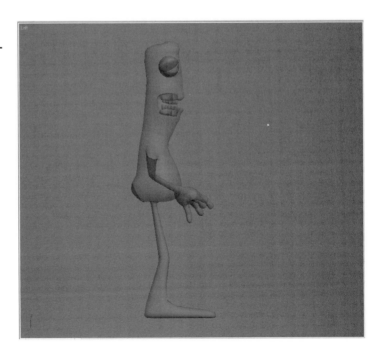

2. Use Zoom Extents in the left viewport so that you can see the entire character. Go to the menu set at the top of 3ds Max's user interface. Under the Character menu, select Bone Tools. The Bone Tools dialog box (see Figure 3-10) will appear.

3. Click the Create Bones button in the Bone Tools dialog box (the button will turn yellow when activated).

4. We are going to create a bone chain constituting the spine of the character. Start by clicking just above where the legs meet the body of the character. This will be the base of the character's spine. Perform three clicks: once midway up the character's back, again around the shoulder area of the character, and under the chin of the character.

5. Right-click at the end the of the bone chain to create the last bone of the spine. The spine chain should contain four bones and look somewhat like that shown in Figure 3-11.

6. Click to turn off Create Bones in the Bone Tools dialog box.

7. If the bones are placed improperly, simply select the Bone Edit Mode button in the Bone Tools dialog box. This will allow you to edit the scale of the bone in the spine chain (as well as the bone's position) without affecting the rest of the bones below it

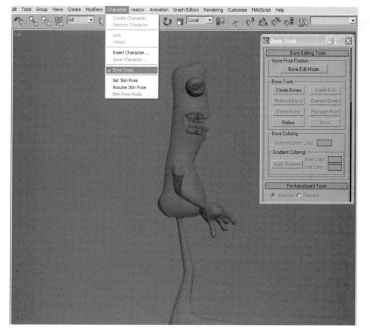

figure | **3-10** |

Bone Tools dialog.

figure | 3-11 |

Create bones in the
Bone Tools dialog.

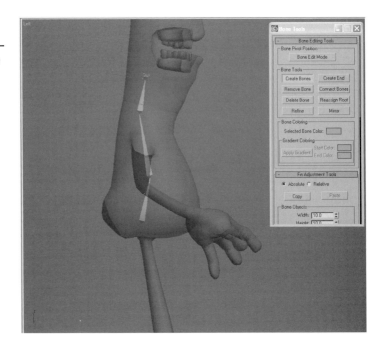

in the hierarchy of that chain. Once you are satisfied with the
position of the bones, deactivate the Bone Edit Mode button.
The spine chain is finished.

There may be times when you do not want to adjust the scale of a
particular bone. You may simply want to rotate or move a bone.
Or you may find it necessary to rotate a chain of bones. In this
case, it may not be necessary to use the Bone Edit Mode feature.
When Bone Edit Mode is turned off, you can edit the position of a
chain of bones or a particular bone using the Rotate tool in 3ds
Max's main user interface. Before you rotate or move bones, make
sure to select Local Reference Coordinate System (Figure 3-12).

▶ Bone Edit Mode

In the Bone Tools dialog, you may also choose Bone Edit Mode to move the
bones to the proper location. The Bone Edit mode button will turn yellow when
activated. The mode is useful if you need to shorten or lengthen a bone. Use the
Move tool only when editing a bone's placement. Do not rotate the bones while
in Bone Edit mode. If you accidentally do so, simply undo. Remember to turn off
Bone Edit mode when finished.

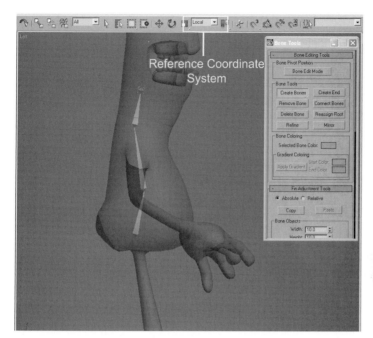
Reference Coordinate
System

figure | 3-12 |

Local Reference
Coordinate System
selected.

An object's local coordinates will align one of the axes down the center of the bone, making rotating the bone much more natural. The animation mesh rotates around the pivot points of the bones, so the placement of the bones is very important for the mesh's deformation. When the bones are properly placed, go back and rename the bones. In any given setup, you may have more than 100 bones and controllers to choose from. Properly labeled bones are much easier to find when you are further into the modeling process. Use whatever naming convention you wish, as long as it is descriptive of the bones' locations. For arms and legs, make sure you distinguish between left side and right side.

Naming the Bones

To name the bones, perform the following steps:

1. Select the first bone that was created at the base of the spine, and in the Create panel change the name from *Bone01* to *Bone_Spine_1* (see Figure 3-13).

2. Select and rename the rest of the bones in the chain as follows:

   ● *Bone_Spine_2*

   ● *Bone_ Neck*

   ● *Bone_ Head*

figure | 3-13 |

Changing the name
of the first bone.

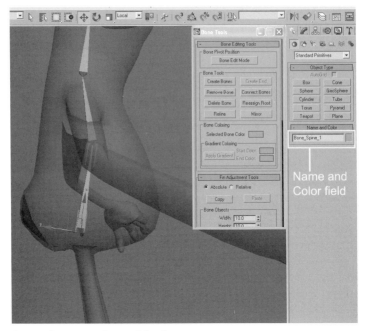

Creating an Arm Chain

To create an arm chain, perform the following steps:

1. Now we will create the bone chain for the right arm of our
   character. This will be done in the Top viewport, so press
   the T key and Zoom the top viewport around the character.

2. With the Bone Tools dialog box activated, click the Create
   Bones button and start the chain for the arm at the shoulder of
   the character.

3. Click at the elbow, then at the wrist, and finally at the center of
   the hand. Right-click to deactivate the tool. The arm chain
   should look something like that shown in Figure 3-14.

4. Now that the bones in the arm chain have been created, name
   them from the shoulder to the hand as follows:

   ● *Bone_Right_Shoulder*

   ● *Bone_Right_Elbow*

   ● *Bone_Right_Hand*

   ● *Bone_Null*

5. Change the view to the Perspective viewport and adjust
   the view using the Arc Rotate tool until you can clearly see

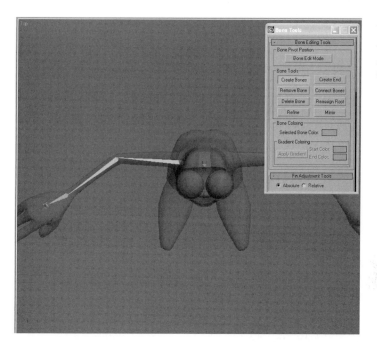

figure | 3-14 |

Arm chain after
step 3.

Bone_Right_Shoulder. Begin to adjust the chain of bones to fit
within the character's geometry by picking and rotating
Bone_Right_Shoulder (see Figure 3-15).

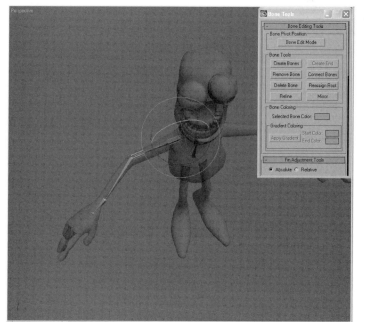

figure | 3-15 |

Adjusting the bones
within the charac-
ter's geometry.

Rotating the chain probably will not center the arm properly in the character's mesh. It may be necessary to use Bone Edit Mode in the Bone Tools dialog box to position the chain. The arm chain should look like that shown in Figure 3-16. Make sure to deactivate the Bone Edit Mode button when done.

Finishing the Arm Chains

To finish both arm chains, perform the following steps:

1. The next step is to attach the arm chain to the spine chain. Select *Bone_Spine_1* at the base of the spine chain and in the Bone Tools dialog box click the Connect Bones button.

2. Drag to the shoulder bone (*Bone_Right_Shoulder*) and then click *Bone_Right_Shoulder*. This will create a bone that runs from the spine to the shoulder, connecting the spine chain with the arm chain. Rename the new bone from *connectBone01* to *Bone_Right_Clavicle*.

3. Let's finish the arm by creating the rest of the hand. In the Top viewport, with the Create Bones button activated, start a chain for the first finger at the knuckle of the character's right hand. The bones will be created from the hand to the tip of the finger.

figure | 3-16 |

Arm chain at
this stage.

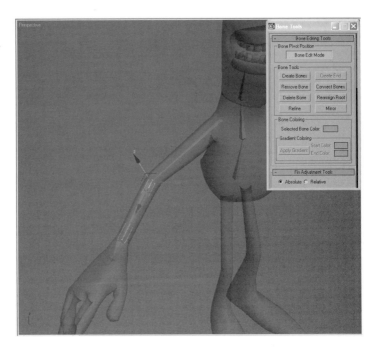

Begin by clicking three times to place the knuckles of the finger, and right-click to end the bone chain. Deactivate the Create Bones tool.

4. This leaves us with four bones in the finger, but we only need three. To delete the extra bone, click the Remove Bone button in the Bone Tools dialog box. This will get rid of the last bone in the chain (see Figure 3-17).

5. Switch to the Perspective viewport and move the chain of bones to the center of the finger. If necessary, use the Bone Edit Mode button to help position it. Name the bones in the finger chain as follows (Bone 1A is the closest to the hand bone, and 1C is at the tip of the character's finger):

- *Bone_Right_Finger_1A*
- *Bone_Right_Finger_1B*
- *Bone_Right_Finger_1C*

6. Now we will duplicate this chain of bones and use it for the rest of the fingers in the hand. Make sure to deactivate the Bone Edit Mode button. Then select all bones in the finger chain. With the Shift key pressed and held, move over the cursor to the next finger in the mesh. Holding down Shift and using the Move tool to position the chain is a quick way of duplicating the skeleton for our

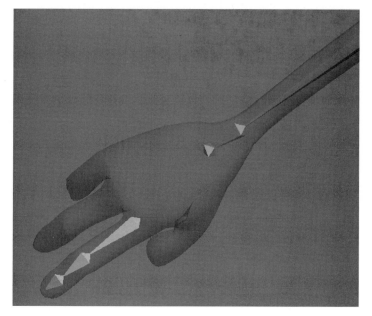

figure | **3-17** |

Getting rid of the last bone in the chain.

finger. The Clone Options dialog box will appear. Use the default settings in this dialog box for the tool by simply clicking OK.

7. Copy the finger chain once more and position the bones for the hand as shown in Figure 3-18. Do not forget to name the two finger chains in accordance with the naming convention as follows:

● *Bone_Right_Finger_2A*

● *Bone_Right_Finger_2B*

● *Bone_Right_Finger_2C*

● *Bone_Right_Finger_3A*

● *Bone_Right_Finger_3B*

● *Bone_Right_Finger_3C*

8. Now that we have positioned the bones that make up the character's fingers, let's finish the hand. Activate the Bone Edit Mode button and the Move tool and then select the small end bone of the arm chain, which should be named *Bone_Null* (see Figure 3-19).

figure | **3-18**

You may have to activate the Bone Edit Mode button again to adjust the finger chains. Just make sure to deactivate it after you are finished positioning the bones.

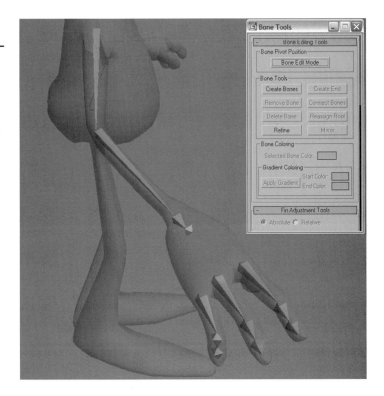

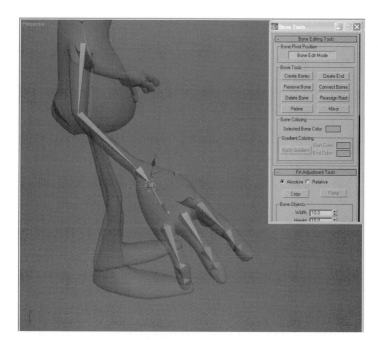

figure | **3-19** |

Small end bone of
the arm chain.

9. Adjust *Bone_Right_Hand* by moving *Bone_Null* down closer to
   the first set of knuckles in the finger bones.

10. Now that we have *Bone_Right_Hand* in position (and, more
    importantly, at the proper size for skinning), we can delete
    Bone_Null. We will not be using it in the skeleton. With
    Bone_Null still selected, use the Delete Bone button in the Bone
    Tools dialog box to delete it from the chain. The skeleton of the
    hand to this point should resemble that shown in Figure 3-20.

11. The final step in completing the hand is to duplicate the finger
    chain once more. This final chain will be for the thumb of the
    character. Use the Move and Rotate tools from the main tool-
    bar to duplicate and place the bones correctly. If necessary, use
    the Bone Edit Mode button in the Bone Tools dialog box to
    properly position the thumb chain. Do not forget to name the
    bone chain as follows:

    ● Bone_Right_Thumb_1A

    ● Bone_Right_Thumb_1B

    ● Bone_Right_Thumb_1C

12. Adjust the position of the thumb chain until the skeleton looks
    like that shown in Figure 3-21.

figure | 3-20 |

Skeleton of hand to
this point.

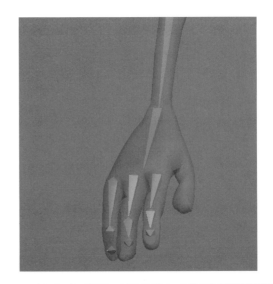

figure | 3-21 |

Position of the
thumb chain.

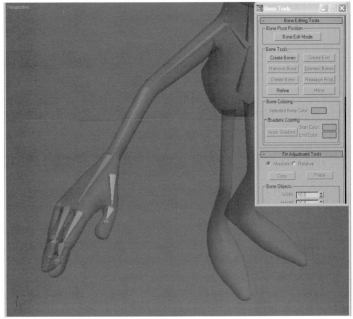

Linking the Bone Chains

We are almost done with the upper body of our character. To finish
the upper body we have just a few things left to do. First, we need
to link the chains of the fingers to the hand using the Link tool.
The Link tool will create a parent/child relationship among the
fingers and the hand chain without creating an extra bone (see
Figure 3-22).

Perspective

Link Tool

figure | 3-22 |

Location of the Link
tool in Max's main
user interface.

1. Select the first bone in the thumb (*Bone_Right_Thumb_1A*),
   and then activate the Link tool. The Link tool is located at the
   top left-hand side of 3ds Max's user interface. The Link tool
   button icon shows two boxes with a chain between them. With
   the Link tool activated, place the cursor over *Bone_
   Right_Thumb1A*. At this point, two boxes should appear. Hold
   down the left mouse button and drag from *Bone_
   Right_Thumb1A* to *Bone_Right_Hand*. A dotted line, as well as
   the two boxes (one solid this time), will appear when the cursor is over *Bone_Right_Hand*. Release the left mouse button
   over *Bone_Right_Hand*. A box should temporarily highlight
   Bone_Right_Hand when you release the button.

2. Test the link by rotating *Bone_Right_Hand*. If the link worked,
   the thumb chain will rotate with it. If the thumb does not
   rotate with the hand, deselect everything and repeat the
   process (see Figure 3-23).

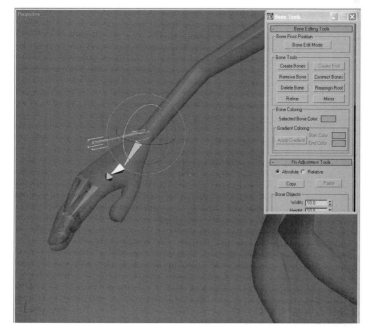

figure | 3-23 |

If the link worked,
the thumb chain
will rotate with it
and appear as it
does here.

> ## The Link Tool
>
> The Link tool groups objects into parent/child relationships. In using the tool, you first select the object you want to be a child in this relationship. Then select the tool and click-drag to select a parent object. The link will be established and the first object becomes a child of the second object. The tool will display two empty boxes when the cursor is held over the first object selected. Hold down the mouse button and place the cursor over a second object. At this point, one colored box and one empty box should appear. There will also be a dotted line that follows the cursor during this process. A box will flash and highlight the parent object when the mouse button is released, indicating that the link was established.
>
> NOTE: You will need to select another tool, such as the Select Object or Move tool, in order to deactivate the Link tool.

3. Undo the rotation and then link the rest of the fingers to *Bone_Right_Hand*. Link each finger chain separately and test the hand after each link by rotating *Bone_Right_Hand* and then undoing the rotation.

Mirroring the Skeleton

With the hand skeleton linked, we are now ready to mirror the right arm to the left side of our model.

1. Select *Bone_Right_Clavicle*. This is the bone that connects *Bone_Right_Shoulder* to *Bone_Spine_1*, as shown in Figure 3-24.

2. Switch to the Perspective viewport and select all bones in the arm chain, making sure to get all fingers in the hand.

3. Go to the Bone Tools dialog box and, with all bones selected, click the Mirror button. The Bone Mirror dialog box will appear, and you should see the arm mirrored at the left side of the character. Click OK. In our scene the default settings for the tool worked perfectly, but you may have to experiment with the Mirror Axis option for the tool to mirror properly for your scene.

4. Rename all of the bones to indicate that they are on the left side of the body.

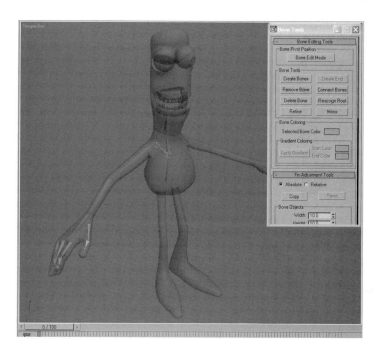

figure | 3-24 |

Connecting bone.

The Final Touches

Now that both arms are properly placed, the skeleton of our character's torso is almost complete. One final step remains. We need to
adjust the bone that will make up our character's head. This will
help speed up the skinning process. We will edit the last bone
(*Bone_Head*) in the character's spine chain. This bone needs to be
longer to better fit the mesh of the character's head.

1. First select *Bone_Head* and then in the Bone Tools dialog box
   click Create End. This will create an extra bone that will allow
   us to edit the size of *Bone_Head*.

2. The bone that was just created by the Create End tool should
   still be selected. If it is not, select it and activate the Move tool
   (W is the hotkey).

3. Activate Bone Edit Mode and adjust the new bone by moving it
   closer to the top of the character's head, as shown in Figure 3-25.

4. Once you are satisfied with the position and size of
   Bone_Head, delete the bone that was created to help adjust it
   and deactivate Bone Edit Mode. The skeleton should look like
   that shown in Figure 3-26.

figure | 3-25 |

Bone moved closer to the top of the character's head.

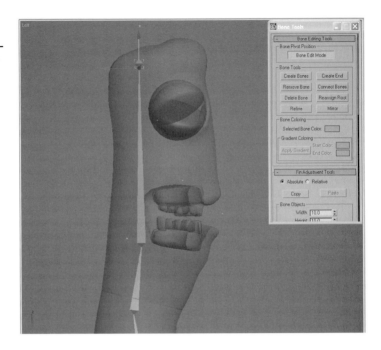

figure | 3-26 |

Skeleton after step 4.

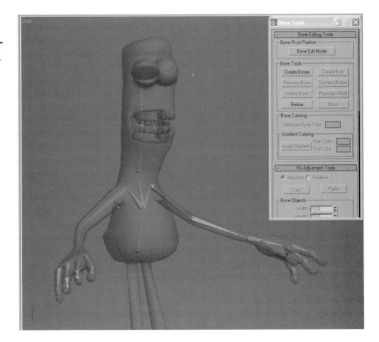

Creating the Leg Chains

We are now ready to move on to the lower part of our character's skeleton, so let's get started on the leg chains.

1. In the Left viewport, click the Create Bones button in the Bone Tools dialog box. Starting at the hip of our character, click the left mouse button once to create the first leg bone.

2. Drag the mouse to the knee and click the left mouse button to create a second bone. Continue down to the ankle of the character and click to create an ankle bone. Then click at the ball of the foot to create a bone there, and finally at the toe of the character to create a toe bone.

3. When you get to the toe, click the right mouse button to end the bone chain.

4. When you are finished, deactivate the Create Bones button. The skeleton for the leg should have five bones in it and should look like that shown in Figure 3-27.

5. Press the P key to switch to the Perspective viewport. Every time you rotate or move a bone, make sure to first select Local Reference Coordinate System (see Figure 3-28). Move and rotate the bones so that they fit within the leg.

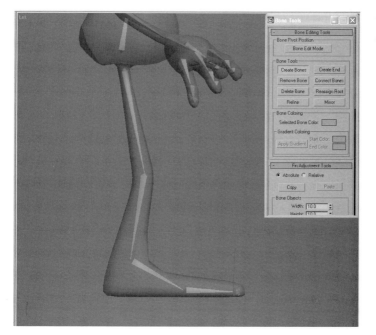

figure | 3-27 |

Skeleton for the leg after step 4.

figure | 3-28 |

The leg chain you have created should resemble this.

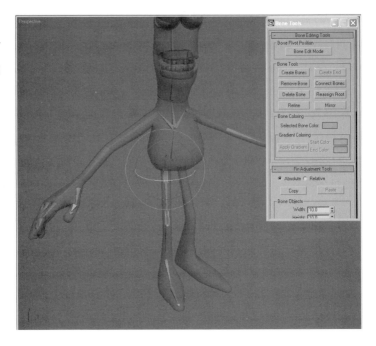

Naming the Leg Chain

Now we need to rename the leg chain.

1. Select *Bone01*. In the Modify panel, change the name from *Bone01* to *Bone_Right_Leg_1*. Select and rename the bones of the chain as follows:

   - *Bone02* to *Bone_Right_Leg_2*

   - *Bone03* to *Bone_Right_Foot_1*

   - *Bone 04* to *Bone_Right_Foot_2*

   - *Bone05* to *Bone_Right_Toe*

Mirroring the Leg

Now that the skeleton for the right leg has been created, let's mirror it for the left side of our character.

1. In the Perspective viewport, select all bones in the right leg. In the Bone Tools dialog box, click the Mirror button. The Bone Mirror dialog box will appear, and the leg should be mirrored but not properly placed in the character's mesh.

2. We need to adjust the leg bones using the Offset attribute in the Bone Mirror dialog box. Click in the Offset field and set it

to about 60. The leg should now be perfectly positioned in the character's mesh. Click OK to continue.

The only thing left to do for the leg chains is to rename the duplicated bones of the left leg. To fit our naming convention, replace the word "*Right*" with "*Left.*" The skeleton should be similar to that shown in Figure 3-29.

Now that we have completed the skeleton, we are ready to start creating some controls for it. Before we do so, we need to discuss two key concepts regarding how these controls will work. These concepts are forward kinematics and inverse kinematics (often referred to as FK and IK), which will play a crucial role in controlling the manipulation of our character's skeleton.

INVERSE KINEMATICS VERSUS FORWARD KINEMATICS

Forward kinematics controls a chain of bones from the top of that chain's hierarchy. Inverse kinematics controls a chain of bones from the bottom of that chain's hierarchy. To demonstrate the differences between forward and inverse kinematics we are going to be using 3ds Max's Bones system to create a chain of bones.

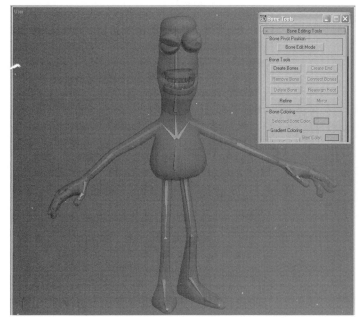

figure | 3-29

Skeleton at this point.

The bones in this chain will create a hierarchy that revolves around a parent/child relationship. Figure 3-30 illustrates the fact that when we animate this chain using the Forward Kinematics feature, the source of the movement is at the top of the hierarchy. For instance, to rotate an entire arm chain, simply rotate the upper arm bone (named *Bicep*) and the forearm and hand bones will move along with it.

This type of movement is much like human locomotion, which is based on arcs. Note the difference in Figure 3-31 when we animate the chain using the Inverse Kinematics feature.

figure | 3-30

Source of movement at the top of the hierarchy.

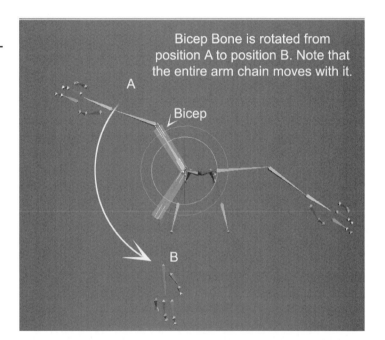

Bicep Bone is rotated from position A to position B. Note that the entire arm chain moves with it.

A

Bicep

B

figure | 3-31

Movement more human-looking after chain animated with Inverse Kinematics.

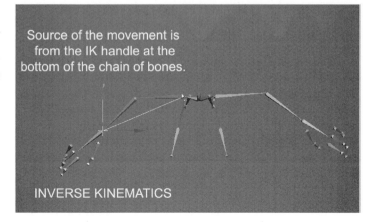

Source of the movement is from the IK handle at the bottom of the chain of bones.

INVERSE KINEMATICS

The source of the movement comes from the bottom of the hierarchy. If the hand of the character is moved, all bones up the chain leading to the shoulder rotate and realign in relation to the position of the hand. Another important fact to be aware of when using IK is that the movement is linear and not based on arcs (see Figure 3-32).

Let's take a closer look at FK. Figure 3-33 shows a chain of bones that make up a character's arm.

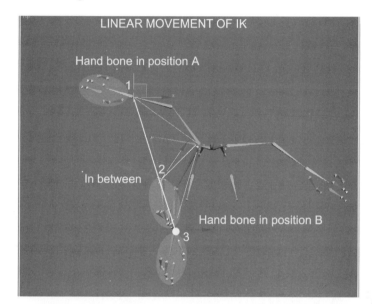

figure | 3-32 |

Using the Inverse
Kinematics feature.

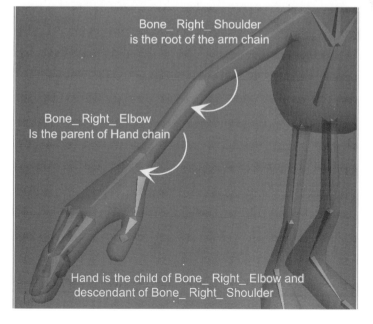

figure | 3-33 |

Chain of bones
constituting the
character's arm.

The first bone in this chain is placed within the bicep of the character's mesh. The bicep bone sits at the top of the chain's hierarchy and is the parent of all other bones in the chain. The second bone in the arm is placed within the forearm of our character and is the child of the bicep bone. The rest of the bones in the chain comprise the hand of our character and are children of the forearm and bicep. By selecting Schematic View you will have a better picture of these parent/child relationships (see Figure 3-34).

This hierarchy of bones is animated by rotating parents in the chain, which are followed by the children of these parent bones. Note in Figure 3-35, for example, that when the bicep bone is rotated the forearm and the hand rotate with it.

figure | 3-34 |

The schematic view gives a visual display of the hierarchy that makes up the character's arm chain.

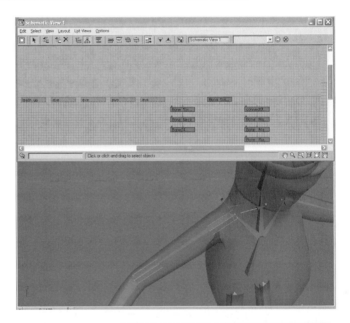

figure | 3-35 |

Forearm and hand rotate with the bicep.

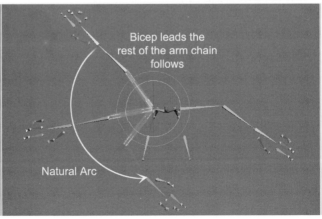

This type of movement is known as forward kinematics. Now let's take the same chain of bones and animate it using inverse kinematics. To do this we will need a tool called an IK handle. The IK handle starts at the shoulder with a line (*vector*), which ends at a crosshair at the wrist. We will refer to the crosshair as a *goal*, which is the attribute of the IK handle used to animate the chain of bones. Note that the goal of the IK handle sits close to the bottom of the chain's hierarchy.

The goal determines how the bicep and forearm bones will rotate during animation, canceling out the parent/child relationship of FK. Thus, the source of the movement in IK comes from the bottom of the chain's hierarchy. Note in Figure 3-36 that when the arm is animated using the IK handle it moves from point A to point B in a linear fashion and has to be manually arced.

So the question is, when do you use FK and when do you use IK to animate your character? A good rule of thumb to follow is that IK is the preferred method of animation when you are creating target animation, or when two surfaces are going to come into contact with each other in 3D space. For example, if your character is going to walk up to a door and open it, you would want to put an IK handle in the character's arm.

Another example would be the feet of a character touching the ground in a walk cycle. This would require IK handles in the legs

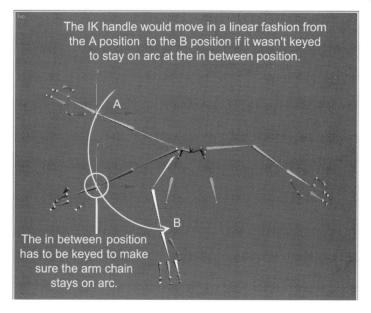

The IK handle would move in a linear fashion from the A position to the B position if it wasn't keyed to stay on arc at the in between position.

A

B

The in between position has to be keyed to make sure the arm chain stays on arc.

figure | **3-36**

Arm moves in a linear fashion from point A to point B.

and feet of the character. However, let's say that during this walk-cycle animation the only thing the arms are going to be doing is swinging back and forth to counterbalance the character. The arms in this case should be animated using FK, not IK. FK has the advantage of being naturally arced. It also provides more control over things such as drag and overlap.

Now that we have a basic understanding of FK and IK, let's put this knowledge to work in our rig. We will begin this process by creating IK controllers for the feet and legs of our character.

Creating IK Handles for the Right Leg

Creating a setup for our character's legs has the potential to become complex. This is due to the fact that the foot must stay planted on the ground even when the body is moving. In addition, when a character is walking, the foot rotates off the heel of the foot, then the ball of the foot, and finally the toe. To accomplish this, we need multiple IK controllers on the foot.

The most common and basic foot control is created via 3 IK Foot Setup. The 3 IK Foot Setup function creates a functional rig for animating feet. However, setting up this rig can be a complicated process. The first step in creating a rig using 3 IK Foot Setup is generating the IK chains. In this example, we are going to create an IK 1 at the ankle, IK 2 at the ball of the foot, and IK 3 at the toe.

When creating IK handles, it is imperative that the bones are not in a straight line. The IK needs to have the angle to solve from. In this example, we want to make sure the knee is bent slightly so that the IK handle knows what angle to solve from for the knee to bend properly.

▶ History-independent Solvers

HI solvers (history-independent solvers) are the recommended IK solver when creating animation. HI solvers' algorithm is history independent. With a history-independent solver, you can create long animation sequences without slowing down the IK due to calculation time. HD solvers (history-dependent solvers) are only recommended for short animations because the HD solvers' algorithm is calculated from the start frame. With an HD solver, the longer the animation sequence the slower the HD solver will become.

1. Go to the Left viewport to create the first IK. Select *Bone_Right_Leg_1*. With *Bone_Right_Leg_1* highlighted, go to 3ds Max's main menu and select Animation > IK Solvers > HI Solver. You will then see a dotted line from the top of *Bone_Right_Leg_1*. Drag the mouse down to *Bone_Right_Foot_1* and click the left mouse button. You have now created the first of three IK handles for the foot rig.

2. Test the IK handle we have placed on the ankle. Select and move the IK handle. If it is working properly the leg will move with it. When finished, press Ctrl+Z to reset the position of the leg bones, as shown in Figure 3-37.

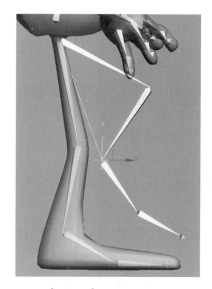

figure | 3-37 |

Test IK chain using Ctrl-Z to reset bone to original location.

It is important to frequently test IK chains as you work. That way, if something goes wrong it will be easier to determine the reason for the mistake.

Now we are going to create the second and third IK chains.

1. Select *Bone_Right_Foot_1*. With *Bone_Right_Foot_1* highlighted, select Animation > IK Solvers > HI Solver, drag the mouse over *Bone_Right_Foot_2*, and click the left mouse button once. This will give you the second IK on the ball of the foot.

2. Repeat the previous step and create an IK from *Bone_Right_Foot_2* to *Bone_Right_Toe*. Rename *IK Chain01, 02,* and *03*, respectively, as follows (see Figure 3-38):

   ● *IK Chain_Right_Heel*

   ● *IK Chain_Right_Ball*

   ● *IK Chain_Right_Toe*

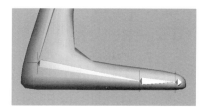

figure | 3-38 |

Placement of the IK solvers on right foot.

Now that we have created all three IK handles for our foot rig, we need to generate controllers for the bones and IKs, but first, let's finish up the IK handles on the left leg.

Creating IK Handles for the Left Leg

Repeat the process for creating IKs for the left leg, using the same naming convention:

- *IK Chain_Left_Heel*
- *IK Chain_Left_Ball*
- *IK Chain_Left_Toe*

Creating the Iconic Controllers

Creating iconic controllers is a vital step in creating a character rig. The controllers are objects on the rig that allow you to easily select and key various aspects of a character's setup. Specifically, we will be creating controllers that will be used to manipulate the entire skeleton. We will create a controller that is the parent of all bones in our skeleton, normally referred to as *Root*. Then we will generate two more controllers, which will allow us to manipulate the hips and feet of our rig.

1. Let's get started by creating the controller that will be the parent of all bones in our rig. Go to the Top viewport by pressing the T key. Click the Zoom Extents button to the view the entire character.

2. In 3ds Max's main menu, go to Create > Shapes > Star, and left mouse click and drag from the center of the character's head until you see a star shape appear. Release the left mouse button once the shape surrounds the body of the character. Then it will be necessary to left mouse click again to adjust the second radius of the star. Try to make the star shape resemble that shown in Figure 3-39.

figure | 3-39 |

Shape desired for the star.

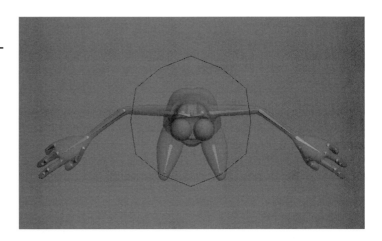

3. With the shape still selected in the Create panel, rename it *Ctrl_Root*. Go ahead and change the color of the shape to black by clicking in the color swatch next to the Name field.

4. Finally, we need to adjust the star's parameters. In the Create panel, click in the Radius 1 and 2 fields and set them both to *140*. The *Root* control is now complete.

5. We will be repeating this same process to create a new control for the hips. Create a second star shape that is smaller than the *Root* control by adjusting the radius fields. They should be set to something like *120*, and do not forget to rename the control to *Ctrl_Hip* and to change the color to black.

6. Switch to a Perspective viewport and move the *Ctrl_Hip* and *Ctrl_Root* controls down around the waist of the character. *Ctrl_Hip* should be closer to the legs than *Ctrl_Root*, as illustrated in Figure 3-40.

Linking the Legs to the Hip Control

To link the legs to the Hip control, perform the following steps;

1. Select *Bone_Right_Leg_1* and activate the Link tool. Left mouse click and drag the cursor over the *Hip* control and release the

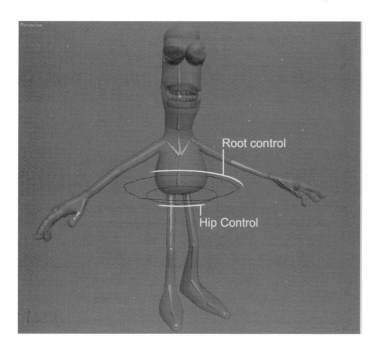

figure | **3-40** |

Ctrl_Hip should be closer to the legs than Ctrl_Root.

Position Constraints

A position constraint allows you to constrain the position of an object to another object. This constraint will enable us to restrict the Hip control's movement to the Root control's movement but not its rotation or scale. The advantage of the position constraint is that it gives us more control when animating by having the ability to rotate the upper and lower part of the character's rig independently.

mouse button to create the parent/child link. *Bone_Right_Leg_1* should now be a child of the *Hip* control. Test this by rotating the *Hip* control. *Bone_Right_Leg_1* should rotate with it. Undo the rotation and deactivate everything.

2. *Select Bone_Left_Leg_1* and activate the Link tool. Left mouse click and drag the cursor over the *Hip* control and release the mouse button to create the parent/child link. *Bone_Left_Leg_1* should now be a child of the *Hip* control. Test this by rotating the *Hip* control.

Now that we have the leg chains linked to the *Hip* control, the next thing we need to do is position-constrain the *Hip* control to the *Root* control.

Constraining the Hip Control

To constrain the Hip control, perform the following steps.

1. In the Top viewport, select *Ctrl_Hip* and in 3ds Max's main menu go to Animation > Constraints > Position Constraint. Drag the cursor over the *Root* control. A crosshair should appear at this point.

2. When you see the crosshair, click the left mouse button. A box will flash, highlighting *Ctrl_Root*. This is an indication that the position constraint has been created.

3. Note that the *Hip* control shifted to align itself with the *Root* control. We need to reset the *Hip* control to its original position.

4. The Motion panel will appear by default when the position constraint is created. Go to the check box named Keep Initial Offset (the last field in the panel, at the bottom) and check it. Note that the *Hip* control is still constrained to the Root control but snaps back to its original position.

Creating Foot Controls

To create controls for the feet, perform the following steps:

1. Make sure you are in the Left viewport. Select Create > Shapes
   > Text from the menu system. Go to the Modify panel and in
   the Parameters rollout replace *MAX Text* with the letter *H* and
   click the left mouse button anywhere in the Left viewport.

2. In the Parameters rollout, change the Size from 100 to *60* and
   change the default color to black. Rename *Text01* to *Ctrl_
   Right_Heel*. Repeat the process and create another helper with
   the letter T. In the Text Parameters rollout, set the color to black
   and rename the letter T *Ctrl_Right_Toe* (see Figure 3-41).

3. Go to Create > Shapes > Circle. Create a circle in the Left viewport, and in the Create panel change the Radius of the circle to
   approximately 30 units. Rename *Circle* to *Ctrl_Right_Circle_Toe*.

4. Now we will create the main foot control, so move to the Top
   viewport by pressing the T key. Go to Create > Shapes >
   Rectangle and simply click and drag to create a rectangle over
   the right foot. The size of the rectangle should be the size of the
   right foot. Change the name *Rectangle01* to *Ctrl_Right_Foot*
   and set the color to black.

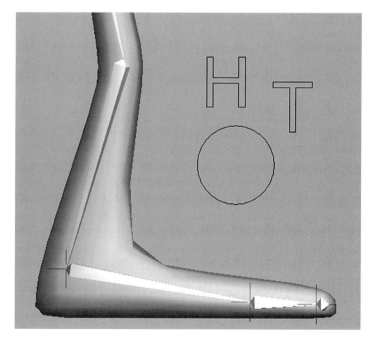

figure | **3-41**

Settings in the Text
Parameters rollout.

5. Go to the Left viewport and move *Ctrl_Right_Foot* to the bottom of the character's right foot (see Figure 3-42). Now that we have created shapes that will be the iconic controllers for our foot, we need to adjust their pivot points.

Adjusting the Pivot Points for the Iconic Controllers

Moving the pivot points for the controllers is an important step for our character's setup. Moving the pivot points changes the placement of rotation for the helpers. For our foot rig, we want to move the pivot for *Ctrl_Right_Heel* and *Ctrl_Right_Toe* to the center of our foot, and move the pivot for *Ctrl_Right_Foot* to the back of the character's heel.

1. In the Left viewport, click *Ctrl_Right_Heel*. Go to the Hierarchy panel and in the Hierarchy rollout activate the Pivot button and select the Affect Pivot Only button (see Figure 3-43).

figure | **3-42** |

Placement of
Ctrl_Right_Foot in
the Left viewport.

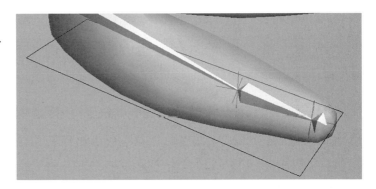

figure | **3-43** |

Adjust the pivot
point to the center
of the controller.

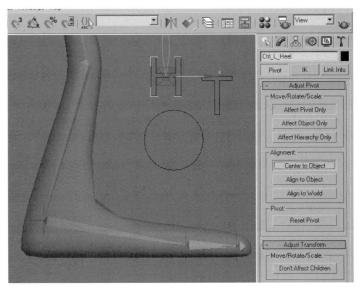

2. Within the same rollout, click the Center to Object button. The pivot of *Ctrl_Right_Heel* is now in the center of the H. In the Left viewport, select *Ctrl_Right_Foot*. With the Affect Pivot Only button highlighted, select and move the pivot point to the back of the heel (see Figure 3-44). Deactivate the Affect Pivot Only button.

Aligning Iconic Controllers

Now that we have all pivot points placed properly, we need to align and link our controllers. Before we link the IK chains to the iconic controllers, we must align the iconic controllers to the foot. We are going to use the Align tool to execute this function. The Align tool is located on the main toolbar next to the Layer Manager tool, as shown in Figure 3-45.

1. Select the *Ctrl_Right_Heel* control and click the Align tool.

2. At the ball of the foot, select the IK chain *IK Chain_Right_Ball*. The *Ctrl_Right_Heel* control should move to the center of the IK chain, as shown in Figure 3-46. In the Align Selection dialog, set

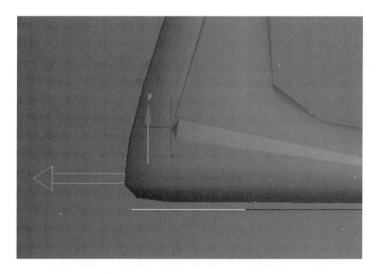

figure | 3-44

Adjust the pivot point of Ctrl_Right_Foot to the back of the controller.

figure | 3-45

Location of the Align tool.

the X, Y, and Z Position options to Pivot Point for both objects. Click OK to continue. Repeat this process to align the circle controller named *Ctrl_Right_Circle_Toe* to *IK Chain_Right_Ball*, as shown in Figure 3-46.

3. Move to the Top viewport and select *Ctrl_Right_Circle_Toe* and *Ctrl_Right_Heel*. Rotate both controllers so that the axes of the two helpers are aligned with the foot bones, as shown in Figure 3-47.

figure | 3-46 |

Align Ctrl_Right_Heel and Ctrl_Right_Circle_Toe with IKChain_Right_Ball.

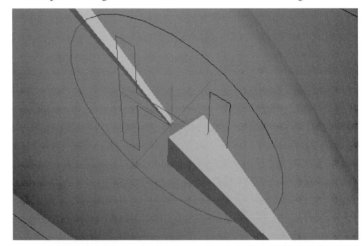

figure | 3-47 |

Rotate Ctrl_Right_ Heel and Ctrl_Right_ Circle_Toe to align with the foot bones.

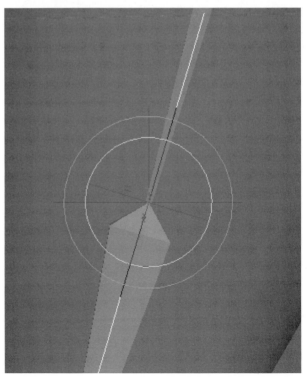

4. Go to the Left viewport and move *Ctrl_Right_Toe* to the toe of the foot.

5. Move to the Top viewport and rotate *Ctrl_Right_Toe* so that the controller is aligned with the foot bones.

6. Select and align *Ctrl_Right_Foot* with the foot bones, as shown in Figure 3-48.

Linking Iconic Controllers

The final step in the foot setup is linking the IKs to the helpers. To link the IKs, perform the following steps:

1. Link *IK Chain_Right_Heel* to *Ctrl_Right_Heel*.

2. Link *IK Chain_Right_Ball* to *Ctrl_Right_Heel* (see Figure 3-49).

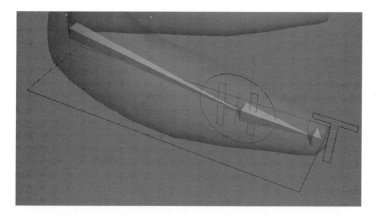

figure | **3-48**

Foot controllers are now aligned with the foot bones.

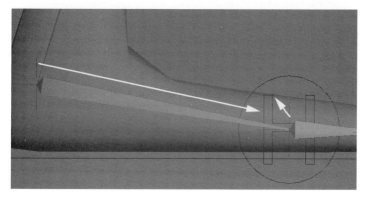

figure | **3-49**

Links established.

3. Link *IK Chain_Right_Toe* to *Ctrl_Right_Circle_Toe* (see Figure 3-50).

To link the iconic controllers, perform the following steps:

1. Link *Ctrl_Right_Heel* to *Ctrl_Right_Toe*.

2. Link *Ctrl_Right_Circle_Toe* to *Ctrl_Right_Toe* (see Figure 3-51).

3. Link *Ctrl_Right_Toe* to *Ctrl_Right_Foot* (see Figure 3-52).

figure | **3-50** |

IK_Chain_Right_Toe
linked to
Ctrl_Right_Circle_Toe.

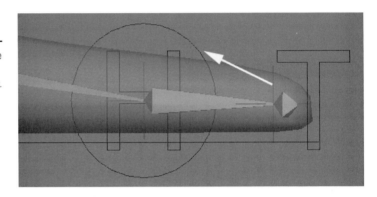

figure | **3-51** |

Links established for
iconic controllers.

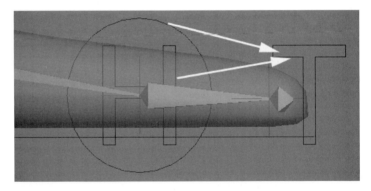

figure | **3-52** |

Ctrl_Right_Toe
linked to
Ctrl_Right_Foot.

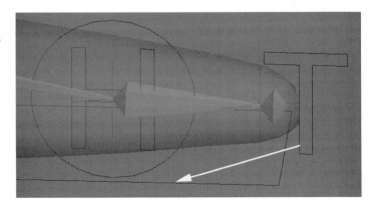

Testing the Controllers

You now have four controls for moving the foot:

- *Ctrl_Right_Heel* moves the heel up and down.

- *Ctrl_Right_Circle_Toe* moves the toe up and down.

- *Ctrl_Right_Toe* moves the foot with the rotate pivot point at the toe.

- *Ctrl_Right_Foot* moves the foot with the rotate pivot point at the heel.

To test the controls, perform the following:

1. To move the knee from side to side, select *IK Chain_ Right_ Heel*.

2. In the Motion Panel > IK Solver Properties rollout, move the spinner arrows for the Swivel Angle field and the knee will move from side to side.

Locking Down Controllers

To minimize the chance of breaking the rig when animating, it is a good idea to lock down rotations or movements of controllers that have undesirable effects. For example, *Ctrl_Right_Circle_Toe* only needs to rotate on the Z local axis. Transforming on X, Y, or Z or rotating on the X or Y axis will result in undesirable effects. Therefore, we want to restrict the movement of that controller. To achieve this, perform the following:

1. Select *Ctrl_Right_Circle_Toe*.

2. In the Hierarchy panel, click the Link Info button.

3. In the Move window, put a check in the boxes for X, Y, and Z.

4. In the Rotate window, put a check in the boxes for X and Y only.

5. Repeat steps 1 through 4 for *Ctrl_Right_Heel* so that you can only rotate the control in the local Z axis, as shown in Figure 3-53.

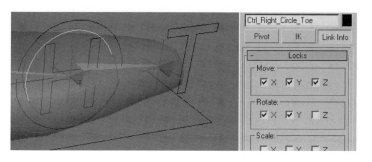

figure | 3-53 |

Lock down Ctrl_Right_Circle_Toe so that you can only rotate it in the Z axis.

Creating Controls for the Left Foot

To create controls for the left foot, you would repeat the process of creating the controls for the right foot. Make sure to follow the naming convention.

Using the Skin Modifier

Skinning the character is an important process for character setup. Skinning the character is the process of making the mesh move with the bones. To do this, we are going to use the Skin modifier.

The Skin modifier influences any vertex on a mesh to any bones you choose. In addition, you can set the amount of influence of any vertex to several bones by a percentage. For example, a vertex around the ankle could be weighted 25 percent to a leg bone and 75 percent to a foot. In this example, the vertex is influenced primarily by the foot bone when animated.

The first way to create weights on your vertices with a Skin modifier is through envelopes. Envelopes are pill-shaped manipulators that help set the amount of influence of vertexes to each bone. Using envelopes is a quick way of weighting vertices. Once the envelopes are adjusted, you can modify individual vertices for improving the skin deformation. Poorly skinned models can cause undesirable effects when animating, so it is important to take the time during setup to skin the character properly.

Creating the Skin Modifier

To apply a Skin modifier, perform the following steps:

1. Continue from the previous exercise, or open *Mr_Blue_Rig_Ready_For_Skin.max*.

▶ Using the Skin Modifier with MeshSmooth

When using the Skin modifier with MeshSmooth, it is best to place the Skin modifier beneath MeshSmooth in the modifier stack. In this order, the Skin modifier drives the low-poly mesh and not the high-poly MeshSmooth. The more vertices the Skin modifier needs to calculate for weighting purposes the slower your file will become. In addition, you can turn off MeshSmooth to speed up working with the file and then turn it back on when you want to render.

2. In the Front viewport, right-click and select Unfreeze All. The mesh can now be edited. A dialog box may appear, stating, "This will unfreeze all objects. Do you want to unfreeze all layers as well?" Click Yes.

3. Under Modify panel > Modifier List > Skin, select the body. The Skin modifier is now added to the mesh.

4. In the Modifier list, move the Skin modifier to a position beneath MeshSmooth Modifier. To do this, click and drag Skin in the modifier stack so that it is beneath MeshSmooth (see Figure 3-54).

Adding Bones to the Skin Modifier

To add bones to the skin modifier, perform the following steps:

1. In the modifier stack, select Skin. In the Parameters rollout, select Add. The Select Bones dialog box will appear. Select all bones in the Select Bones dialog box except *Bone_Head* and *Bone_Neck*.

2. In the Modifier list, select the plus sign next to Skin to expand the modifier. In the Parameters rollout, select Edit Envelopes (see Figure 3-55).

Envelopes are a quick visual way of controlling and manipulating the weights of vertices on the mesh. Generally, envelopes are pill shaped

figure | **3-54**

The Skin modifier should be placed beneath the MeshSmooth modifier.

<figure>figure **3-55**</figure>

Location of edit envelopes in the skin modifier.

and each has an inner and outer ring. Each bone has an envelope. In general, the larger the envelope on a bone the more influence the envelope will have on nearby vertices. As the level of influence increases on the vertexes, the vertex will change in color from blue to red. Overlapping envelopes will average the weight of their influence on a given vertex by proximity to each influenced envelope. For example, an ankle may have a lower leg bone envelope and a foot bone envelope that both overlap at the ankle. The vertices in the overlapping area will be influenced by location. The vertices closer to the foot will be influenced more by the foot envelope due to it proximity. In general, you want to overlap envelopes around joints or other areas of the mesh that deform.

Editing the Envelopes

To edit the envelopes, perform the following steps.

1. With Edit Envelopes activated, select *Bone_Right_Shoulder*. Once the bone is selected, the envelope for that bone will be displayed (see Figure 3-56).

   If you look closely, you will notice that the envelope consists of an inner and outer ring. At two locations on the rings are circles with four small squares on them. The four squares on the circles are manipulators that change the size of the envelope. In addition, you will see two additional squares in the center of the envelope on both sides. The two in the center are manipulators that move the envelope.

2. Adjust the envelope by moving the manipulators so that the envelope looks like that shown in Figure 3-57.

3. Rotate *Bone_Right_Shoulder* to examine the deformation of the skin. As you can see, the skin around the upper arm moves with the bone. However, the skin around the hands is not working because the envelopes need to be adjusted (see Figure 3-58). To move the arm, you must exit Envelope mode. Undo your rotation actions to move the arm back to its original location.

4. Continue adjusting the envelopes on the right hand and fingers. The mesh starts to turn red as you increase the size of the envelope, signaling that the envelope will influence the mesh. Once you have adjusted the envelopes on the right hand and fingers, test the skin by moving the arm and hand (see Figure 3-59).

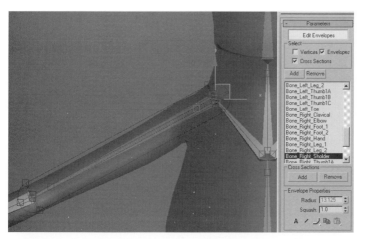

figure | 3-56 |

Envelope for bone.

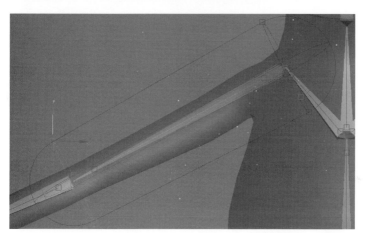

figure | 3-57 |

Adjustment to envelope by moving the manipulators.

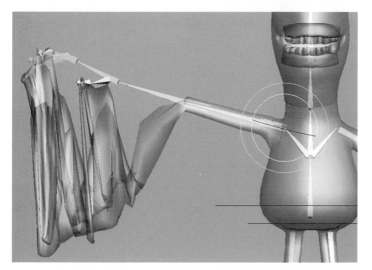

figure | 3-58 |

The envelopes around the hand need to be adjusted.

figure | 3-59 |

Adjusting the
envelopes for the
right arm.

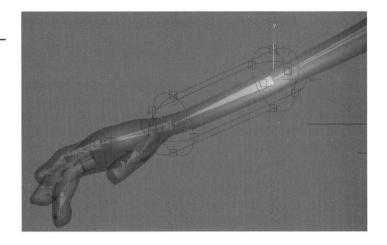

▶ Temporary Animation When Editing Envelopes

When editing envelopes, it is a good idea to put some temporary animation on
the bones to test the deformation of the skin. Putting animation on the bones
helps in two ways. First, it sets the position for the bind pose, allowing you to
return to the original pose after moving the bones around. Second, it speeds up
editing the envelopes and painting (i.e., establishing, discussed in the section
following) weights because you can see the way the skin reacts to the movement without having to exit Edit Envelopes mode to rotate the bones.

Painting Weights for the Hand

As you rotate the hand, you will notice that some of the vertices are
not deforming properly, as shown in Figure 3-60.

To fix these types of problems, we are going to use the Paint Weights
tool. The Paint Weights tool is a quick visual way of editing the
weight of vertices.

1. Select the mesh and press Alt+X to exit See-Through mode.
   Now it should be easier to examine the weighted colors on the
   envelopes.

2. In the Skin modifier's Parameters rollout, select Edit Envelopes.

3. Select *Bone_Right_Hand*. The hand should turn red and yellow.

4. Select the Paint Weights button at the bottom of the Parameters
   rollout. Click the small button with the three dots (ellipsis) next to

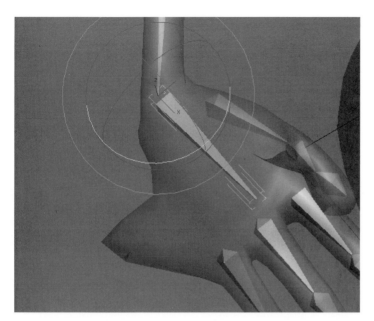

figure | 3-60 |

The envelopes around the hand need to be adjusted.

it to open the Painter Options dialog box. In the Painter Options dialog box, change the brush's Max Size to *30* (see Figure 3-61).

5. To paint weights, simply click and hold down the left mouse button and move the paint brush cursor over the area for which you want to increase vertex weights (see Figure 3-62).

Editing Envelopes for the Spine and Rest of the Body

For the spine, you may want to add cross sections in the envelope to modify the shape to conform more closely to the shape of the body. To add a cross section in an envelope, select the Add button in the Cross

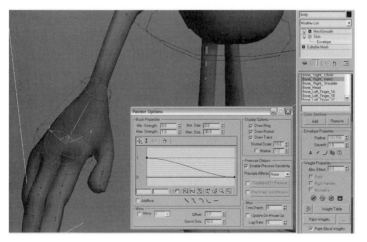

figure | 3-61 |

Adjusting the envelopes for the right hand.

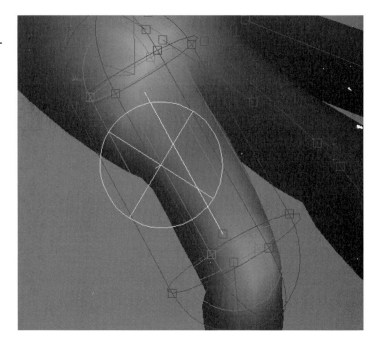

Sections area of the Parameters rollout. Once the Add button is selected, you can click on the yellow center line of the envelope to add cross sections (see Figure 3-63). Make sure to deactivate the Add button when finished. Continue editing envelopes for the rest of the body.

Weighing Individual Vertices Manually

After adjusting envelopes and painting weights, often you will find a few vertices that are not deforming properly. To fix this, we are going to manually set the weight for these vertices.

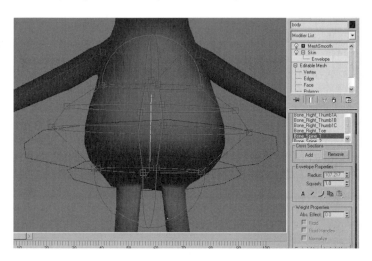

Figure 3-64 shows two vertices that are weighted too much to the leg bone. In this example, we want the two vertices to have more influence on the foot and less on the leg. To see the vertices better, we deleted the MeshSmooth modifier on the body and will add it back later. Sometimes when editing vertices it is easier to view the mesh in Edge Faces mode. To switch to Edge Faces mode, press F4.

To adjust the vertices manually, perform the following steps:

1. Select the body. In the modifier stack, delete MeshSmooth.

2. Select Edit Envelopes in the Skin modifier.

3. In the Envelope Parameters rollout, check the box for Select Vertices.

4. Select *Bone_Right_Foot_1*.

5. Click-drag the mouse over the vertices you want to modify.

6. In the Parameters rollout > Weight Properties section, you will see a field labeled Abs Effect. In the Abs Effect box, type *0.9* (see Figure 3-65).

Facial Rigging

For the character's head, we are going to use the same tools as used for the body. If you look closely, you will see that the teeth and eyes are

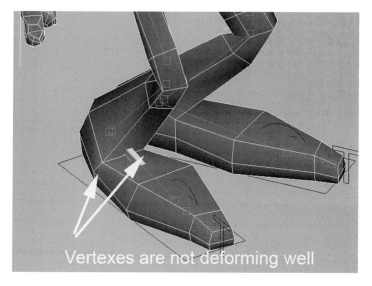

figure | **3-64** |

Two vertices weighted too much to the leg bone.

figure | 3-65 |

Setting two vertices manually to have 90% influence from Bone_Right_Foot.

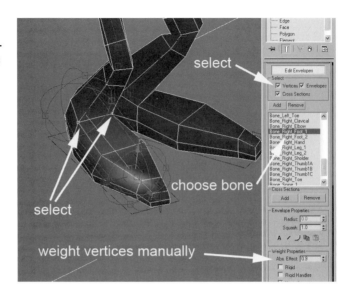

select

choose bone

select

weight vertices manually

pieces of geometry independent of the head. To rig the head, we are going to use the Skin modifier and link the teeth and eyes to *Bone_Head*.

Linking Teeth

To link the teeth, perform the following steps:

1. Use the Layer menu to freeze the *head*.

2. Link *teeth_up* to *Bone_Head*.

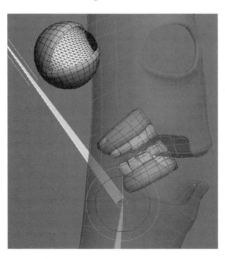

figure | 3-66 |

Test your linking of eyes and teeth by moving the neck bones.

3. Link *teeth_Dwn* to *Bone_ Head*.

4. Select *teeth_Dwn*. In the Hierarchy panel, click the Link Info button, and lock down Move in XYZ and Rotate in YZ.

5. Repeat steps 1 through 4 for *teeth_up*.

6. Link the eyeballs and eyelids to *Bone_Head*, which will result in six objects total (see Figure 3-66).

Skinning the Head

Use the Skin modifier to skin the head.

1. Unfreeze the head.

2. Add the Skin modifier to the head.

3. Place the Skin modifier beneath the MeshSmooth modifier, as shown in Figure 3-67.

4. Add *Bone_Head*, *Bone_Neck*, and *Bone_Spline_2* to the Skin modifier.

5. Adjust the envelopes and paint weights. On the bottom row of vertices on the head, manually weight the vertices at 100 percent to *Bone_Spine_2*. That way you will not get a crease between the head and body (see Figure 3-68).

figure | **3-67** |

Move the Skin modifier to a position beneath the MeshSmooth modifier.

Creating Iconic Controllers for the Head

The head is now fully functional. However, you may want to add iconic controllers to the head. That way you can select it faster when animating. Also, we can set up the eyes to always look at an object.

1. In the Front viewport, create three dummies and move them so that they match Figure 3-69. To create a dummy object (which is the same as an iconic controller), go to Create > Helpers > Dummy.

2. Select *Bone_Head*. In the main menu, select Animation > Constraints > Orientation Constraint. Constrain *Head_Bone*

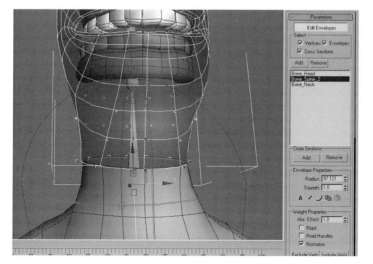

figure | **3-68** |

Make sure the bottom row of vertices is weighted 100% to Bone_Spine_2.

figure | 3-69 |

Creating the head
controllers.

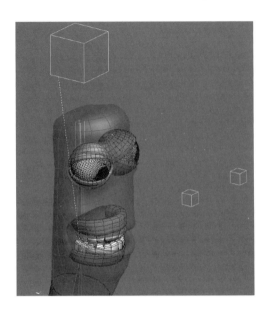

to the new dummy over the head. Make sure to check the box
Keep Initial Offset, which is in the Orientation Constraint
rollout.

3. Select *Eye*. Under the main menu, select Animation >
   Constraints > LookAt Constraint. Constrain *Right Eyeball* to
   the new dummy in front of the eye. Make sure to check the box
   Keep Initial Offset, which is in the LookAt Constraint rollout.

4. Repeat steps 1 through 3 for *Left Eyeball*.

The Morpher Modifier

The Morpher modifier lets you change the shape of one object
into the shape of another. When rigging a character, this modifier
is great for facial animation. Setting up a face's attitude, expressions, and phonemes can be achieved quickly and easily with this
tool. In this example, we will use the Morpher modifier to make
Mr. Blue smile.

1. Open the file *Chapter03/Mr_Blue_Rig_Morpher.max*.

2. In the Perspective viewport, select just the head of the character.
   It is the only piece of geometry to which we will be applying the
   Morpher modifier.

3. With the head still selected, activate the Move tool, hold down the Shift key, and move the head along the X axis to create a copy of it. Make sure to copy only the head (*not* the teeth or eyes) of Mr. Blue.

4. The Clone Options box will appear. Make sure to select Copy (not Instance or Reference) and name the duplicate head *Smile*. This name will be important when we apply the Morpher modifier to the original head.

5. With Smile still selected, right-click in the viewport and a quad menu should appear. From this menu, select Hide Unselected. The only thing you should see in the Perspective viewport is *Smile*. The rest of the geometry should be hidden. This will allow us to more easily focus on the job of modeling our new target shape.

6. Press the L key to move to the Left viewport, and then press the Z key to zoom extents around Smile. Now we are ready to create the target shape for the Morpher modifier.

7. Right-click in the Left viewport, and from the quad menu select the Vertex option (see Figure 3-70). This will allow us to access and adjust the surface points (vertices) of the duplicated head.

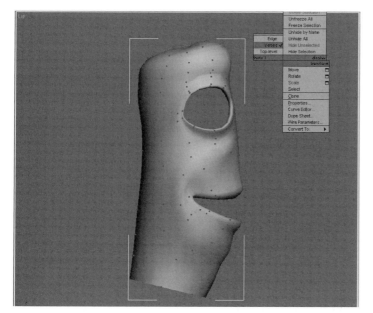

figure | 3-70 |

Vertex option.

8. This next step is a little tricky, as you can see the vertices have now shown up as small dots all over the duplicated head. Activate the Select Object tool and click and drag a marquee around the vertices that surround the top edge of the mouth. When the vertices are selected, they will indicate this by changing to a red color, as shown in Figure 3-71.

9. It is important to note that you need to marquee select the vertices, not select them individually. By marquee selecting the vertices through the geometry of the head, you are able to adjust the vertices on both sides of the head symmetrically. You can double-check that you have selected the vertices correctly by going to the Perspective viewport and checking that the reciprocal vertices on both sides of Smile are highlighted red. If they are not, go back to the Left viewport and deselect the vertices by clicking on nothing and repeating step 8.

10. Once you are satisfied with the your selection of the vertices, we need to manipulate these vertices with the Move, Rotate, and Scale tools until it appears as though Mr. Blue is smiling. First, we will move the vertices up in the Y axis.

11. In the Left viewport, with the vertices still selected, activate the Move tool. Move the vertices up in the Y axis until you see them collide with the unselected vertices that surround Mr. Blue's lower eye. The surface surrounding the selection of vertices should buckle and crease just slightly.

figure | 3-71 |

Vertices indicating that they are selected.

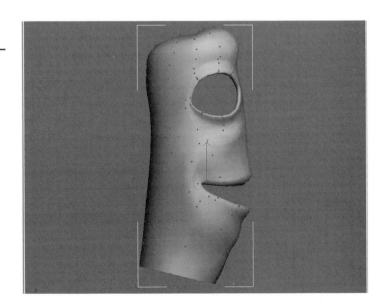

12. Activate the Rotate tool by pressing the E key and rotate the selection of vertices until it appears as though Mr. Blue is smiling, as shown in Figure 3-72.

13. Activate the Scale tool and then scale the selection of vertices in the X axis to widen the grin slightly. This should finish the target shape for *Smile* and prepare us for the Morpher modifier.

14. Deactivate everything and right-click to access the fly-out quad menu again. Select Unhide All. The geometry of Mr. Blue previously hidden should reappear. In the Modify panel, select Editable Mesh to get out of vertex sub-object mode.

15. Select the original head of Mr. Blue and go to the Modify panel. In the Modifier list, select Morpher.

16. The Morpher rollouts will appear in the Modify panel to the right. Scroll down in the Modify panel until you get to the Channel List rollout. Click the Load Multiple Targets button. A selection dialog box will appear and the target shape Smile (which we just modeled) will appear in the list. Select it and click Load, as shown in Figure 3-73.

17. *Smile* will now show up in the selected field within the Channel List rollout in the Modify panel. By adjusting the value next to the *Smile* slider, the face of Mr. Blue will update and smile. The target *Smile* can now be deleted without affecting the Morpher modifier, as indicated in Figure 3-74.

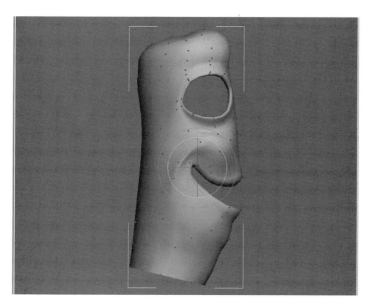

figure | **3-72** |

Vertices rotated to make Mr. Blue smile.

figure | 3-73 |

Load option.

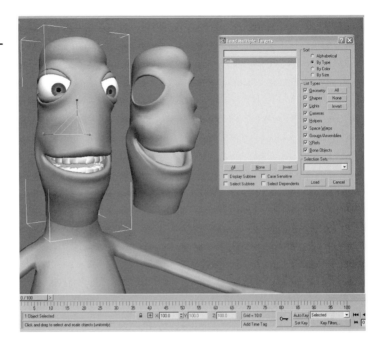

figure | 3-74 |

Smile target can
now be deleted.

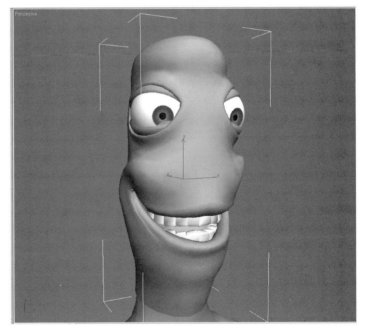

It does not take much imagination to realize the potential the Morpher modifier offers for rigging a face. The possibilities of this modifier are endless. To demonstrate a few examples, we have included a set of phonemes and facial controls in file *Chapter03/Mr_Blue_Rig_Complete.max* on the companion CD-ROM for you to experiment with in your own animations.

SUMMARY

In this chapter we have discussed some key concepts that will help you create an efficient and effective rig in 3ds Max 8. However, the basic concepts covered in this chapter (such as skinning, iconic controls, constraints, and bones) are common in other 3D packages. The knowledge gained in this chapter will help you begin to explore character setup. Remember to storyboard your scene before you rig. Take some time to experiment with a tool once you have learned its use. This will help you create rigs that are eay to animate.

in review

1. What is an edge loop?

2. What role does the Bones system in 3ds Max play when rigging a character?

3. When creating a rig, what are the advantages of using iconic controls?

4. How does an orientation constraint differ from a position constraint?

5. What is the purpose of Schematic View?

6. Define the terms *inverse kinematics* and *forward kinematics.*

7. What is an IK handle and when is it an appropriate tool for use in your rig?

8. What is the Link tool in 3ds Max used for and why would you use it instead of a position or orientation constraint?

9. What does the Morpher modifier do in 3ds Max 8?

↗ EXPLORING ON YOUR OWN

1. Research the human skeletal system and note which joints are ball-and-socket and which are hinge joints. Then apply this knowledge to the next computer-generated character's bone system you create.

2. Research creating sliders to control the movement of fingers. To do this, you will need to research Wire Parameters and the Reaction manager options.

ADVENTURES IN DESIGN

RENDERING TO ELEMENTS

Introduction

Okay, so this does not really have to do with animating per se, but rendering to elements is a technique that can help make compositing complex animation and special effects sequences a lot easier. You will find that when you begin producing very intricate scenes, it may be increasingly difficult to make subtle adjustments to the final frames. Rendering to Elements is a feature within 3ds Max that splits a rendered frame into separate parts. For instance, you can designate certain aspects of your scene to be rendered as individual images, which allows you to render mesh objects, lighting, atmospheric effects, shadows, reflections, mattes, and alpha channels (to name a few of the different types of render separations you can designate).

Tweaking Your Frames

In the animation industry, it is common practice to run the final animation sequences through a postproduction process, which includes scene editing, color adjustments, and compositing. Compositing is a big aspect of postproduction, especially if your 3D animation is being incorporated with live-action film or video footage. In order to composite, you need access to software such as Adobe After Effects or Discreet's Combustion. This software allows you to arrange the rendered aspects of your scene for the final composite as layers, much like a Photoshop document. This enables you to make adjustments to each layer independently, which would be impossible with each frame as a single image.

By splitting each rendered image into multiple aspects, you have much greater control over what the final frame will look like. You can perform color adjustments on the diffuse element, make contrast corrections on reflection elements, increase or decrease opacity on atmospheric elements, or virtually any other type of adjustment you can think of. The bottom line is that greater control over each rendered element will give you a much better look in the resulting composite frame. The best part is that it is very easy to set up a 3D scene to render elements.

Setting Up the Renderer

You may be surprised at how easy it is to set up the 3ds Max renderer to output element images. Within a minute, you can assign the aspects you wish to separate from the complete render.

1. Open the elements.max file from the Render Elements folder within the Adventures in Design directory

of the CD-ROM. You will see our friend, Mr. Blue, standing in a dark stony corridor with some reflective urns behind him, as well as some volumetric fog. We will designate the element separations from this file (see Figure A-1).

2. Go to Rendering > Render to open the Render Scene dialog box.

3. Click the Render Elements tab to access the Elements dialog box.

4. Click the Add button at the top of the Render Elements settings. This will open a small dialog box that will allow you to choose which elements you would like to separate from the scene during render time.

5. From the list, select Atmosphere. Click OK. You should now see Atmosphere in the main Elements settings (see Figure A-2).

6. Repeat step 5 and add Diffuse, Lighting, and Reflection to the Elements list.

7. Now that we have designated the separations we want, we can tell 3ds Max where to save those separations when we render the scene. Highlight one of the elements from the list and within the Selected Element Parameters section found below the main list, click the button with three dots ("..."). This will open a Save dialog box that will enable you to choose an image format for the rendered element. Once you have selected a location to save the file, give it a file name and save it as a .tiff image. Repeat this for the remainder of the elements you designated.

8. At this point, the element separations are set up and we are ready to go. Make sure the Camera view is active, and then click the Render button.

9. Max will first render the frame image as a whole, and then separate the elements into different files once the render is complete. Although this does not necessarily speed up the rendering process, it will provide you more control over the final frame composites during postproduction. The resulting rendered elements can be seen in Figures A-3 through A-6.

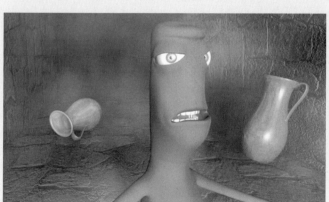

Figure A-1
Rendered frame of the scene with all elements rendered as one image frame.

Now that you know how to output your animations with element separations, as well as how to make adjustments during the compositing process, you will be able to achieve better quality in your final frames.

Figure A-2
Render Elements dialog and Elements list.

Figure A-3
The rendered Diffuse element.

Figure A-4
The rendered
Lighting element.

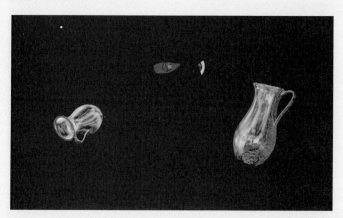

Figure A-5
The rendered
Reflections
element.

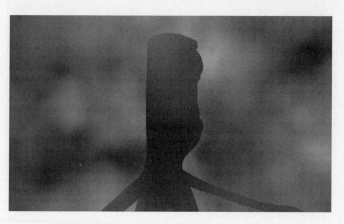

Figure A-6
The rendered
Atmospherics
element.

charting your course

Computer-generated characters can be found in feature films and in advertising, and are most prevalent in the ever-growing field of computer gaming. Movies such as Pixar's *Toy Story*—and games such as "Grand Theft Auto" and "Halo"—would be much less appealing without the realistic movements the characters display throughout the entertainment experience. Character animation has always been an area of computer graphics many artists strive to become proficient at, yet it can be a difficult genre to master. Years are often spent learning the craft of character movement before an artist can consistently create a flowing and accurate series of motions that are realistic. 3ds Max makes this road a bit shorter with the inclusion of Character Studio in its base package.

Character Studio consists of two parts: the Biped system and the Physique modifier. Bipeds are parametrically built, customizable humanoid bone arrangements used as an internal structure for a more complex, high-polygon-count 3D model. You can quickly create an intricate character hierarchy in a matter of a few clicks of the mouse. Bipeds can be complex; for example, they can have five multi-jointed fingers and toes, a long neck, a tail, a ponytail, and even an extra leg joint. They can also be simpler, with a single finger, no tail or ponytails, and normal legs. They can even be created without any arms at all. Bipeds can be customized to match nearly any character configuration you can imagine. Bipeds represent a quick way of creating a hierarchy (i.e., without manually rigging and making IK chains) similar to one that can be created with the Bones system discussed in Chapter 3. Bones, however, can augment any biped to add wings, tusks, or any other attributes the biped does not already have.

Rather than animating the vertex-dense model, the biped is animated. The Physique modifier, similar to the Skin modifier covered in Chapter 3, is the link between the biped and the model. After applying it to the model, the model's vertex locations are driven by their proximity to the biped's structure. As the biped moves, the model deforms to match. You can refine which biped bones control which model vertices through the use of envelopes (the cylindrical pockets that define the limits of a biped bone's influence). Using a biped and the Physique modifier efficiently, you can significantly reduce the time it takes to rig and animate a character.

 *chapter objectives*

- **Understand bipeds**
- **Create and modify a biped**
- **Load and save biped structures**
- **Animate a biped**
- **Load and save animation**
- **Understand the Physique modifier**
- **Skin a model to a biped with the Physique modifier**
- **Adjust bone envelopes**

UNDERSTANDING BIPEDS

To understand a biped, you must understand the concept of hierarchies as they apply in 3ds Max. A hierarchy is an organization of objects linked in parent/child relationships. Take the human arm as an example: the forearm is a child of the upper arm and a parent of the hand. The hand has five child objects, the first bone in each finger, and each of these is a parent as well. Transforms (Move, Rotate, and Scale) applied to a parent object are passed down the chain to their children. This mimics, for example, the fact that when you raise your upper arm until it is parallel to the ground, your forearm, hand, and fingers all raise as well. The terminology used in hierarchies is similar to the terminology used in a family tree or flow chart.

- *Parent:* An object whose transforms control one or more child objects.

- *Child:* An object that receives the transforms by a parent object. A child can also be a parent to several other objects, but it can only have one parent.

- *Ancestor:* A parent object two or more levels above a child object. In a biped, the upper arm and clavicle are both ancestors of the hand and finger links.

- *Descendant:* A child object two or more levels below a parent. The head is a descendant of the spine links in a biped.

- *Root:* The object that resides at the top of the hierarchical tree and has no parent object.

Figure 4-1 shows part of a default biped hierarchy as seen in the Controller window of the Curve editor. The *Bip01* object is the hierarchy's root object.

All transforms occur at an object's pivot point. When an object or selection is rotated or scaled, it is rotated about (or scaled from) its pivot point. This is most evident with nonsymmetrical objects or selections. When an object is moved, in reality the pivot point is moved and the surrounding geometry or features move with it. In character animation, the proper location of an object's pivot point location is essential to the success of the transform in a hierarchy. Looking one more time at the human arm example, the upper arm rotates around the shoulder and not the elbow. If the reverse were the case, rotating the upper arm would either detach the arm from the body or lift the body from the ground.

figure 4-1

A biped hierarchy showing parent/child relationships.

Bipeds are preformed hierarchies of objects that initially begin as a humanoid form. They have arms, legs, torsos, necks, heads, and so on, with the parent/child linkage already assembled and the pivot points properly located. Bipeds can have their parameters adjusted at the structure level to establish the number of finger, toe, and leg links (bones); the addition of a ponytail and tail links; height; body type; and several other features. Rather than changing the biped's parameters in the Modify panel, the standard for most other 3ds Max objects, a biped's parameters are modified in the Motion panel. Figure 4-2 shows the four body type choices and their default parameters.

Bipeds can be further modified using the transform tools. These are applied directly on the bone objects to achieve the desired appearance to match the model they will eventually be associated with (via

figure | 4-2 |

The four biped body type options from left to right are Skeleton, Male, Female, and Classic. Classic was the only choice in previous versions of Character Studio.

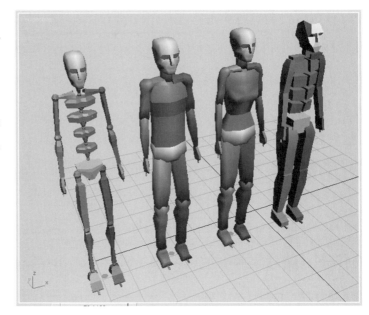

the Physique modifier). When a bone is moved or rotated, it can be done in any transform coordinate system, although Local often gives you the best results. When scaling a bone, the Local transform coordinate system must be used so that the transform axis is relative to the orientation of the bone rather than to the World space. This causes a bone's length to be adjusted when dragging the Z axis handle of the Scale transform gizmo, rather than becoming wider or thicker depending on the bone's initial orientation.

3ds Max assists this process in Figure mode by automatically locking in the Local transform coordinate system whenever a biped object is selected and the Scale transform tool is activated (see Figure 4-3). Figure mode is discussed later in this chapter. In addition to being a structure a model can be associated with, bipeds are easily animated. This animation is passed along to the model.

CREATING AND MODIFYING A BIPED

Rather than being considered geometry, bipeds are a system of objects; therefore, their creation begins with the Systems tab rather than the Geometry tab of the Create panel.

figure | 4-3 |

Using the transform tools, bipeds can be adjusted to resemble almost anything—from a feline-like villain to a barrel-chested hero or even an ostrich.

Creating a Biped and Modifying Its Structure

1. In the Command panel, select Create > Systems and then click the Biped button. The Biped button highlights and the Create Biped rollout (see Figure 4-4) appears, displaying the default parameters.

2. Click in the Perspective viewport to set the location for the biped, and then drag the cursor to set the height (as shown in Figure 4-5). The biped is created using the default parameters, and it is color-coded so that objects on the biped's right side are colored green and objects on its left side are colored blue.

3. At the bottom of the Create Biped rollout are the controls for adjusting the structure of the biped. Increase the number of fingers to four and the number of finger links to three (see Figure 4-6). The second finger added to a biped is always an opposable thumb. This will create the hand structure for a typical four-fingered cartoon character.

NOTE: How many fingers and toes you need will depend on the character and what it is doing. If it is wearing mittens or shoes, or is constantly gripping an object, a single finger and thumb or a single

figure | 4-4 |

The Create Biped rollout appears, displaying the default parameters.

figure | 4-5 |

Click and drag in
the viewport to
create the biped.

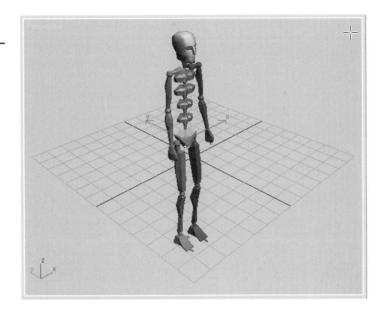

figure | 4-6 |

Adjust the number
of fingers and finger
links for the biped.

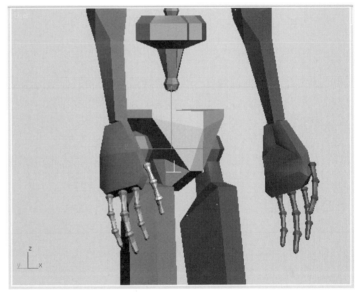

toe may be adequate. The middle finger and toe can be scaled to be wide enough to control the position of the character's remaining digits when fine-motor movements are not required.

4. Deselect the biped and then select it again. Click the Modify panel tab. Where are the biped rollouts and parameters? Unlike most other objects in 3ds Max, the biped controls are not located in the Modify panel but are in the Motion panel. Click

the Motion tab in the Command panel to display the biped's controls.

5. Bipeds are controlled in one of several modes, including Figure mode and Footstep mode. The Figure Mode button must be active whenever a biped's structure or configuration is changed. Any changes to a biped's pose performed when not in Figure mode will be lost when the Figure Mode function is next accessed. This is a common error made by users when they begin working with Character Studio.

6. Click the Figure Mode button at the top of the Biped rollout. The Motion panel adjusts to display the Figure-mode-specific rollouts. Click the plus sign to expand the Structure rollout and reveal the controls for the biped's structure.

7. Add a ponytail by increasing the Ponytail1 Links value and add a tail by increasing the Tail Links value (see Figure 4-7).

Modifying a Biped's Proportions

The biped's proportions are based on standard human proportions and are driven by the initial Height value. The length of the character's arms, legs, and torso and the shape of its head and other parts will rarely match the biped's default features. A close fit between your biped and your model is essential to clean and efficient animation, and you will find yourself tweaking the size and pose of your biped to match your model.

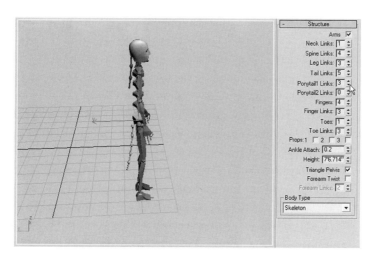

figure | 4-7 |

Add a ponytail and tail in the Structure rollout of the biped's Figure mode options.

1. Continue with the previous exercise or open *Biped Proportions.max* from the companion CD-ROM.

2. Select any part of the biped. If you are not in Figure mode yet, click the Figure Mode button. Click the small plus sign next to Modes and Display and on the gray line that runs along the bottom of the Biped rollout. This will display additional biped modes and display options.

3. In the Name field, enter a new name for your biped. Entering a name here will change the name of the root object and propagate that name as a prefix for all of its descendants (see Figure 4-8). Be aware that selecting the root object and changing its name using any other method will rename the root, but not the other objects in the hierarchy. The biped's name will remain *Bip01*. Feel free to rename it.

figure | 4-8 |

Entering a name in the Name field renames the root object and all of its descendants.

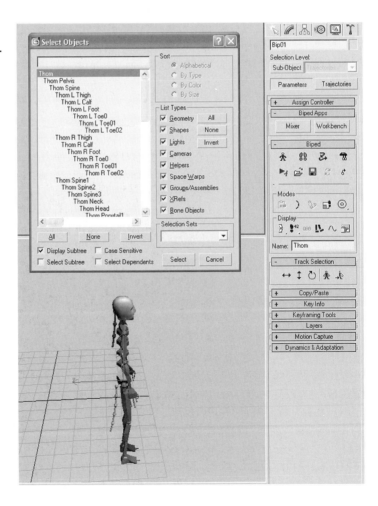

4. We need to adjust the biped's height. Expand the Structure rollout and then enter 6'-0" in the Height field. The biped's height changes, as well as the proportions of its features.

5. Select the biped's right calf and then activate the Scale tool in the Main toolbar. The reference coordinate system changes to Local and then grays out. Scale transforms on biped parts must be performed in the Local reference coordinate system. 3ds Max ensures this by automatically changing to the Local reference coordinate system whenever the Scale transform (see Figure 4-9) is selected. The Reference Coordinate System field is grayed out, making it unchangeable.

6. Click and drag the Y axis handle to extend the length of the calf. Click and drag the X and Z axes handles to make the calf thicker and wider.

7. Repeat the process on the biped's right thigh.

8. The biped's right leg has been modified, but the same appearance must be reflected on the opposite side of its body. Rather than repeating the steps, which may result in unexpected differences in the body's two halves as well as a lack of symmetry, we will use a different technique. 3ds Max contains tools for copying a pose or structure from one side of a biped to the other.

9. Select the biped's right calf and thigh. Click the plus sign to expand the Copy/Paste rollout, and then click the Copy Posture button. A graphic displaying the copied parts appears in the window at the bottom of the rollout, as shown in Figure 4-10.

10. Click the Paste Posture Opposite button. The left calf and thigh change to match the modifications made to the right calf and thigh (see Figure 4-11).

NOTE: The Copy and Paste features in the Copy/Paste rollout are not restricted to use within the same biped. The

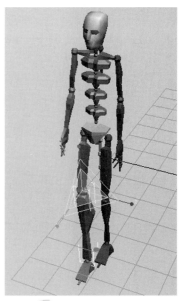

figure |4-9|

Use the Scale transform to change the proportions of a biped part.

figure |4-10|

The window in the Copy/Paste rollout displays the copied objects.

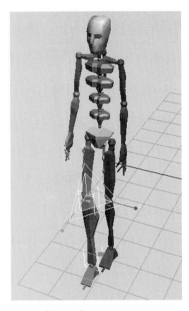

structure can be copied from one biped and pasted into another. Use Paste Posture, rather than Paste Posture Opposite, when pasting to the same side of another biped.

11. When the biped's legs were lengthened, they extended below the grid to where, in all likelihood, the floor will be created. To move the biped's initial location in the scene, you must use the Body Horizontal and Body Vertical buttons (see Figure 4-12) in the Track Selection rollout. Click the Body Vertical button and then click and drag the Z axis handle of the Move transform to move up the biped in the scene. Turn on the grid in the Front or Left viewport (using the G shortcut key) if needed to help guide the biped's location.

figure |4-11|

Paste Posture Opposite copies the appearance of the copied objects to the selected objects.

Modifying a Biped's Pose

When a model is created, it is best done in a pose that presents access to the individual vertices with a minimum of visual obstruction from other sections

figure |4-12|

Use Body Vertical to move the biped's initial location up in the Z axis.

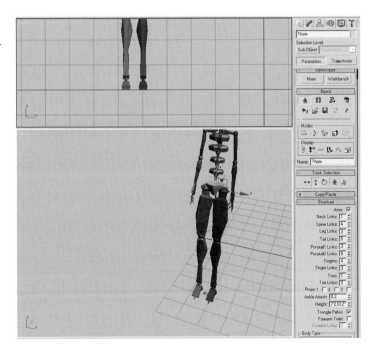

of the same model. It is common practice to create the model in what is often called the reference position (or the "da Vinci pose"): feet shoulder-width apart and arms extended from the body straight out or at a slight downward angle, with a bend at the elbow and the fingers extended. In this pose, specific vertices or polygons can be quickly selected and manipulated with a minimum of unwanted selections. Your biped must be posed to match the model, and the steps that follow are used to achieve this, but can also be used to animate your biped.

1. Select the biped's right upper arm and then activate the Rotate transform in the Main toolbar. Click and drag the Y transform handle until the arm rotates away from the body, as shown in Figure 4-13. The lower objects in the hierarchy rotate as well.

2. Select the right forearm and in the Top viewport rotate the forearm as shown in Figure 4-14. You may need to switch the viewport's rendering mode to Wireframe to effectively select the objects.

3. Select both the right upper arm and right forearm and copy the posture in the Copy/Paste rollout. Select the left upper arm and forearm and paste the posture using the Paste Posture Opposite button in the Copy/Paste rollout.

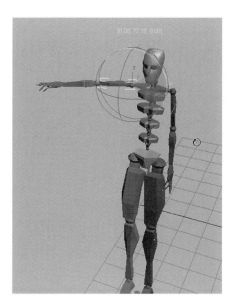

figure | 4-13 |

Use the Rotate transform to orient the upper arm.

figure | 4-14 |

Rotate the forearm to give it a natural bend.

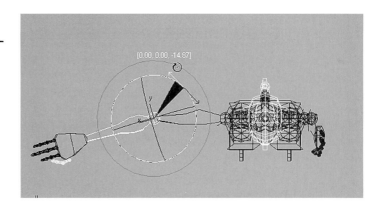

SAVING AND LOADING BIPED STRUCTURES

When there are several echelons of similar enemy soldiers or a mass of attacking aliens, their structures are often similar or identical. In 3ds Max you can save a biped's structure and pose to a *.fig* file that can be applied to any other biped you select. You can also apply it to your current biped to restore any structure or pose that was lost.

1. Select any part of the biped. In Figure mode, click on the Save File button in the Biped rollout.

2. The Save As dialog box opens. Select a location for the *.fig* file, enter a name in the File name field, and then click Save (see Figure 4-15).

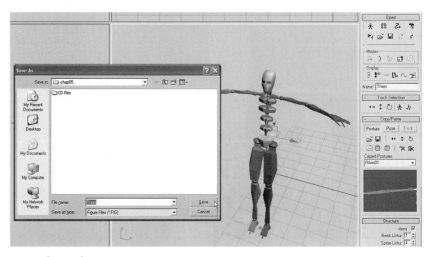

figure | 4-15 |

Save the biped's structure as a *.fig* file.

3. Create a new biped in the scene. Activate the Figure Mode button and then click the Load File button in the Biped rollout.

4. In the Open dialog box that appears, select the *.fig* file you just created and click Open.

5. At first, it appears that the new biped disappears. In fact, it is just occupying the same location and pose of the first biped you created. Click the Body Horizontal button in the Copy/Paste rollout to move the new biped away from the old one. As you can see, the two bipeds have identical structures (see Figure 4-16).

ANIMATING A BIPED

This is where the fun with Character Studio begins. Bipeds use footstep-driven actions to animate the locations of their feet at any point in time. Whenever and wherever a left or right footstep is located in a scene, the biped's appropriate foot will impact it regardless of the contortions required to achieve the movement. In addition to setting animation keys for the feet, keys are created for any biped parts affected by the foot movements. For example, stepping forward with the left foot causes a sway in the hips, a twist throughout the torso, and rotations of the joints of both arms. A massive number of keys can be created automatically just by giving the biped a simple walk cycle.

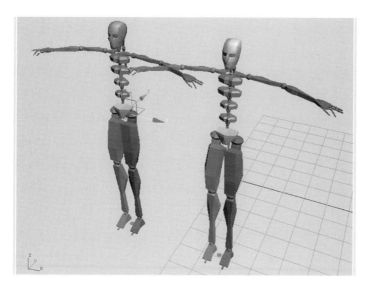

figure | 4-16 |

You can use *.fig* files to transfer entire biped structures, including poses, from one biped to another.

Assigning a Walk Cycle

1. Continue with the previous exercise or open the *Biped Walk.max* file from the companion CD-ROM.

2. Select the biped. In the Motion panel's Biped rollout, click the Footstep Mode button at the top of the panel.

3. In the Footstep Creation rollout, ensure that Walk at the right side of the rollout is active and then click Create Multiple Footsteps on the left-hand side (see Figure 4-17).

4. The Create Multiple Footsteps dialog box opens (see Figure 4-18), defining the parameters (based on the biped's height) for the footsteps that will be created. Enter *10* in the Number of Footsteps field and then click OK.

5. The footsteps appear in front of the biped, but they are not yet associated with it. In the Footstep Operations rollout, click the Create Keys for Inactive Footsteps button (see Figure 4-19). Note that the footsteps are color-coded to match the color coding of the biped.

6. The biped's arms drop because that is not the normal position for a character that is walking. Click the Play Animation button in the Playback Controls section at the bottom of the user interface. The biped walks, complete with arm movements and swinging tail and ponytail (see Figure 4-20).

figure

Click on Walk on the right-hand side of the rollout and then on Create Multiple Footsteps on the left.

figure | 4-18 |

The Create Multiple Footsteps field sets the parameters for the biped's footsteps to be created.

Create Multiple Footsteps: Walk

General
Start Left ⦿   Number of Footsteps: 10   OK
Start Right ⦾   Parametric Stride Width: 1.0   Cancel
Alternate ☑   Actual Stride Width: 0'6.99"   Default
Total Distance: 24'5.779"

Timing
Auto Timing ☑   Start after last footstep ⦾
Interpolate ☐   Start at current frame ⦿

First Step
Parametric Stride Length: 0.75
Actual Stride Length: 3'0.722"
Actual Stride Height: 0'0.0"
Time to next Footstep: 15
Speed (units per frame): 2.45
Walk Footstep 18
Double Support 3

Last Step
Parametric Stride Length: 0.75
Actual Stride Length: 3'0.722"
Actual Stride Height: 0'0.0"
Time to next Footstep: 15
Speed (units per frame): 2.45
Walk Footstep 18
Double Support 3

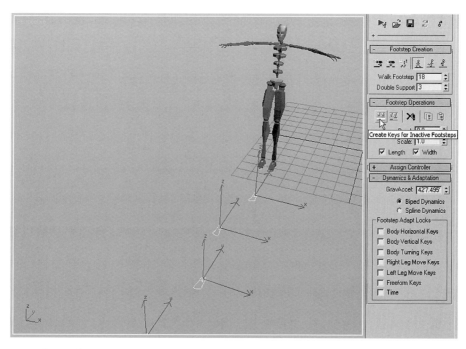

figure | 4-19 |

Click on the Create Keys for Inactive Footsteps button to associate the footsteps with the biped and to create animation keys.

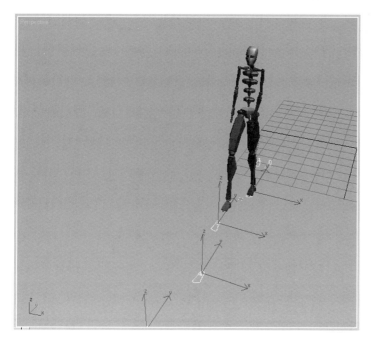

figure | 4-20 |

The biped moves to match the footsteps created.

NOTE: A walk, run, or jump cycle can be added as footsteps for a biped. During a walk cycle, the biped always has either one or two feet on the ground at a time. A run cycle consists of either one foot on the ground or both feet in the air at any point, and during a jump cycle either both feet are on the ground or both are in the air.

7. Experiment by adding walk, run, or jump cycles to the biped's movement. Remember to click the Create Keys for Inactive Footsteps button to append the new footsteps to the end of the existing footsteps. 3ds Max will extend the active time segment for your scene to accommodate any footsteps you add.

Moving Footsteps and Adding Free-Form Animation

The footsteps produced via the Create Multiple Footsteps dialog box are always created in a straight line, alternated from left to right and evenly spaced. Using the transform tools, these footsteps can be moved and rotated to achieve any movement required, including skipping, standing, and even dancing.

Moving Footsteps

1. Continue with the previous exercise or open the *Move Footsteps.max* file from the companion CD-ROM.

2. Select the biped and then activate the Footstep Mode button.

3. Right-click in the Top viewport and then click Zoom Extents in the viewport controls to display all of the footsteps and the biped.

4. The footsteps are actually sub-objects of the biped, and entering Footstep mode accesses these sub-objects. Use the Move tool to select and move the footsteps until they surround the biped.

5. Activate the Rotate tool and then rotate the footsteps individually to add some personality to our biped's movements (see Figure 4-21). Be aware of how much a footstep is rotated and compare it to how much a real person could rotate their foot between each step.

6. Click the Play Animation button to check the biped's movements and make any adjustments required.

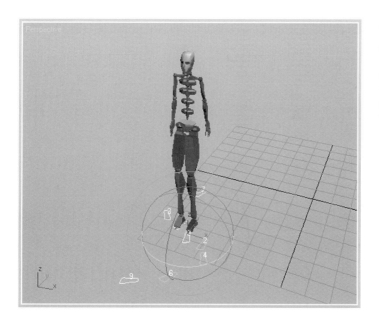

figure |4-21|

Use the Move and
Rotate transforms
to relocate and
reorient the
footsteps.

Adding Free-Form Animation

The movement and animation keys created automatically by
Character Studio provide a standard, and slightly stiff, motion for
the biped. This is not a fixed motion, and you can adjust, move,
add, or delete any keys necessary to accomplish your animation
goals. By deleting a block of shoulder-rotation keys and replacing
them with keys you create, for example, you can turn a simple arm
swing into a wave or a throw.

1. Select the biped's left upper arm.

2. Drag the Time slider until it is near the middle of the active
   time segment.

3. Select three or four keys in the trackbar (see Figure 4-22) at the
   bottom of the user interface. Right-click one key and then
   select *Delete selected keys* from the pop-up menu. All selected
   keys up to this key will be deleted.

4. Click the Auto Key button to activate Auto Key mode.

5. Rotate the biped's upper arm, in all three axes, until it is
   extended above its head at the top of a wave pose. A key is created at the current time. Move the Time slider forward and
   rotate the upper arm and forearm to create the wave. Move the

figure | 4-22 |

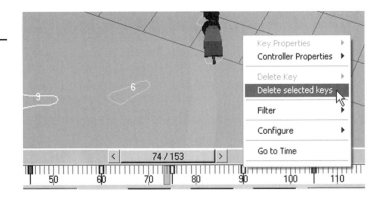

Delete selected keys from the trackbar.

Time slider forward again and rotate the arm in a manner similar to that performed for its initial raised position. Your scene and trackbar should look similar to those shown in Figure 4-23.

6. Turn off Auto Key mode and then scrub the Time slider to check your animation and make any changes required. The keys on either side of the keys you just created will dictate the arm's location before and after the wave cycle.

Subtle movements are what make a character's motion look realistic. Turning its head as it approaches a turn in a corridor or straightening its back before lifting a heavy load are examples of the type of free-form animation you should strive to add to your animations.

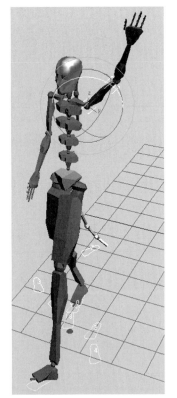

LOADING AND SAVING BIPED ANIMATION

Similar to *.fig* files, which contain the structure and appearance of a biped, *.bip* files hold the information regarding a biped's motion. This includes any animation automatically generated by the Create Keys for Inactive Footsteps button and any that were manually created.

By creating a dancing sequence with only one character and then saving it as a *.bip* file, you can open that file and copy the motion to all the monsters in your dance troupe. The motion is relative to the size of the biped. Therefore, a mouse and an elephant can share the same *.bip* file. However, the mouse's steps will be much smaller. 3ds Max ships with a significant library of *.bip*

figure | 4-23 |

Create keys for a wave cycle.

files for your use. Perform a file search at and below the 3ds Max root folder and you will find .*bip* files located in several file folders.

1. Continue with the previous exercise or open the *Copy Animation.max* file from the companion CD-ROM.

2. Select the biped. In the Motion panel, ensure that you are not in Figure or Footstep mode.

3. In the Biped rollout, click the Save File button.

4. Enter a name for the .*bip* file in the *File name* field in the Save As dialog box (see Figure 4-24) that opens and then click Save.

5. Create another biped in the scene and make it significantly larger or smaller than the existing biped. Adjust its structure and appearance so that it differs from the existing biped.

6. Select the Motion panel. In the Biped rollout, click the Load File button to open the Open dialog box (see Figure 4-25).

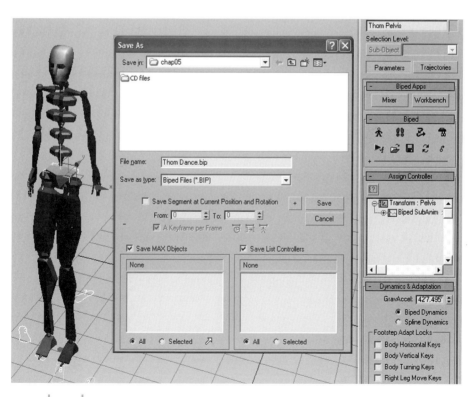

figure | 4-24 |

Name the .bip file you want to save.

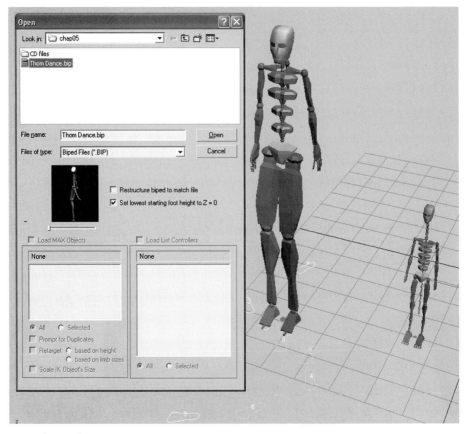

figure | 4-25 |

Load a *.bip* file into your existing biped using the Open dialog.

NOTE: The Open dialog box contains a preview window for discovering what motions a *.bip* file contains. Simply drag the slider beneath the window to see several sample frames of the biped animation.

7. Select the *.bip* file to be loaded and then click the Open button. The new biped co-locates with the old biped and new footsteps are created that parallel those of the old biped, but at a different scale.

8. Enter Footstep mode and select all of the footsteps for the new biped. Move the footsteps away from the older biped so that their animations do not cause collisions, as shown in Figure 4-26.

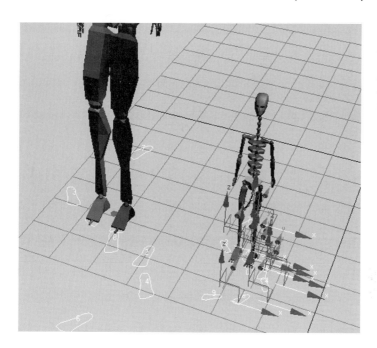

figure 4-26

Select and move
the footsteps and
the biped will move
with them.

9. Exit Footstep mode and then click the Play
   Animation button (or scrub the Time slider) to
   review the animation. The bipeds share the same
   animation, but at scales appropriate to their relative sizes (see Figure 4-27).

UNDERSTANDING THE PHYSIQUE MODIFIER

Chapter 3 discussed and explained the Skin modifier
and its ability to drive a model's vertex locations based
on their proximity to bones located within a mesh.
The Physique modifier performs the same functionality as the Skin modifier (and there are several similar-
ities between them) but is designed specifically to be
implemented with a Biped system. *Biped system* refers
to the low-polygon-count, easily animated bones
within a model that are not meant to be seen.

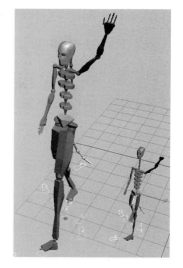

figure 4-27

The bipeds share the same animation saved to the *.bip* file.

Once a biped has been adjusted to fit within a model, the Physique
modifier is applied to the model and then associated with the
biped's root object. Any poses or actions performed by the biped

are reflected in the model's movements. Just before rendering, select and hide the biped objects so that any parts that poke through the model's surfaces are not rendered and do not become part of the final image. If there is a MeshSmooth modifier at the top of the modifier stack, be sure to place the Physique modifier below it so that the Physique modifier drives the low-polygon model rather than the higher-polygon model created with MeshSmooth.

SKINNING A MODEL TO A BIPED WITH THE PHYSIQUE MODEL

Once your model is completed, you can start the character animation process by creating and modifying a biped so that it fits snuggly within your model. It is acceptable that a certain number of your biped's objects extend beyond the surface of the model, as long as they are not near a surface they should not influence.

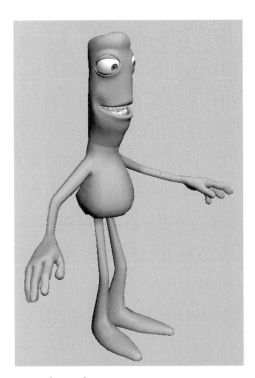

Creating and Adjusting the Biped

To create and adjust a biped for animation purposes, perform the following:

1. Open the *Mr_Blue_CS.max* file from the companion CD-ROM (see Figure 4-28). This consists of the same model that was skinned with the Skin modifier in Chapter 3.

2. Select all objects in the scene and then press the Alt+X keys to place those objects in See-Through mode.

3. Right-click in the viewport and select Freeze Selection from the quad menu to prevent the model from being inadvertently selected during the biped modification procedure.

figure | 4-28 |

Mr. Blue before the biped is created.

4. In the Top viewport, create a biped at approximately the same height as the model. As you can see in Figure 4-29, the proportions of Mr. Blue are significantly different than those of the biped. The model's head is much longer and its torso is short compared with the legs.

5. The movements of the biped spring from the pelvis, and thus the pelvis's location in the model is crucial. Select the root object (named *Bip01* if the object has not been renamed), and then click the Motion tab and then the Figure Mode button.

6. Using the Body Horizontal and Body Vertical buttons found in the Track Selection rollout, move the biped so that its pelvis is centered on the model's pelvic area. Check the location in all viewports for accuracy (see Figure 4-30 and Figure 4-31).

7. Select the pelvis and scale it in the Z axis until the biped's legs are centered on the model's legs.

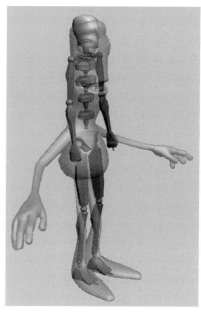

figure | **4-29** |

The biped's proportions do not match those of the model.

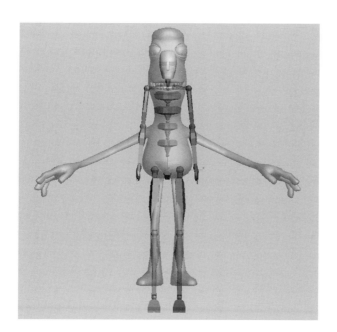

figure | **4-30** |

The biped's pelvis is properly located in the Front viewport.

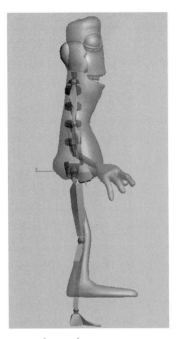

figure | 4-31 |

The biped's pelvis is properly located in the Left viewport.

8. Using the techniques discussed in the "Creating and Modifying a Biped" section, use the Scale and Rotate transforms to adjust the length, width, and orientation of one leg and then copy/paste the posture to the other leg (see Figure 4-32). Be sure to locate the biped's knee joints at the same location as the model's knees.

9. Select one of the feet and rotate and scale it to match the model's foot. A single toe with one Toe Link is adequate to animate this model. Ensure that the biped's toes and toe links values are set to 1 in the Structure rollout, and then scale the toe properly. If you scale the foot in the X axis, making it taller, you may need to rescale the calf to relocate the foot.

10. If necessary, change the Ankle Attach value in the Structure rollout to reposition the foot toward the front or back of the leg. Select the leg and foot and then copy/paste the structure to the other side. The legs and feet should look similar to those shown in Figure 4-33.

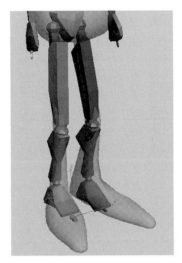

figure | 4-32 |

Adjust the biped's legs to match the model.

figure | 4-33 |

The biped's legs and feet match the model's.

11. Continue the setup by working on the biped's back. The spine links should be scaled down in the X axis (until the clavicles are properly located) and then scaled larger until they fill the model, as shown in Figure 4-34 and Figure 4-35. Rotate the spine links to match the contour of the torso. If necessary, scale the pelvis's depth to match the model.

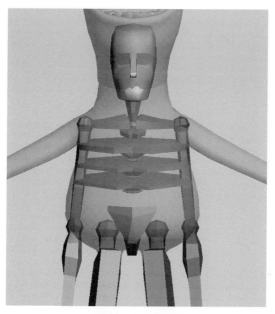

figure | 4-34 |

The biped's spine is scaled to match the torso's height and width.

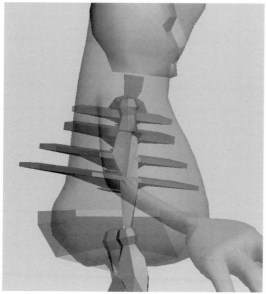

figure | 4-35 |

The biped's spine is scaled and rotated to match the torso's depth and posture.

12. Adjust the biped's arms and hands to match those of the model, being sure to properly locate the elbow. In the Structure rollout, set the Fingers value to 4 and the Finger Links value to 3 to give the model sufficient dexterity. Be sure to select the Local reference coordinate system when moving or rotating the fingers and finger links. Mr. Blue is not perfectly symmetrical, so you may need to make minor adjustments after pasting the posture to the other side (see Figure 4-36).

NOTE: Double-clicking on any single biped component selects all of its children and descendants.

13. Add a neck link and then scale and rotate the neck link to fill the model's throat area.

14. Scale and slightly rotate the biped's head to fit the model as closely as possible. Your biped and model combination should look similar to those shown in Figure 4-37.

figure | 4-36 |

The biped's spine, arms, hands, and fingers are adjusted to fit the model.

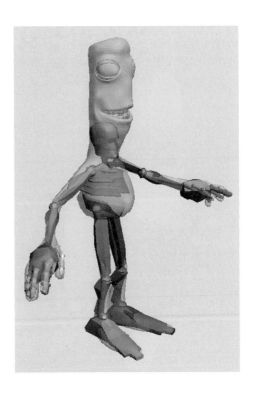

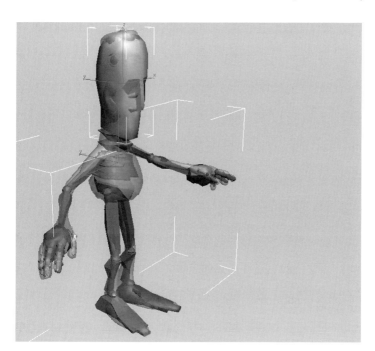

figure | 4-37 |

The completed
biped and model.

Applying the Physique Modifier

Now that the biped is complete, it is time to associate it to the model using the Physique modifier.

1. Continue with the previous exercise or open the *Mt_Blue_CS_Physique.max* file from the companion CD-ROM.

2. Right-click in the viewport and select Unfreeze All from the quad menu to unfreeze the model's components (see Figure 4-38).

3. Select the head and body objects. Click the Modify tab. In the Modifier list, select Physique. In the modifier stack, drag the Physique modifier to a position below the MeshSmooth modifier (see Figure 4-39).

4. In the Physique rollout, click the Attach to Node button (see Figure 4-40) and then select the root object of the hierarchy to be associated with the Physique modifier. It is easiest, after clicking the Attach to Node button, to press the H key to open the Pick Object dialog box. Here, the root object can be selected by name, eliminating the possibility of selecting the incorrect object.

5. In the Physique Initialization dialog box that appears, click Initialize to accept the default settings. The cursor changes to a coffee cup icon until the initialization is complete.

figure | 4-38 |

Unfreeze the model
using the quad menu.

figure 4-39

Select the head and body and then apply the Physique modifier.

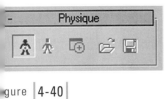

gure 4-40

ick the Attach to Node button and en select the biped's root object.

6. Select a biped part and then assign a walk cycle to the biped, as discussed earlier in this chapter. Play the animation. The eyes and teeth remain in place and there may appear to be portions of the model that do no properly follow the biped.

7. Return the Time slider to frame 0 and then select the eye and teeth objects. Move them, if required, to their proper locations.

8. Click the Select and Link button in the Main toolbar and link the selected objects to the biped's head component. These are linked to the head, rather than skinned with the Physique modifier, to avoid any distortion the modifier may cause.

9. Play the animation again to ensure that the objects follow the model properly.

ADJUSTING BONE ENVELOPES

The areas that do not properly follow the biped's movement are caused by the biped not being close enough to the model's vertices to dictate their location. This is common near a biped's extremities. This can be fixed by refining the area the biped's objects affect by adjusting their envelopes. Envelopes are sub-objects of the Physique modifier and consist of two offsct capsule-shaped gizmos that define the limits of any selected biped's influence.

Vertices located within the inner envelope are completely controlled by the selected bone. Vertices located outside the outer envelope are not affected by the selected bone. Vertices located between the envelopes receive a variable amount of influence depending on their proximity to either envelope. The following controls in the Modify panel affect the shape and size of envelopes.

- The Inner, Outer, and Both buttons determine whether the controls described in the following bulleted items affect the inner envelope, the outer envelope, or both envelopes. The default is Both.

- Radial Scale defines the size of an envelope's cross section.

- Parent Overlap adjusts how far the end of an envelope extends over the selected bone's hierarchical parent.

- Child Overlap adjusts how far the end of an envelope extends over the selected bone's hierarchical child.

To adjust bone envelopes, perform the following:

1. Take note of which areas are not following the biped. Select the biped and then access Figure mode.

2. Select the body object and in the modifier stack click the plus sign next to the Physique modifier to expose its sub-objects. Select the Envelope sub-object (see Figure 4-41).

3. Click the biped component closest to the offending vertices to display its envelopes (see Figure 4-42).

4. In the Modify Panel > Blending Envelopes roll-out, adjust the Radial Scale and Child Overlap parameters until the envelopes encompass the offending vertices completely (see Figure 4-43).

5. Select Physique in the modifier stack to exit the sub-object mode. Select the biped. In the Motion panel, exit Figure mode to see if the envelope modification was successful.

6. Repeat steps 1 through 5 to fix any other unresponsive areas.

7. Exit any sub-object modes and deselect all objects. Press the H key to open the Select Objects dialog box. Select all of the biped objects and be sure not to select any of the model objects, including the eyes and teeth linked to the biped's head.

figure |**4-41**|

Select the Envelope subobject level of the Physique modifier.

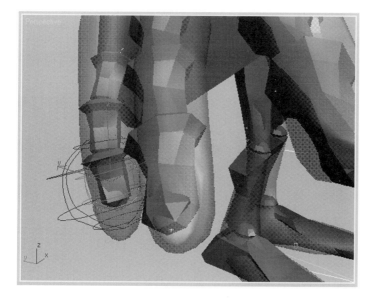

figure |**4-42**|

Select the bone to display its envelopes.

figure | 4-43 |

Adjust the envelopes until they encompass the model's finger.

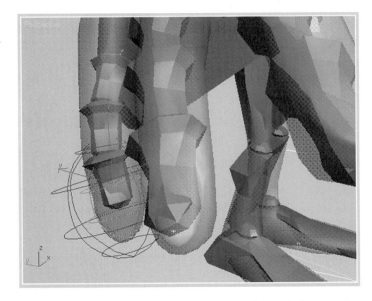

8. Right-click in the viewport and, to hide all biped objects, select Hide Selection from the quad menu that opens.

9. Select all remaining objects in the scene and then press the Alt+X keys to turn off See-Through mode.

10. Play the animation to watch your skinned and animated character move cleanly through the scene.

Study the files *Mr_Blue_CS_Complete.max* and *Mr_Blue_CS_Complete. avi* on the companion CD-ROM for an example of the completed model and biped.

SUMMARY

Character Studio is a powerful feature of 3ds Max that can significantly reduce the amount of time it takes to rig and skin a bipedal character. In this chapter you learned how to create and adjust biped systems and how to add walk cycles and free-form animation to a biped. You also learned how to save a biped's structure and animation to files that can be loaded into other bipeds. We also covered applying the Physique modifier to a model and the procedure for adjusting Physique's envelopes to tweak the biped's control over the model's vertices.

1. What are the different body type choices for a biped?

2. What type of file contains a biped's structural information?

3. How do you save a biped's animation to a file?

4. How do you quickly rename all objects in a biped?

5. What is the difference between Figure mode and Footstep mode?

6. Which reference coordinate system should be used when adjusting biped components?

7. What object should be selected after clicking Physique's Attach to Node button?

8. What is the purpose of envelopes and how are they adjusted?

↗ EXPLORING ON YOUR OWN

1. Explore the library of *.bip* files that ship with 3ds Max by loading them into the Mr. Blue character you created and skinned.

2. 3ds Max's standard Bones systems can be used in conjunction with Character Studio. Add bones to your scene to represent wings or another set of arms and link them to your biped. Complete the process by creating additional geometry and skinning it to the new bones.

3. Character Studio's tool set is extensive, and only the basics were covered in this chapter. Research Motion Flow mode and Mixer mode and how they can augment your Character Studio skills.

charting your course

To this point you have learned how to animate objects using various animation tools, such as the Dope Sheet and Curve editor. You have also gained experience in character design and rigging. In this chapter, we will explore how to animate other aspects of a 3D scene, including materials, lights, and cameras. You will also be introduced to the 3ds Max Video Post utility, which allows you to add basic special effects to an animation. With these additional animation techniques, you will be able to add those finishing touches to your scenes that will really make your animations look spectacular.

 chapter objectives

- **Animate an object along a spline path**
- **Create and animate multiple cameras in a scene**
- **Set up and animate light objects**
- **Generate animated procedural materials**
- **Apply Video Post effects to 3D objects**
- **Animate post effects**

ANIMATING ALONG A PATH

Throughout the course of animating a 3D scene, you may encounter situations in which animating certain objects would be achieved easier by having them follow a predetermined path. This can be an extremely helpful approach when animating things such as missiles firing, ships sailing, and airplanes flying, or cameras following other objects. Throughout the course of this chapter, we will animate a single scene by first animating a caveman's car moving through a shrubbery labyrinth and then adding some animated materials to objects at the center of the maze.

Once that is complete, a camera will be set up and animated along a path, which will allow us to see the scene from a bird's-eye view of the animation. A second camera will also be animated, and the two camera shots will be combined in postproduction. The next step will be to set up an animated light to add ambience to the scene. Finally, 3ds Max's Video Post features will allow us to cut between the two animated cameras, as well as add some basic special effects to the objects that have animated materials applied to them. Once finished, the completed scene will be ready to be rendered.

GETTING THE CAVEMAN ROLLING

It is time to begin by leading the caveman through the labyrinth by animating it along a path. Normally when animating vehicles, it would be necessary to set up controllers to animate the wheels' rotation as the vehicle travels along the path. For this exercise, we will forego this process for simplicity's sake.

1. Open the *maze_car.max* file located in the *Chapter 5* folder of the companion CD-ROM.

2. Upon opening the file, you will see a ground plane, a maze, two spheres in the center of the maze (a smaller sphere within a larger sphere), and a cute little caveman car at the entrance of the maze, as well as a spotlight object (see Figure 5-1). We will first draw a path from the car to the maze exit. Activate the Top viewport and maximize the view to make it full screen. This will make it easier to draw our path. Using the Line tool, draw a path through the maze, starting at the middle of the car. Convert the corners to Beziers to round out the turns by going into the vertex sub-object mode. Refer to Figure 5-2 to see the finished path.

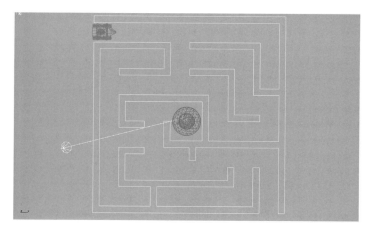

figure |5-1|

The scene before
the car path has
been added.

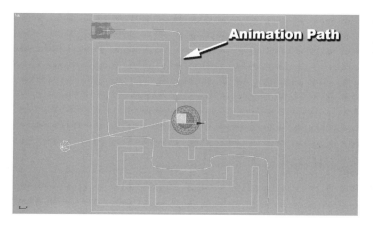

figure |5-2|

The scene with the
path added.

3. Once the path has been drawn, press the Alt+W keys to toggle back to the four viewports. Use the Move Transform Type-In tool to raise the spline off the ground plane by entering 10.5 as the Absolute World value in the Z axis (be sure you have exited the vertex sub-object mode first). If we did not raise the spline off the ground, the car would move through the ground plane once we assigned the car to the path. Name the spline *car path*.

4. Set up the timeline by making some adjustments within the Time Configuration dialog box. Open the Time Configuration dialog box and set Frame Rate to Custom and Frames per Second (FPS) to 15. Enter a Frame Count value of *255* within the Animation settings to set the length of the animation to 254 frames (see Figure 5-3).

figure | 5-3 |

Settings in the
Time Configuration
dialog.

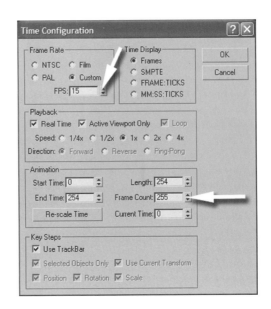

5. Select the *caveman car* object and go to the Motion panel. Within the Assign Controller rollout, select the Position transform and click the Assign Controller button. From the controller list, select Path Constraint. Click OK (see Figure 5-4).

figure | 5-4 |

Adding a Path
Constraint
controller to the
position transform
of the caveman car.

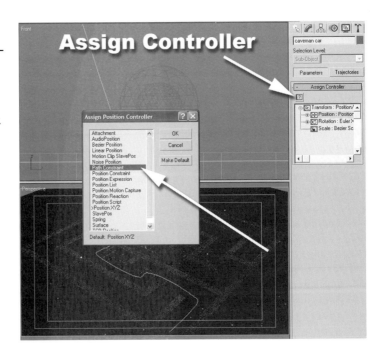

6. Within the Path Parameters rollout (see Figure 5-5), activate the Add Path button and click on the *car path* to select it. This tells the car to follow the path of the spline object. Deactivate the Add Path button and check the box next to Follow. This will reorient the car as it makes the turns throughout the maze.

7. Because we will be adding camera motion and some fade-ins and fade-outs during postproduction, we are going to move the path animation keyframes to accommodate this. With the caveman car still selected, click the key at frame 0 on the trackbar and move it to frame 75. Move the last keyframe to frame 224. Now the car will not move until five seconds into the scene, and will stop at frame 224 to allow for a one-second pause and a one-second fade-out.

8. Play the animation to see Mr. Caveman drive his way through the maze. Save your work to your local hard drive.

Note: Be sure to copy the maps from the *Chapter 5* folder of the companion CD-ROM to the directory where you saved your Max scene. Otherwise, the materials will not show up at render time.

figure | 5-5 |

Path Parameters rollout.

Fantastic! We have successfully helped our little caveman friend find his way through the garden labyrinth. Using a simple process, we can generate an animation very quickly, which would have taken much longer to do had we used standard keyframing approaches. Next, we will create some animated materials for those spheres at the center of the maze.

ANIMATING MATERIALS AND TEXTURES

Animated materials are extremely useful tools in an animator's creative arsenal. They are great for producing countless effects for various particle system setups. For instance, a particle system can be made to look like water, steam, smoke, or fire simply by changing the type of material applied to the particle system. In this exercise, we are going to transform the spheres at the center of the maze into energized balls of weird plasma.

To achieve this effect, we will animate a couple of procedural textures and apply them to the spheres. We think you will be pleasantly surprised by how dramatic the change will be in the spheres once we generate and apply the animated materials. Let's get started!

GENERATING PLASMA

As stated previously, we are going to transform those boring spheres in the maze into a-*maze*-ing balls of plasma! This will be done by using procedural noise maps and then animating the Phase value to produce the look of volatile plasma. In addition, we will animate a Noise modifier that will be applied to the inner sphere (small plasma sphere) to enhance the volatile nature of the plasma.

1. Open the *maze_materials.max* file found in the *Chapter 5* folder of the companion CD-ROM, or use the file you saved from the previous exercise.

2. Open the Material editor (M key). You will see three materials already in the editor, which have already been applied to the objects in the scene (minus the two plasma sphere objects). Select an empty material slot and rename the material *Purple Plasma*.

3. Under the Blinn Basic Parameters rollout, change the Self-Illumination value to *100*.

4. Within the Maps rollout, click the map slot in the Diffuse Color channel. From the Material Map browser, select a noise map (see Figure 5-6).

figure 5-6

Adding a noise map to the Diffuse Color channel.

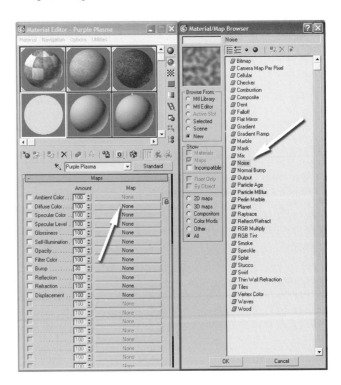

5. Within the Noise map parameters, under the Coordinates roll-out set the Blur value to *0.01*.

6. In the Noise Parameters rollout, set Noise Type to Turbulence. Under Noise Threshold, set High to *0.125*, Levels to *1.4*, and Size to *7.0* (see Figure 5-7).

7. Click the Swap button next to the Color 1 and Color 2 swatches and set Color 1 to a medium purple (R-166, G-0, B-141).

8. Now to animate the noise. Move the Time slider to the last frame (frame 254) and activate the Auto Key button. Under Noise Parameters, set Phase to *6.25*. Deactivate the Auto Key button. You have just created your first animated material!

9. Now to finish off the *Purple Plasma* material. This texture will be applied to the large outer sphere, so we need to find a way to see the inner sphere through the larger one. To accomplish this, we will utilize an opacity map. Continue with the following steps.

10. Click the Go to Parent button in the Material editor to return to the Maps rollout. Click and drag the noise map from the Diffuse Color channel to the Opacity channel. When prompted, select Copy. You have now duplicated the noise previously set up and put it in the Opacity channel. Open the Opacity Noise map and change Color 1 to white (R-255, G-255, B-255). This will cause the purple areas of the diffuse color to be opaque and the black areas to be transparent, allowing us to see the small inner sphere.

11. Click the Go to Parent button to return to the root of the material. Select the Show Map in Viewport button in the Material Editor tools. This will allow you to see the material in the

figure | **5-7** |

Noise Parameters settings for *Purple Plasma*.

shaded viewports once the material has been applied to an object (see Figure 5-8). Select the *large plasma sphere* object and assign the *Purple Plasma* material to the selected object.

12. Now we will create another animated material for the inner sphere, but this time we will make it yellow. We can use the *Purple Plasma* material as the foundation for the new *Yellow Plasma*. Drag the *Purple Plasma* sample slot into an empty material slot. Rename the copied material *Yellow Plasma*.

13. Click the Noise map in the Diffuse Color slot and within Noise Threshold set High to *0.48*, Low to *0.1*, Levels to *10*, and Size to *20*. Change Color 1 to a bright yellow (R-246, G-255, B-0) (see Figure 5-9).

14. Activate the Auto Key button and move the Time slider to the last frame in the animation. Set Phase to *4.75*. Deactivate the Auto

figure **5-8**

The animated transparent material applied to the large sphere. (The figure is shown using the Smooth & Highlights viewport shader.)

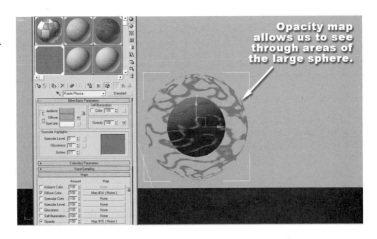

figure **5-9**

Noise Parameters settings for *Yellow Plasma*.

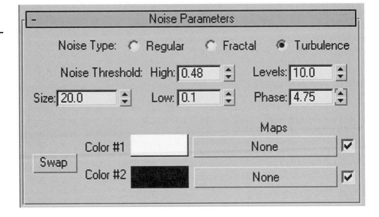

Key button. We have just slowed the motion of the noise, which will add some nice variation to the different plasma spheres.

15. Click the Go to Parent button to return to the Maps rollout. Drag the Noise map in the Diffuse Color channel to the Opacity channel to overwrite the old Opacity Noise map from the *Purple Plasma*. Make the new Opacity map a copy. In the Noise Parameters for the Opacity map, change the yellow color to white.

16. Select the *small plasma sphere* object and assign the *Yellow Plasma* material to it (see Figure 5-10).

17. Close the Material editor. Play the animation to see the new animated plasma materials in motion in the scene. Be sure your viewport is set to Smooth & Highlight so that you can see the materials on the objects.

18. To make the inner ball of plasma appear more volatile, we are going to add a Noise modifier to the sphere mesh. Select the *small plasma sphere* object, and in the Modify panel add a Noise modifier.

19. In the Parameters rollout (see Figure 5-11), set Scale to *36.0* and activate the Fractal option. In the Strength settings, set the X, Y, and Z strength settings to *20.0*. Under Animation, check the Animate Noise box and set Frequency to *0.1*. Now we have some nice volatile plasma! Be sure to save your work to your hard drive.

Note: When previewing animations that contain animated materials, close the Material editor. When the Material editor is open, 3ds Max will try to update the sample slots for every frame, which will slow the playback of the viewport. By closing the Material editor you will get faster playback.

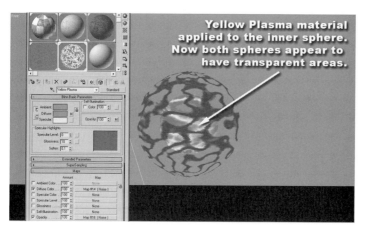

Yellow Plasma material applied to the inner sphere. Now both spheres appear to have transparent areas.

figure | 5-10 |

Yellow Plasma material applied to the smaller, inner sphere.

figure | 5-11 |

The Noise modi-
fier's Parameters
settings.

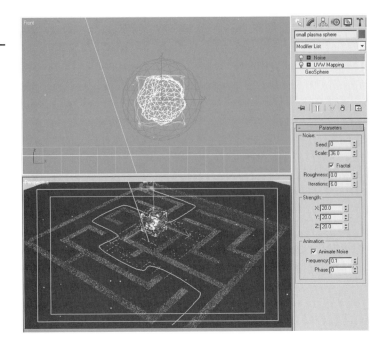

Great job! You now have some really cool animated materials in
your project. This scene is really starting to shape up nicely. Next,
we will add an Omni light object and animate its Multiplier value
(light intensity), which will give the illusion that the plasma spheres
are emitting light in the scene.

ANIMATING LIGHTS

Animated lights can really be helpful within a scene. You can create
disco lights, simulate a flickering fire, or in our case simulate the
effect of illuminated plasma throwing erratic light in the scene. In
addition to animating the actual physical position of a light, a
light's parameters can be animated in much the same way the material parameters were animated.

CREATING A FLICKERING LIGHT

To create the appearance that the balls of plasma are emitting light,
we will animate the Multiplier value of an Omni light. The
Multiplier of a light object controls how bright or dim the light is.
The higher the Multiplier value the brighter the light. By assigning a
negative value via the Multiplier, you can actually create darkness

with a light object. In the following exercise, we will animate an erratic Multiplier value in order to simulate the effect that the plasma is casting light into the scene.

1. Open the *maze_lights.max* file from the *Chapter 5* folder of the companion CD-ROM, or continue with the file you saved from the previous exercise.

2. In the Top viewport, create an Omni light directly on top of the plasma spheres. In the Front viewport, use the Move tool to move the Omni light up the Y axis until the light is positioned directly above the largest sphere (see Figure 5-12). Name the new Omni light *plasma light*. (In our example, the Omni light has an Absolute World Z coordinate of 65.)

3. Within the *plasma light's* General Parameters rollout (the light must be selected and you must go to the Modify panel), check the box next to On in the Shadows area. We will use the default Shadow Map type for these shadows.

4. Click the Exclude button to open the Exclude/Include dialog box. Select the *large plasma sphere* and the *small plasma sphere* objects and click the ">>" button in the middle of the dialog box. This will move the two plasma spheres to the Exclude list. Leave the settings at their default to exclude the spheres from both illumination and shadow casting (see Figure 5-13).

5. Under the Intensity > Color > Attenuation rollout, set Multiplier to *2.5* and click the white color swatch to change the color of the light to a bright magenta (R-222, G-0, B-255). We need to try to match the color of the light to the color of the outer plasma, in that the plasma color would have a bearing on what the light color is if the sphere were actually emitting this

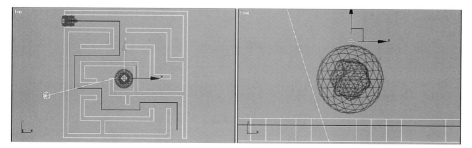

figure | 5-12 |

Omni light position within our scene.

figure | 5-13 |

Excluding the plasma spheres from illumination and shadow casting.

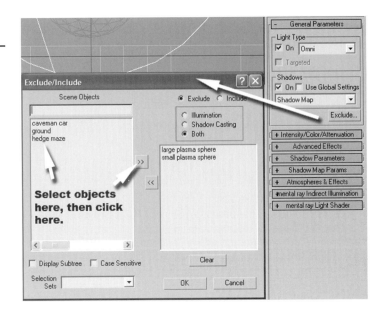

light (although we will brighten the light color to be more noticeable in the scene).

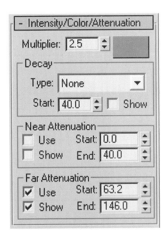

figure | 5-14 |

Settings used in the Intensity > Color > Attenuation rollout.

6. Under Far Attenuation, check the boxes next to Show and Use. Set Start to *63.2* and End to *146.0*. This will cause the light to gradually fade as it travels over distance. We want to try to keep the light emitted from the plasma isolated within a general area of the maze (see Figure 5-14).

7. Under the Shadow Parameters rollout, change the color of the shadows from black to a very dark gray (R-27, G-27, B-27). Set Dens. to *0.9*.

8. In the Shadow Map Params rollout, set Size to *1024* and Sample Range to *15.0*. This will increase the shadow's resolution and soften the shadow edges (see Figure 5-15).

9. Now that the light is set up, we can set up the animation for the multiplier. To do this, we will utilize a controller assigned to the Multiplier track in the Curve editor. Open the Curve editor and click the Filters button.

10. In the Filters dialog box, in the Hide By Category section at the right-hand side of the dialog box, check the box next to Geometry (see Figure 5-16).

Filters button

figure |5-15|

Settings used within
the Shadow
Parameters and
Shadow Map
Params rollouts.

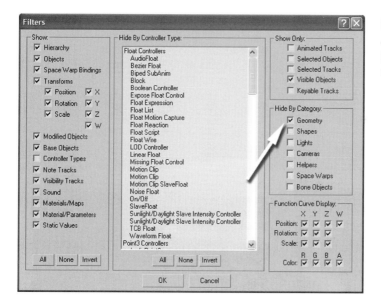

figure |5-16|

Filters dialog
settings.

11. Expand the list under the Object (Omni Light) in the track list
    to expand the *plasma light*'s setting tracks. Select the Multiplier
    track (see Figure 5-17).

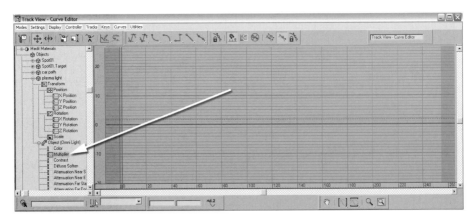

figure | 5-17 |

Selecting the Multiplier track in the Curve editor.

12. From the Track View menus, select Controller > Assign to open the Assign Controller dialog box. From the list of controllers, select Noise Float. Click OK. This will open the Noise Controller dialog box.

13. In the Noise Controller dialog box, set Strength to 3.221, check the box next to ">0", set Frequency to 0.045, and leave Fractal Noise unchecked (see Figure 5-18).

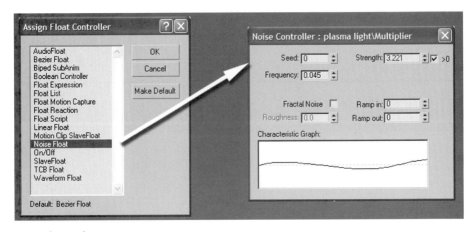

figure | 5-18 |

The Assign Controller and Noise Controller dialogs.

14. We now have a function curve for the Multiplier track (see Figure 5-19). Close the Track View and save your work to your hard drive. If you like, you can render an *.avi* movie of the animation so far to see what the animated light looks like.

By assigning a Noise controller to the Multiplier of the light, we were able to quickly create a nice erratic effect to the light's brightness, without the need of keyframing any parameter values. Next, we will add some interest by adding and animating some cameras to the scene.

ANIMATED CAMERAS

Including animated cameras in your scene can add drama and interest to your animated scenes. By animating a camera, you can create an architectural walkthrough, simulate a first-person point of view, have a camera follow another object moving in a scene for a third-person point of view, and simulate real-world camera moves used in the film industry. In the following exercise, we will create animated cameras to add interest to the final animation.

CAMERA MOVEMENTS

We already have some fantastic animation in our little labyrinth scene, including cool animated materials, a neat animated light object, and a cute animated caveman car. To add further interest, in the final animation we are going to add two animated cameras to the scene.

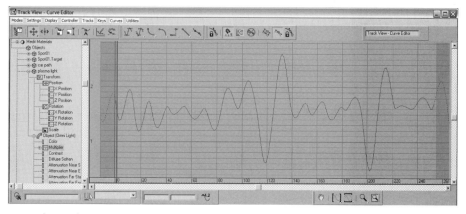

figure | 5-19 |

The new Multiplier function curve created with the Noise Float controller.

The first camera will be used to create a shot that "sets the stage" for the animation. It will start with a close-up shot of the caveman car and will then pull back to show the maze environment. A second animated camera will then be used to pan around the maze as the car travels through the labyrinth. Once the cameras have been animated, we will use the Video Post tools to make a camera cut from the first camera to the second.

1. Open the *maze_cameras.max* file from the *Chapter 5* folder of the companion CD-ROM, or use the file saved from the previous exercise.

2. The first camera we will create will be animated by setting up a couple of keyframes. Create a Free Camera in the Front viewport. Name the camera object *intro camera*. In the Move Transform Type-In function, set the Absolute World coordinates as follows: X = –43.688, Y = 49.094, and Z = 38.086 (you can use the transform type-ins at the bottom of the user interface). This will reposition the camera to the starting position of the animation (see Figure 5-20).

3. Now we will tilt the camera to finish the first establishing shot of the caveman car. Right-click the Rotate tool to open the Rotate Transform Type-In dialog box. Enter the following Absolute World values: X = 80.0, Y = 0, Z = 50.0. This creates the correct angle for the camera (see Figure 5-21).

Set Keys button

4. Now that the camera position and angle have been set up, we can begin assigning keys to the camera. Make sure the *intro camera* object is selected. Activate the Set Key animation button (found beneath the Auto Key button). On frame 0, click the Set Keys button to add a key to the timeline. Move the Time slider to frame 15 and click the Set Keys button to add another key. This will produce a hold on the camera, which will keep it from moving until frame 16.

figure | 5-20 |
_____

Move Transform
Type-In settings for
the Free Camera.

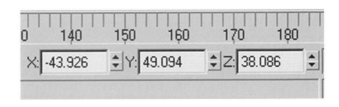

figure 5-21

The Rotate Transform Type-In values for the camera.

5. Move the Time slider to frame 40. In the Move Transform Type-In function, set the Absolute World coordinates as follows: X = 170.817, Y = −60.093, Z = 55.985.

NOTE: Entering transform type-in values is more efficiently done through the use of the coordinate text fields at the bottom of the 3ds Max interface, rather than opening a separate Transform Type-In dialog box. These fields can be used to enter Move, Rotate, or Scale values on a particular axis. If you wish to enter a precise position for an object, make sure the Move tool is active. If you wish to enter rotational information, be sure the Rotate tool is active. For Scale values, activate the Scale tool before entering values into these text fields.

6. In the Rotate Transform Type-In dialog box, set the Absolute World rotation values as follows: X = 80.0, Y = 0, Z = 60.0. Click the Set Keys button to add a key on frame 40.

7. Move the Time slider to frame 75. In the Move Transform Type-In dialog box, set the Absolute World coordinates to the following: X = 215.436, Y = −427.931, Z = 232.916.

8. In the Rotate Transform Type-In dialog box, enter the following Absolute World values to reorient the angle of the camera: X = 60.99, Y = −0.708, Z = 28.198.

9. Click the Set Keys button to set a keyframe for the new camera position on frame 75. Deactivate the Set Key button. Activate the Perspective viewport and press the C key to switch to the Camera view. Click the Play Animation button to preview the newly animated camera (see Figure 5-22). (Change to Wireframe mode for smoother playback.) Save your work so far to the local hard drive of your computer.

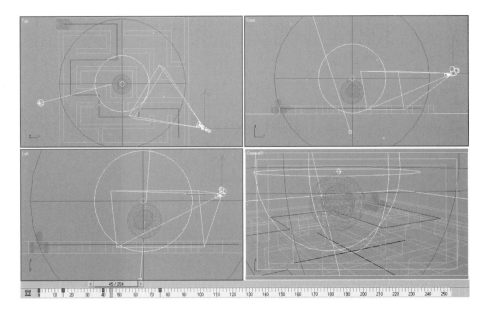

figure | 5-22 |

The newly created animated camera.

Now we will create and animate the second camera for the scene. This time, instead of setting keyframes for the animation, we will assign the second camera to an animation path, just as we did with the caveman car. In addition to applying a path constraint to attach a second camera to a path, we will apply a LookAt controller to keep the focal point of the camera on the plasma spheres.

1. In the Top viewport, create a Line spline with four vertices, starting at the top of the maze and drawing the line toward the bottom of the maze (see Figure 5-23). Name the new spline *main camera path*.

figure | 5-23 |

Creation of the main camera animation path.

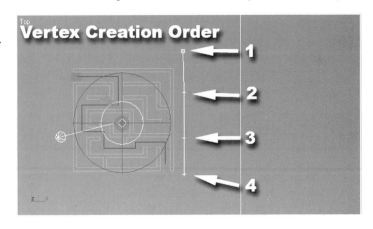

2. In the Modify panel, activate the vertex sub-object mode, select each vertex (starting with the first vertex at the top), and use the Move Transform Type-In dialog box to reposition each of the vertices into its appropriate location (see Figure 5-24). Use the following Absolute World coordinates:

- *Vertex 1:* X = 63.879,   Y = 452.367,   Z = 93.427
- *Vertex 2:* X = 327.789, Y = 176.442,   Z = 162.846
- *Vertex 3:* X = 438.648, Y = –154.729, Z = 93.427
- *Vertex 4:* X = 244.994, Y = –285.899, Z = 75.31

3. Right-click the second and third vertices and convert them to Bezier vertices. Using the various viewports, adjust the Bezier handles until the *main camera path* line resembles that shown in Figure 5-25. Once the line has been adjusted, deactivate the vertex sub-object mode.

4. Now to create a camera. In the Front viewport, create a Free Camera. Name the new camera *main camera*. In the Motion panel, within the Assign Controller rollout, select Position

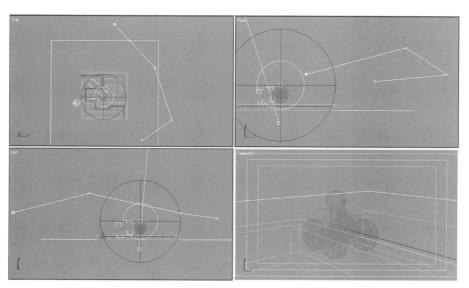

figure | 5-24 |

Path after the vertices have been repositioned.

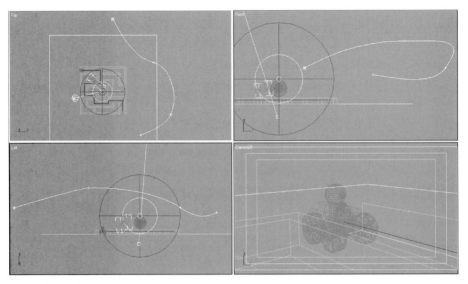

figure | 5-25 |

Camera path after it has been smoothed out using Beziers.

from the Transform list and click the Assign Controller button. Select Path Constraint from the Assign Position Controller dialog box.

5. Under the Path Parameters rollout, activate the Add Path button and select the *main camera path* object. We will not have the camera's rotation follow the path, because we will have the camera focus on the maze.

6. Select the Rotation transform under the Assign Controller rollout. Click the Assign Controller button and select LookAt Constraint from the Assign Rotation Controller dialog box.

7. Under the LookAt Constraint rollout, activate the Add LookAt Target button and select the *hedge maze* object. Deactivate the Add LookAt Target button.

8. Set the Select LookAt Axis to Z and check the box next to Flip.

9. Under Source/Upnode Alignment, set Source Axis to Y and Upnode Axis to Z. This will correctly orient the camera and keep the camera pointed to the maze object's pivot point as the camera travels along the path. Refer to Figure 5-26 for the LookAt Controller settings.

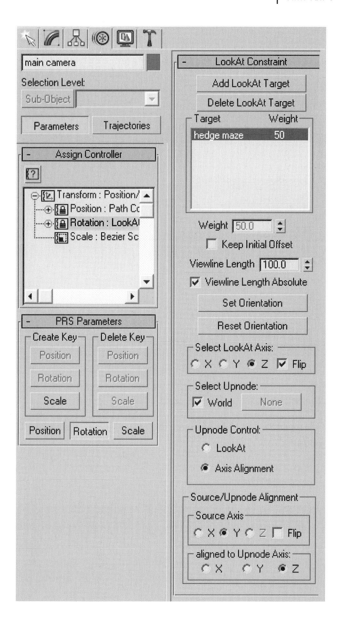

figure | 5-26 |

Settings and param-
eters used for the
camera's LookAt
constraint.

10. Now all we have to do is adjust the length of the animation for
    the main camera. Make sure the *main camera* object is selected.
    In the trackbar, select the keyframe on frame 0 and move it to
    frame 76.

11. Select the last keyframe on frame 254 and move it to frame 234.

12. Activate the *main camera* viewport and preview the animation
    (see Figure 5-27). Save your work to your computer.

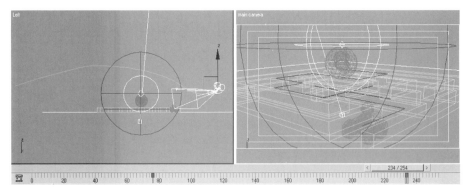

figure | 5-27 |

Keyframes of the *main camera* path animation moved to their new frame positions within the trackbar.

Great job! We now have two animated cameras in our scene. In the next exercise, we will set up 3ds Max to render both cameras in one video file, as well as add some special effects to the plasma balls. You can see how animated cameras can add a lot of interest to a fairly boring animation. This simple animation now appears to be much more complex than it really is, and it was fairly easy to set up.

SPECIAL EFFECTS AND CAMERA CUTS WITH VIDEO POST

Once the animation process has been completed on a project, the animation usually undergoes additional work during postproduction, where special effects are added and editing is performed. 3ds Max includes a utility known as Video Post, which allows some of these effects to be applied, although many effects are added via third-party software such as Autodesk's Combustion or Adobe's AfterEffects. Max's Video Post will allow us to add glow effects to our plasma spheres, as well as cut between the two animated cameras that exist in our scene. Figure 5-28 shows the Video Post dialog box.

We will not spend a lot of time describing every aspect of the Video Post interface. However, we will identify some of the main tools used to achieve the results we need to put the finishing touches on our labyrinth animation. Video Post utilizes *events*, which 3ds Max uses to composite elements into a final image frame. An event can include scene geometry, bitmap images, video files, or effects generated with

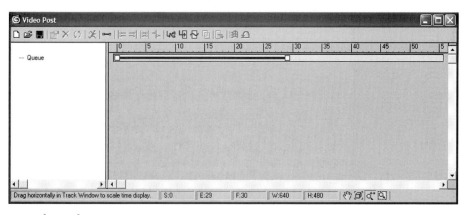

figure | 5-28 |

Video Post interface.

Video Post itself. These events are listed in a hierarchical list in the Video Post queue (see Figure 5-29).

Even though this is only an introductory look at the Video Post features, it is still important to take a look at some of the commonly used tools within the Video Post toolbar, some of which we will be using for our final composite (see Figure 5-30).

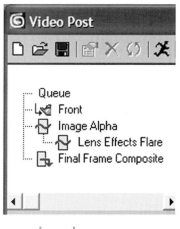

figure | 5-29 |

Video Post queue.

- *Add Scene Event:* This tool adds the current 3ds Max scene to the queue, which will render the Max scene in addition to any other effects to be executed from the queue.

- *Add Image Input Event:* This adds a previously saved still image or movie file to the scene.

- *Add Image Output Event:* This allows you to specify the file type for the executed result from the Video Post queue.

- *Edit Range Bar:* Similar to editing animation ranges, this tool allows you to edit the length of a particular event within the event tracks area.

- *Add Image Filter Event:* This tool allows you to add image-processing filters to an image or scene. Effects such as lens flares, glows, contrast adjustments, and fade effects are just some of the filters that can be applied.

figure | 5-30 |

Some of the more commonly used Video Post tools.

- *Execute Sequence:* Involved in the final step of a postproduction setup, this tool works in a manner similar to the Render Scene function, although it is possible to execute a video post-sequence without rendering the 3ds Max scene. By clicking on this tool, 3ds Max will execute the events found in the queue.

Now that you have a basic understanding of some of the most commonly used tools in the Video Post dialog box, it is time to set up the labyrinth scene's queue.

COMPOSITING THE FINAL RENDER

In the following exercise, we will set up the Video Post queue to render *intro camera* and *main camera*, as well as add glow effects to the plasma spheres. We will also add fade effects to the queue to produce a fade in and a fade out. Finally, an image output event will be used to produce a finished video file.

1. Open the *maze_post.max* file from the *Chapter 5* folder of the companion CD-ROM, or open the file saved from the previous exercise.

2. Go to Rendering > Video Post to open the Video Post dialog box. Click the Add Scene Event button from the Video Post toolbar. Under View, select *intro camera* from the drop-down list. Under Video Post Parameters, set VP End Time to *75* (see Figure 5-31). Once you have set up the event, click OK.

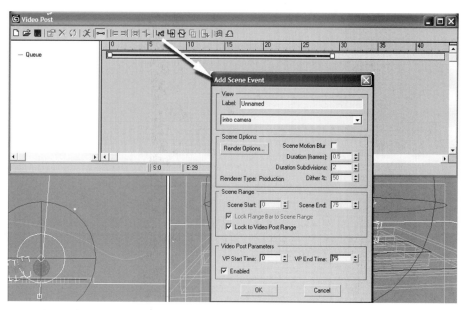

figure | 5-31 |

Settings for the *intro camera* scene event.

3. Repeat step 2, but this time select *main camera* from the drop-down list to add a second scene event to the queue. Under Video Post Parameters, set VP Start Time to *76*. Now we have both cameras set up as scene events.

4. Next, we will set up a glow effect for the plasma. Before we add another event to the queue, we need to change the Material Effects channel of the *Purple Plasma* material. Open the Material editor (M key) and select the *Purple Plasma* sample slot. In the Material editor's toolbar, click and hold the Material Effects Channel button and change the number from 0 to *1* (see Figure 5-32). Close the Material editor.

5. In the Video Post dialog box, click the Add Image Filter Event button. In the Add Image Filter Event dialog box, change the Label name to *Plasma*. From the Filter Plug-in drop-down list, select Lens Effects Glow. (It should be noted that lens effects can also be added as rendering effects without the use of Video Post.) Click the Setup button to open the Lens Effects Glow dialog box.

figure | 5-32 |

Changing the
Material Effects
channel of the
Purple Plasma
material.

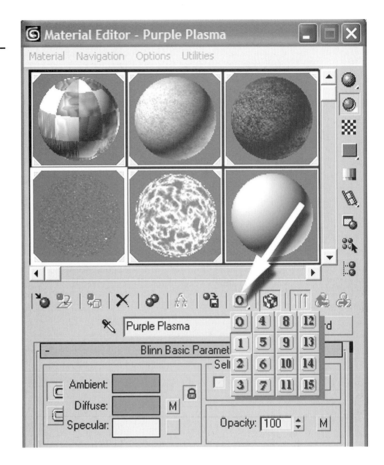

6. In the Properties tab, uncheck Object ID and check the box next to Effects ID. This will apply the glow to any object whose Material Effects channel has been set to 1.

7. In the Preferences tab, set Size to *3.0*. Click the Preview button to see how the glow will look (see Figure 5-33). Note that a generic scene will be rendered to show the effect. We will not view how this looks on the actual plasma objects yet (although you can choose to render a preview of the effect as it will appear in the scene by clicking on the VP Queue button, next to the Preview button, after the effect has been set up). Click on OK to accept the Lens Effects Glow settings.

8. After you set up the glow effect, click somewhere in the queue to deselect the *Plasma* event. Click the Add Image Filter Event button and name the new event *Fade In*. Select Fade from the drop-down list and then click the Setup button. Select In and then click OK.

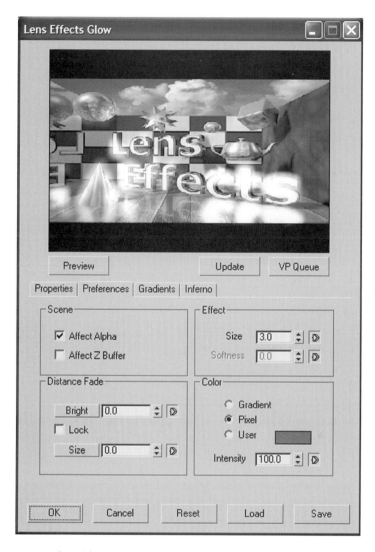

figure |5-33|

Lens Effects
Glow dialog.

9. Under Video Post Parameters, set VP End Time to *15*. Click OK to close the dialog box.

10. Repeat steps 8 and 9, but label the filter event *Fade Out* and set VP Start Time to *239*. (Do not forget to click the Setup button and select Out.)

11. Now for the last event. Click the Add Image Output Event button. In the dialog box, name the event *Final Composite*. Click the Files button. In the Select Image File for the Video Post Output dialog box, set *Save as type* to AVI File, name the file *Labyrinth_Final*, and then click Save. When the AVI File Compression Setup dialog box appears, feel free to use whatever

video compression codec you wish. After setting up the compression, click OK to close the output event.

12. Activate the Zoom Time tool at the bottom right-hand corner of the Video Post dialog box, and drag to the left to zoom the event tracks area until you can see all track ranges. You should have something that resembles that shown in Figure 5-34.

13. Click the Execute Sequence button. In the Execute Video Post dialog box, under Output Size select *35mm 1.85:1 (cine)* from the drop-down list and set Width to *400*. Press Enter (see Figure 5-35).

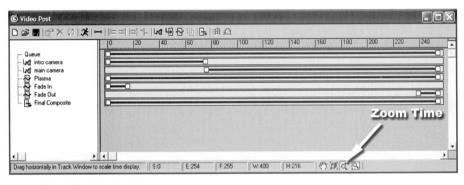

figure | 5-34 |

Video Post queue with all of the events.

figure | 5-35 |

Execute Video Post dialog settings.

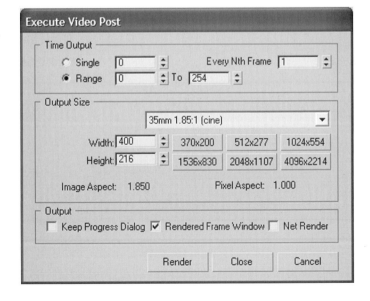

14. Click the Render button to produce the final .*avi* movie. Once the rendering process is complete, you may locate the movie file on your hard drive and play the final result (see Figure 5-36). If you wish, you may add lights to the scene to brighten it up a bit. Save your work.

Congratulations! We have completed a really cool little animation using a variety of techniques, including video post-compositing and effects processing. Now you can add those finishing touches to your own animations.

SUMMARY

Now that you have had some exposure to path animation, animated lights and materials, and video postproduction, we hope you can see the benefit of these additional animation techniques. These methods are widely used in the industry and can prove to be a huge time saver. Try using these approaches in your own animations and you will surely find them to be an invaluable way of animating various aspects of your 3D scenes.

figure | 5-36 |

Frame from the final animation.

in review

1. List at least three scenarios in which a path animation would be a good approach.

2. Describe what a LookAt constraint is used for.

3. What is a Material Effects channel?

4. What does a Noise Float controller do when applied to an animation track?

5. What is a video post-event? How is it used?

↗ EXPLORING ON YOUR OWN

1. Create a number of different light objects and experiment with animating various light properties other than the Multiplier. Try animating shadows, light color, attenuation, and so on.

2. Attempt more complex animated materials by animating aspects of the material such as self-illumination and shader parameters.

ADVENTURES IN DESIGN

USING VIDEOS AS MATERIALS

Introduction

When it comes to 3D animation, the animator needs to be as much a magician as he is an animator. Often, many of the effects created for a final animation shot are done using tricks and shortcuts in order to produce an effect that otherwise might have taken many long hours to accomplish using other methods. One such shortcut is the use of videos as object materials. By using video clips as a material, an animator can save a tremendous amount of time when it comes to producing certain types of effects. Video materials can be used to apply video images on a television model, or be used as a background environment map when animating 3D characters with live-action footage.

Importing a Video into the Material Editor

Importing videos into the 3ds Max Material editor is as easy as loading a bitmap image into a material map slot. The imported video acts and behaves in much the same way as an image file, giving you the same type of tiling and positioning control you would have with a static image. Let's try importing a video clip into an empty material slot and applying it to a basic object.

1. Start a new Max scene. In the Top viewport, create a box with a length, width, and height of 75.

2. Open the Time Configuration dialog box (see Figure B-1). Set the frame rate under Custom to *15* fps. Set the animation Length to *200*.

3. Open the Material editor and select an empty material sample slot.

4. Keep the default Blinn shader parameters as they are and open the Maps rollout. In the Diffuse Color map channel, click the large None button to open the Material/Map browser.

5. From the material list, select Bitmap. From the Select Bitmap Image File dialog box, select the *fireball.avi* movie from the *AID Video* folder located on the companion CD-ROM. Click OK to load the file.

6. You will see that the sample sphere turns black, but because the video clip depicts an animated explosion, initially we will not see anything. If you scrub the Time slider or click Play in the animation playback controls, you will be able to view the explosion in the material sample slot (see Figure B-2).

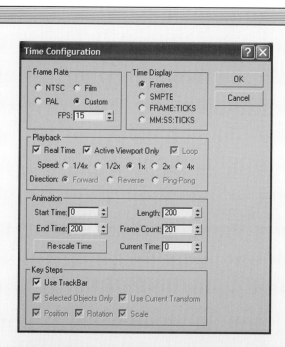

Figure B-1.
Time
Configuration
dialog settings.

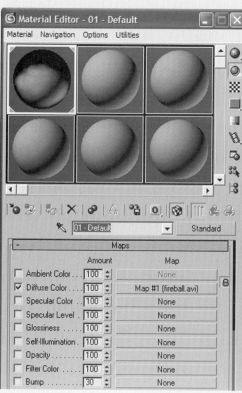

Figure B-2.
The imported
video appears in
the sample
sphere, as seen
on frame 6.

7. Click the Go to Parent button in the Material editor tools and activate the Show Map in Viewport button. This will allow us to see the video material in the viewport.

8. Apply the material to the cube object in your scene.

9. We can now see the material on our cube. However, the video will not play in our viewport (although the material will be updated if we move to different frames in the timeline). To see the final result (see Figure B-3), go to Rendering > Environment and in the Environment dialog box set the Background color to something other than black. (Because the material starts as black, changing

the color of the background will allow us to better see the object.)

10. Select Rendering > Render to open the Render Scene dialog box. Select Active Time Segment within the Time Output section. Set Output Size to *320 x 240*.

11. Under Render Output, click the Files button to open a Render Output File dialog box. Under Save as Type, select AVI and give your movie a file name. Save it to a location on your hard drive. Click OK.

12. When prompted, select the compression you would like to use. We used the Cinepak codec by Radius in our final AVI. Click OK once the compression has been set.

Figure B-3. Material applied to the cube, as seen on frame 20.

13. Click the Render button to render the scene. The finished rendered AVI movie will depict the box object with the video material applied to it.

That is all there is to it! You can easily incorporate motion graphics into your materials as easily as you do static images. You can even use static image sequences if you like. To load an image sequence, known as an *.ifl* (Image File List) file, select Bitmap from the Material/Map browser and select the first image in the sequence. Within the Select Bitmap Image File dialog box, check the box next to Sequence, and the images following in the sequence will be loaded in as an animated material.

6

charting your course

A rainstorm or snowstorm, a spray of water from a hose, smoke billowing from a burning vehicle, and a large flock of birds all have one thing in common: when created in a 3D environment they can be composed of a massive number of objects. Trying to animate and control a large amount of objects can be unwieldy and unproductive, especially if they all have similar movement and properties. To the rescue are particle systems. Particle systems are a selection of tools that create and define the emission of a potentially large number of particles from a single source. The particle can be rendered in a variety of 2D and 3D shapes and can even appear as copies of geometry already located, even hidden, in your scene.

Space warps are forces (such as gravity or a vortex) that can alter a particle's direction and speed based on the parameters set for the space warp. Deflectors are planes, spheres, or even scene objects that, surprisingly, deflect any particles that impact them. Particles can bounce, stop, or even spawn new particles when they collide with a deflector. Using particle systems in conjunction with space warps and deflectors, you can make your storm of hailstones, gold coins, or spacecraft debris rain down upon the earth, bouncing off buildings and cars and coming to a rest on the ground.

chapter objectives

- **Understand particle systems**
- **Create a Super Spray particle system**
- **Define particle speed and quantity**
- **Specify a particle type to render**
- **Adjust particle spawning to create additional particles**
- **Load and save particle presets**
- **Alter particle directions with space warps**
- **Bounce particles with deflectors**

UNDERSTANDING PARTICLE SYSTEMS

Particle systems come in two different types: event driven and non-event driven. Event-driven particle systems use a system of tests and operators, partitioned in groups called events, to determine the actions of the particles. Operators are features (such as shape, size, and material) that define the particle. They are placed in sequential order according to how they are to be applied to particles. Tests are conditions that must be met before a particle can continue to the next event.

Tests can look at a particle's age (how long the particle exists), its size, whether it has impacted a deflector, or many other occurrences within the scene. 3ds Max has a robust event-driven particle system called Particle Flow (see Figure 6-1), which uses a flow chart analogy for laying out the events, operators, and tests in a 3ds Max scene. In the Particle View window, operators and tests (which link one event to the next) are dragged from a depot into events. Unfortunately, Particle Flow is extensive and beyond the scope of this book. See the section "Adventures in Design – Particle Flow" for an example of Particle Flow in action.

Non-event-driven particle systems use a series of value-based parameters to determine the appearance of the particles as well as size, speed, and other characteristics. All of the non-event-driven particle systems in 3ds Max have two common features: an emitter and the

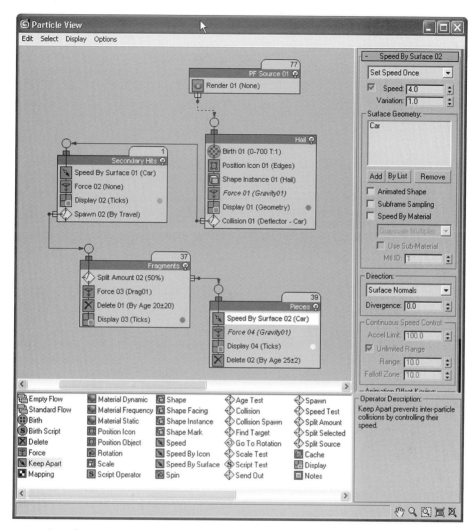

figure | 6-1 |

The Particle View window is used to lay out the events, operators, and tests of a Particle Flow particle system.

particles themselves. The emitter (see Figure 6-2) is a non-rendering object used as the location where the particles begin their lives. Depending on the particle system selected, the emitter can be one of a variety of shapes, including planes, boxes, cylinders, and emitter-specific icons. When using the PArray or PCloud particle systems, the system emitter can act only as an icon in the viewport, whereas selected geometry in the scene can actually emit the particles.

figure | 6-2 |

From left to right, the emitters for a Spray, Snow, Particle Cloud, and Super Spray particle system.

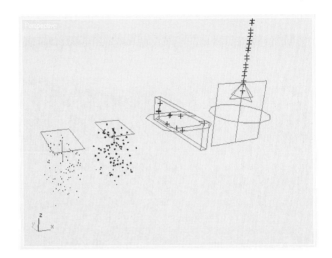

The real meat of a particle system is the particles. You create particle systems to generate a large number of objects that follow roughly the same course, and you have a great deal of control over what those particles do and how they appear. The most important aspect of the particles is how they look, also known as the type of particle emitted. Depending on the particle systems selected, the particles can be 2D or 3D and can appear in a variety of standard shapes, including triangles, stars, tetrahedrons, cubes, and spheres. A special 2D particle shape, called a "facing" particle, consists of a square shape that is constantly oriented toward the camera or viewport. Using a facing particle, with an opacity-mapped material applied to the particle system, you can quickly create the appearance of smoke, dust, or snowflakes without the need for a massive number of particles. For the purpose of viewport speed, the quantity and type of particles shown in the viewports can be different from those shown in the rendered frames.

Two of the more powerful and entertaining particle-type options available are MetaParticle and Instanced Geometry. Metaparticles, based on metaball technology, are spherical particles, each of which has an area of influence around it. Whenever two areas of influence intersect, the metaparticles change their shapes so that they pull toward each other and appear to meld together. This gives the appearance of blobs of fluid intermixing in the particle stream. When paired with a shiny or reflective material, the metaparticles can add an amazing look to your scene.

NOTE: Metaparticles are computationally intensive, and they can add significant time to your renderings, especially when used with ray-traced material.

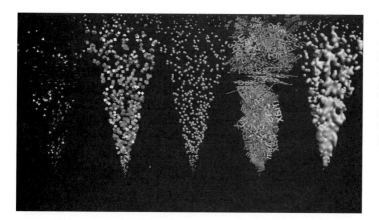

From left to right, the particles types selected are Triangle, Cube, Sphere, Instanced Geometry, and MetaParticle.

When you select Instanced Geometry as the particle type, any 3D object in your scene (even hidden geometry) can be substituted for each particle at rendering time. This gives you the ability to shoot bullets out of one end of a weapon with one particle system and eject shell casings out of the side with another. When a group is selected as the instanced object, 3ds Max will randomly select a group member for each particle emitted. Figure 6-3 shows examples of some of the particle types available to the Super Spray particle system.

PARTICLE SYSTEM TYPES

3ds Max comes packaged with a variety of particle systems, several of which can be classified as "legacy" because their functionality has been included in some of the more capable systems. The two oldest, and the first to be included with 3ds Max, are Spray and Snow. Although these still function as they have for several years, their capabilities have been eclipsed with the Super Spray and Blizzard particle systems, both of which were formerly third-party programs purchased separately from Max. The greatest drawbacks of the legacy particle systems are their limited particle selections and particle control. The non-event-driven particle systems included with 3ds Max are as follows:

● *Spray:* A very basic particle system, in Spray particles are emitted from a plane-shaped emitter with a choice of rendering either tetrahedron or facing particles.

● *Snow:* Similar to the Spray particle system, Snow has additional controls for adding a tumble factor to each 2D particle emitted. This can give the star, triangle, or facing particles the rotational randomness found in falling snow or blowing leaves.

- *Super Spray:* This has a large amount of control over the emission, motion, and type of particles and whether particles can spawn additional particles upon collisions. Many features have Variation parameters that add randomness to the particles' motion or appearance. Particle parameters can be saved as presets and loaded into other 3ds Max scenes.

- *Blizzard:* This system is an updated version of the Snow particle system with much of the control found in the Super Spray particle system.

- *PArray: This* uses an existing geometry object in the scene as the emitter. Particles can be emitted from the object's edges, vertices, or faces.

- *PCloud:* This system restricts the location of the particles to the volume of the PCloud icon or a selected geometry object.

CREATING A SUPER SPRAY PARTICLE SYSTEM

When creating a linear spray of particles, with non-event-driven particle systems, the Super Spray system is generally the most common particle system used. Its control over the spread, speed, timing, particle type, and particle motion meets the needs of most particle situations. In the following exercises you will create a Super Spray particle system that emits particles from the back of a deep-welled object and around another object.

Creating the Emitter

To create an emitter, perform the following steps:

1. From the companion CD-ROM, open the file *Super Spray.max.*

2. In the Command panel, select Create > Geometry > Particle Systems from the drop-down list and then click the Super Spray button (see Figure 6-4).

3. In the Left viewport, click and drag to create the Super Spray emitter (see Figure 6-5). The initial direction of the particles is always in the positive Z direction of the viewport in which they are created.

4. Move the emitter to the back of the box-shaped object.

5. Drag the Time slider and watch the particles as they exit the emitter, flow in a straight line, and then disappear.

DEFINING THE PARTICLE SPEED AND QUANTITY

As you see when you drag the Time slider, the particles leave the emitter from a single point, travel in a straight line, and then vanish before they approach the end of the box. There are a limited number of particles in a scene, and each particle has a predetermined life span measured in frames. Once a particle has exhausted its allotment of frames, it dies and is recycled in the particle system to be reemitted. Two parameters define the distance a particle travels before it dies: Life and Speed. To increase the distance a particle travels, either increase the Life setting (the object travels at the same velocity for a longer amount of time) or the Speed setting (the object travels for the same amount of time but at a greater velocity), or both.

figure |6-4|

Select Super Spray from the Command panel.

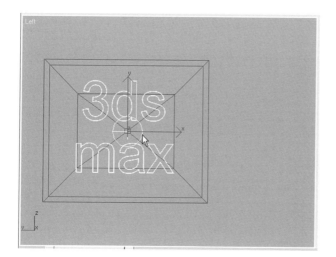

figure |6-5|

Create the Super Spray particle system in the Left viewport.

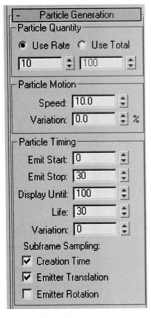

Particle quantity and speed are
set in the Particle Generation
rollout.

You should also notice that the emitter discontinues discharging particles soon after it starts. The Super Spray particle system only emits particles over the range of time defined by the Emit Start and Emit Stop parameters in the Particle Generation rollout (see Figure 6-6). Particles begin emitting at the Emit Start frame and end at the Emit Stop frame, allowing you to bracket the particles during a specific time frame. The Display Until parameter determines at which frame 3ds Max will stop displaying and rendering particles regardless of the Emit Stop setting. For example, if Emit Stop is set to 300 but Display Until is set to 200, no particle will be visible after frame 200.

Finally, the density of particles in the rendered scene and in the viewports must be addressed. The Particle Quantity section has two options: Use Rate and Use Total, each with a spinner for entering a quantity value. Use Rate determines the number of particles emitted during each frame, whereas Use Total sets the number of particles emitted over the life of the system. Use Rate is more commonly used and is the preferred option for creating a constant stream of particles.

Viewport performance can take a significant hit when you are trying to display a large number of objects, especially when the objects are animated. To keep your performance from degrading while particle systems are visible, only display in the viewports a fraction of the number of particles emitted and rendered. The Percentage of Particles setting in the Basic Parameters rollout determines the percentage of particles, as defined by the Use Rate or Use Total setting, displayed in the viewports. All particles emitted are shown when the scene is rendered.

Setting the Life and Speed

To establish the Life and Speed parameters of the particle system, perform the following steps:

1. Continue with the previous exercise or open the file *Super Spray Speed.max* from the companion CD-ROM.

2. Drag the Time slider to frame 100.

3. Select the particle system and then increase the Emit Stop and Display Until values to *200*. This will force the particle system to emit and display particles for the current length of the animation in the scene (see Figure 6-7). The particles still only travel half the distance to the opening of the box.

4. Increase the Speed to 15 to boost the velocity by 50 percent.

5. Increase the Life value until the particles pass beyond the text object at the mouth of the box.

6. Click the Play Animation button at the bottom of the user interface to ensure that a constant flow of particles emits toward the mouth of the box.

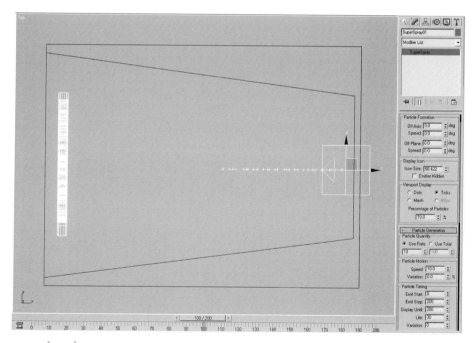

figure | 6-7 |

Setting the Emit Stop and Display Until parameters extends the amount of time particles will be emitted and displayed.

Setting the Quantity and Spread

Setting the number of particles to be emitted determines the density of the particles in the system. A Use Rate of 10 may be fine at the beginning of a project, but as the Speed or Life is increased, the Use Rate may also need to be increased to maintain the particle density. To establish quantity and spread, perform the following steps:

1. In the Particle Generation rollout, set the Use Rate to *15*.

2. Set the Percentage of Particles to *100*, temporarily, to see the actual number of particles to be emitted.

3. Increase the two Spread values in the Particle Formation section of the Basic Parameters rollout until the particles are emitted in a pattern slightly wider than the inside of the box, similar to the particle system shown in Figure 6-8. Off Axis Spread fans the particles out horizontally and Off Plane Spread fans the particles vertically.

4. Set the Percentage of Particles back to *10*.

SELECTING A PARTICLE TYPE

When selecting a particle type, there are two areas to consider: how the particles are to appear in the viewports and how they are to appear in the rendered frames. There are four viewport particle display options, found in the Viewport Display section (see Figure 6-9) of the Basic Parameters rollout, that balance display information with display speed. Dots and Ticks represent the particles in the scene as dots or

figure | 6-8 |

With Percentage of Particles set to 100, the total number of particles is shown in the viewports.

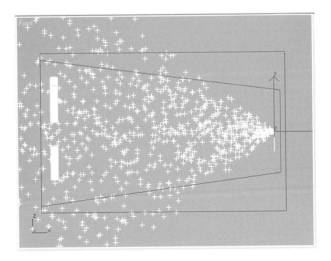

crosses in the viewports. Both of these options efficiently display the particles with a minimum of resources required. However, the Ticks option generally presents the particles in a manner that is a bit easier to follow in the viewports.

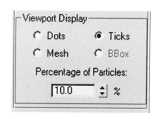

figure |6-9|

The Mesh and BBox options display the particles as 3D mesh objects. The Mesh option shows all polygons of the objects at the selected rendering level of each viewport (see Figure 6-10), and the BBox option shows each particle (see Figure 6-11) as a bounding box (i.e., the smallest possible box the object could completely fit within). Mesh can provide an accurate picture of where and how the particles are dispersed in the scene and how they interact with the other geometry. This is even more helpful when Instanced Geometry (discussed

Set the particle viewport display option in the Viewport Display section.

figure |6-10|

With the viewport display set to Mesh, each particle's geometry is shown in each viewport.

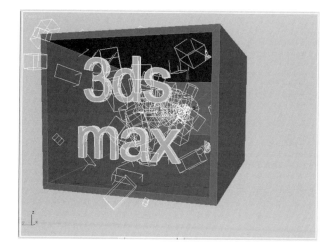

figure |6-11|

With the viewport display set to BBox, only the bounding box for each particle is shown.

in material to follow) is selected as the particle type. Although BBox is not nearly the offender that Mesh is, both options can cause a significant degradation of performance in your scene. Refrain from using either of these options, especially when complex particle geometry or a large number of particles is used.

NOTE: The Mesh option presents an idea of where the particles flow in the scene, but this is only an approximate result. When the Percentage of Particles parameter is set to a value less than 100, only a portion of the particles (even when displayed as mesh objects) is shown.

Setting the Rendered Particle Size and Type

Particle size is dependent on the type of particle selected, as well as on the geometry size when instanced geometry or the Tension setting of metaparticles is used. Particles that are too small may not be visible or may not give the impression of volume that they should, and particles that are too large may overlap one another in an unwanted manner.

Like many other features found in a Super Spray particle system, Size is teamed up with a Variation parameter that can introduce a random difference in particle size. The Variation value is a percentage greater than or less than the Size value, which represents a range for the particles' allowable dimensions.

Using Standard Particles

To experiment with using standard particles, perform the following steps:

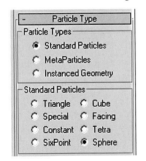

figure | 6-12 |

Select Standard Particles and Sphere to define the particle shape.

1. Continue with the previous exercise or open *Super Spray Type.max* from the companion CD-ROM and move the Time slider to frame 100.

2. Select the particle system and open the Modify panel.

3. In the Particle Type rollout, select Standard Particles in the Particle Types section and then select Sphere as the Standard Particle type (see Figure 6-12).

4. Render the Camera viewport. Where are the particles? They are there, but they are difficult to see because their default Size value of 1.0 is too small for the size of the objects in the scene and the proximity of the camera.

5. In the Particle Generation rollout, set the Size value to about 20 and then render the viewport again.

6. Now the particles are visible and a good size for this exercise (see Figure 6-13). Verify that the Variation value is set to 0.0 and then note that the particles vary in size. This is not caused by the Variation setting but by the Grow For and Fade For settings. Grow For defines the number of frames by which the particles grow, from a size of 0.0 to the value specified by the Size parameter. The Fade For setting defines the number of frames, at the end of the particles' lives, by which they shrink (down to zero).

7. Set Fade For to 0, but leave Grow For at 10 so that the spheres will expand in size rather than just appearing at the emitter fully grown.

8. Try experimenting with the other Standard Particle types to see how they look in your scene.

Using Metaparticles

As previously mentioned, a metaparticle has a sphere of influence around it that determines (when it is near another metaparticle from the same particle system) whether the geometry around it should be drawn together to form a blob. Metaparticles are the particle of choice when making fluid animation such as lava lamps, amorphous-shaped attackers, or the occasional zero-gravity alien blood effect. The Tension setting influences the effect of the metaparticle setting's blending. The greater the tension, the more likely the particles are to blend. Continue with the previous exercise by performing the following steps:

1. In the Particle Type rollout, select MetaParticles.

2. Render the viewport.

figure | 6-13 |

With the Size set to 20, the particles are now visible.

Using Instanced Geometry

The instanced geometry particle type allows you to select geometry objects in the scene as substitutes for the particles emitted. Using instanced geometry, your particle system can appear to be emitting anything from text to characters to spaceships. Only one object can be selected as the instanced geometry object. However, if the selected object is a group, each member of that group will be randomly emitted from the particle system.

Using a group with a significant Variation value can create the appearance of many more objects being emitted than there actually are. When using the instanced geometry particle type, the Size parameter has a different outcome regarding the size of the objects emitted. Rather than an ambiguous value, the Size value becomes a multiplier of the actual size of the object. For example, if a cylinder (used as instanced geometry) has a radius of 7 units and the Size parameter is set to 8, the emitted cylinders would have a radius of 56 units. To practice using instanced geometry, perform the following steps:

1. Right-click in an empty area of a viewport to open the quad menu. Click Unhide All to unhide the apple-shaped object that will soon be emitted by the particle system (see Figure 6-14).

2. In the Particle Type rollout, select Instanced Geometry as the particle type.

3. In the Instancing Parameters section, click the Pick Object button (see Figure 6-15) and then select the apple located behind the box.

4. Render the scene. Your Rendered Frame window shows only a slight change of color in the green spectrum. This is because the Size setting is multiplying the size of the apple, already a good size in the scene, to 20 times its original.

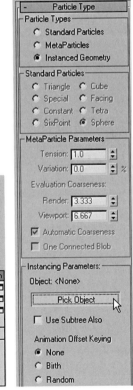

figure | 6-14 |

figure | 6-15 |

Select Unhide All to unhide the geometry that will be emitted.

Select Instanced Geometry and then click on the Pick Object button.

figure | 6-16 |

Setting the Size value lower than 1.0 reduces the size of the instanced geometry object.

5. In the Particle Generation rollout, set the size to 0.25 and then render the scene again. This produces a flow of apple particles that is much more appealing and manageable (see Figure 6-16).

6. Hide the Apple object. It does not need to be visible to act as the instanced geometry object.

ALTERING PARTICLE DIRECTION WITH DEFLECTORS AND SPACE WARPS

Space warps are non-rendering objects in 3ds Max that can influence the appearance of geometry or the motion of the particles in a particle system, the latter of which is the focus of this section. Space warps can affect particle systems in several ways, including altering the direction and speed of the particles, introducing randomness to the motion, and causing particles to bounce off objects in the scene. Space warps can improve the appearance of a particle system by altering the (often linear) movement of particles and can create the impression of an external force, such as wind, gravity, or an obstruction impeding the flow of particles. The space warps that can affect particle systems in 3ds Max include forces and deflector types. Forces include the following:

● *Motor:* Creates a rotational force to the particles that approach it, altering their motion to spin around the Motor gizmo in the scene.

● *Vortex:* Similar to the Motor space warp, Vortex adds a rotational spin to the particle stream. However, the particles are also drawn together and down the length of the Vortex gizmo in a swirling pattern similar to water going around a sink and down a drain.

- *Path Follow:* Causes the particles to follow the contiguous segments of a selected shape in the scene. The particles can follow the path for their entire life, or the path's influence time frame can be determined by parameters set in the space warp's Modify panel.

- *Wind:* Adds a linear influence to the particles to simulate the effect of wind. Randomness can be added to the Wind effect using the Turbulence parameters.

- *Push:* Used to evenly scatter the particles in a direction perpendicular to the orientation of the space warp's gizmo.

- *Drag:* Works in the opposite manner as the Push space warp. Particle motion is slowed and the particles bunch as if they have entered a denser material or an area of greater resistance.

- *PBomb:* Used to disperse particles as if the particle system has been exploded. Can be used with the PArray particle system to simulate blowing up a mesh object.

- *Gravity:* Applies a linear or spherical force, similar to Wind, but with fewer controls for turbulence or randomness.

Deflector types include the following:

- *Deflector:* Causes particles that impact the deflectors to bounce at the reciprocal angle that they hit the deflector. The Bounce parameter acts as a multiplier regarding the speed of the particles as they exit the deflector relative to their speed when they impact it. Deflectors are planar and SDeflectors are spherical. A UDeflector allows the selection of a scene object to act as a deflector.

- *OmniFlector:* Improved version of the deflector, with additional controls for refracting and spawning particles and the ability to turn the deflection capability on and off. Omniflectors can be created as planes (POmniFlect) or spheres (SOmniFlect), or they can specify a scene object as the deflector (UOmniFlect).

- *DynaFlector:* Similar to OmniFlectors, DynaFlectors allow the particles to affect scene geometry. For example, you could use particles to knock objects off a shelf or to spin a target that they impact.

The presence of a space warp in a scene does not immediately cause it to influence all of the particle systems. The particle systems must be associated, or bound, to the space warp using the Bind to Space Warp button in the Main toolbar (see Figure 6-17). Simply click the button, click on the particle system, and then drag and release over the space warp. The space warp will temporarily turn white to indicate a successful binding process. To verify or delete the binding, select the particle system and then open the Modify panel. All space warp bindings appear in the Stack View window above all modifiers that may be applied. To temporarily discontinue the space warp's effect, simply click the light bulb icon (see Figure 6-18) to the left of the space warp's binding; to delete the binding, select the binding, right-click, and then select Delete from the context menu that opens. To modify the parameters for the space warp, you must select the space warp in the viewports rather than selecting the binding in the particle system's Modify panel.

NOTE: Unlike the linking procedure in 3ds Max, there is no parent/child relationship between the particle system and the space warp. The order of the objects selected when you click-drag-release to bind the space warp does not matter.

Adding Gravity and Wind to a Particle System

To add gravity and wind to a particle system, perform the following steps:

1. Continue with the previous exercise or open *Super Spray SWarps.max* from the companion CD-ROM.

2. Drag the Time slider to frame 100 so that the effects of the space warps will be apparent.

3. Go to Create > Space Warps > Forces in the Command panel and then click the Gravity button (see Figure 6-19).

4. Click, drag, and then release in the Top viewport to create the Gravity icon. The location and size of the icon does not matter, but the orientation does. Creating it in the Top viewport causes the Gravity space warp to be oriented in the World negative Z direction, as indicated by the direction arrow at the base of the icon.

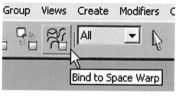

figure | 6-17 |

Use the Bind to Space Warp button to cause the space warp to influence the particle system.

figure | 6-18 |

The light bulb icon indicates that the space warp binding is currently turned on.

figure | 6-19 |

Select Gravity in the Create panel.

5. Click the Bind to Space Warp button, click on the particle system, and then drag and release over the Gravity space warp. A dashed rubber-banding line appears between the particle system, and the cursor changes to indicate that a binding is taking place. The cursor will have a white box when it is over a valid bindable object and an X inside when it is not (see Figure 6-20).

6. The Front viewport best shows the effect of the Gravity space warp on the particles. They drop through the box and off the screen. This will be fixed in the next section using deflectors.

7. Select the Gravity space warp and in the Modify panel set the Strength value to 0.75 and ensure that the Planar gravity type is selected.

8. Go to Create > Space Warps in the Command panel and click the Wind button. Create a Wind space warp in the Front viewport. This will cause the Wind space warp to push the particles across the box.

9. Rotate the Wind space warp 180 degrees around the Z axis in the Top viewport so that the particles are blown from left to right as they exit the emitter. The space warp can be relocated to a more convenient location, if required, but its actual location does not matter.

figure | 6-20 |

A white box appears in the bind cursor when it is over an object type that can be bound to.

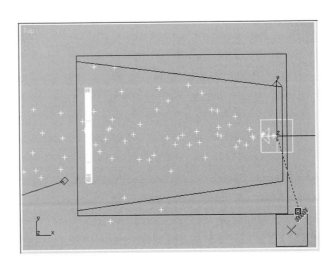

10. Bind the Wind space warp to the particle system using the procedure in step 3. The particles are pushed out of the box toward the top of the screen in the Top viewport.

11. Set the Strength to 0.5 and the Turbulence to 4.0 to reduce the influence of the Wind space warp and to introduce randomness to the Wind space warp's effect (see Figure 6-21).

Adding Deflectors to the Particle System

The Gravity and Wind space warps have accomplished their goals of moving the particle stream downward and to the side of the box, but the particles exit the box through the sides and bottom, rather than through the mouth as they should. This will be rectified by creating deflectors to restrict and control the particle motion by forcing the particles to bounce off the walls and the text object.

1. Continue with the previous exercise or open the *Super Spray SWarps2.max* file from the companion CD-ROM.

2. Drag the Time slider to frame 100 so that the effects of the deflectors on the particles will be apparent.

3. Go to Create > Space Warps > Deflectors in the Command panel and then click the UOmniFlect button (see Figure 6-22).

4. Click and drag in a viewport to create the deflector icon. Its location and orientation are irrelevant.

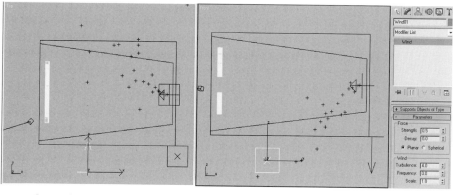

figure |6-21|

After binding and rotating the Wind space warp, adjust the Strength and Turbulence parameters to alter the Wind space warp's effect on the particles.

figure | 6-22 |

Click on the UOmniFlect button to create a deflector that uses a scene object as a deflector.

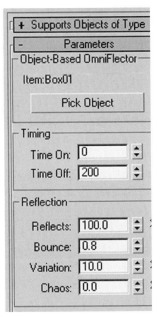

figure | 6-23 |

Set the UOmniFlect parameters to utilize the box as a deflector and to set the particles' resultant motion after impacting the deflector.

5. In the Parameters rollout, click the Pick Object button and then click on the box object. The box will flash white temporarily to indicate the selection is successful, and the name of the object will appear above the Pick Object button.

6. In the Timing section, set the Time On value to 0 and the Time Off value to 200. This will cause the particles to be deflected for the entire animation length of the scene.

7. Set the Bounce parameter to 0.8 so that the particles will bounce off a wall at only 80 percent of the velocity that they impact the wall (see Figure 6-23). Change the Variation setting to 10.0, allowing the actual bounce speed to vary between 70 percent and 90 percent of the impact speed and to establish a small amount of randomness.

NOTE: Be aware that the Bounce value is cumulative for each time a particle collides with a deflector. For example, if Bounce is set to 0.5 and a particle collides with a deflector, or several deflectors, 3 times the final velocity of the particle will be 0.125 (12.5 percent) of its original.

8. Bind the Deflector to the particle system in the same manner you bound the space warps. The particles are still pushed downward and away by the Gravity and Wind space warps, but the box object, acting as a deflector, prevents the particles from escaping (see Figure 6-24).

9. Render the Camera viewport (see Figure 6-25).

10. Hold down the Shift key and move the UOmniFlect deflector to create a clone of it. In the Clone Options dialog box, select the Copy option and then click OK.

11. Click the Pick Object button and then click on the text object. This will cause the text object to act as a deflector as well, and will prevent the instanced apples from passing through the surfaces of the text.

12. When bound space warps are cloned, the binding itself is not. Bind the new UOmniFlect deflector to the particle system.

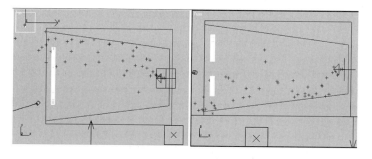

figure | 6-24 |

After binding the deflector to the particle system, the particles no longer flow through the walls of the box.

figure | 6-25 |

The apples now only leave the box through the mouth.

13. Render the scene one more time and you see that the apples no longer pass through the text.

ADJUSTING PARTICLE SPAWNING TO CREATE ADDITIONAL PARTICLES

Spawning is the creation of new particles when a particle collides with a deflector to which the particle system is bound. The original particle can die at the point of collision, be unaffected, or die a specified variable amount of time after the collision. The spawned particles can be created at the first collision only, or at a specified number of collisions.

When the collisions occur, any number of particles can be generated from each collision, so caution must be used so that an unwieldy number of new particles are not spawned. For example, a particle system composed of 1,000 particles (each particle of which spawns 10 particles at each of its 5 collisions with the deflectors) can create 50,000 particles in the scene in a short amount of time. If these particles are composed of instanced geometry objects, each with 48 faces,

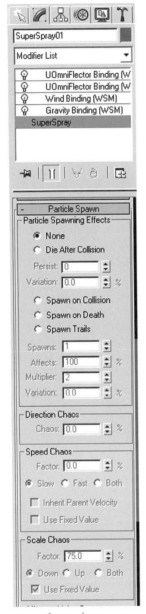

figure | 6-26 |

After selecting the particle system in the viewports, select the SuperSpray entry in the modifier stack and then expand the Particle Spawn rollout.

2,400,000 faces will be quickly added to a scene. To create additional particles, perform the following steps:

1. Continue with the exercise or open the *Super Spray Spawn.max* file from the companion CD-ROM.

2. Leave or move the Time slider to frame 0. This will allow you to make changes to the particle system without degrading the system performance while the particle quantity updates.

3. Select the particle system and then open the Modify panel.

4. In the modifier stack, highlight the SuperSpray entry and then scroll down and expand the Particle Spawn rollout (see Figure 6-26).

5. In the Particle Spawning Effects section, select the Spawn on Collision option to cause new particles to be spawned.

NOTE: Be careful when using the Spawn Trails option, as this will generate new particles at each frame of the particle's life and can create an immense number of particles.

6. Enter 2 in the Spawns field to create spawned particles for the first two collisions for each particle and leave Affects set to 100% so that all particles involved in collisions are spawned.

7. Set the Multiplier to 2 to create two particles at each collision with a deflector; in this case, the sides of the box.

8. In the Scale Chaos section, set the Factor parameter to 75, causing each spawned particle to be 75 percent the size of the particle that spawned it (see Figure 6-27).

9. Move the Time slider to frame 100 and then render the Camera viewport.

As you can see, adding a spawn factor to your particle system can give the appearance of your particles breaking into smaller (or even larger) versions of themselves after they impact with a deflector. Particle spawning can be used in the creation of 3ds Max fireworks by using Spawn Trails to simulate the rocket exhaust as the particle zooms into the air and spawns particles to reproduce the effect of the exploding ordnance.

figure | 6-27 |

After they collide
with a deflector, the
initial particles die
and are replaced
with two spawned
particles that are
75% the size of the
original.

LOADING AND SAVING PARTICLE PRESETS

When considering the many parameters that can be set in a particle system (including Particle Quantity, Life, Size, Particle Type, Spawning, and the numerous others), setting up several similar particle systems can be tedious. Particle presets can significantly reduce the number of repetitive settings that must be identified, located, and reproduced by storing the parameter values as a single named value. Once the particle parameters are saved, they can be loaded into any other particle system, overwriting any existing parameters.

The loaded parameters are not locked to the original preset and can be altered to fit the needs of each specific particle system. For example, after the Hose preset is assigned to several particle systems representing fire hoses, each can be modified to give them individuality so that they do not appear to be clones of one another. Particle presets only affect the emission of particles and do not replicate the effects from space warps, which must be separately bound to each particle system they are to affect. The following exercise covers loading and saving a particle preset using a Super Spray particle system to create a magic wand.

Loading a Particle Preset

To load a particle preset, perform the following steps:

1. Open the *Presets.max* file from the companion CD-ROM. This consists of a magic wand with a star-shaped head linked to the wand's shaft. Any movement of the shaft will result in the head moving as well.

2. In the Top viewport, create a Super Spray particle system. The emitter size does not matter. This parameter is controlled by the particle preset that will be loaded.

3. With the Super Spray still selected, click the Align button in the main toolbar. The Align tool moves and orients one object, called the Current Object, in relation to a selected Target Object (see Figure 6-28).

4. Move the cursor, which now looks like the Align tool's button icon, over the star object and then select it. This opens the Align Selection dialog box, where the parameters for the alignment are specified.

5. The goal is to center the particle system with the star. In the Align Selection dialog box, check the X, Y, and Z Position boxes at the top to instruct 3ds Max to move the Current Object, the particle system, in all three axes.

6. Select Center in both the Current Object and Target Object sections. This aligns the center of the particle system's bounding box to the center of the star's bounding box (see Figure 6-29). In conjunction with the Position boxes selected in step 5, the particle system will be centered on the star. Click the OK button to complete the alignment.

7. The particle system must move and change its orientation to match the changes in the star. Click the Select and Link button in the Main toolbar, click on the particle system, and then drag and release over the star. The star will flash white briefly to indicate that the link was successful. The linkage can also be verified by moving or rotating the wand's shaft (see Figure 6-30).

8. Click the Modify tab to display the particle system's rollouts and parameters.

9. Scroll to the bottom of the Command panel and then expand the Load/Save Presets rollout. Highlight the Trail preset option in the Saved Presets field and then click the Load button (see Figure 6-31).

10. Move and rotate the magic wand's shaft. The Trail preset emits particles as a trail that follows the particle system wherever it goes (see Figure 6-32).

Saving a Particle Preset

To save a particle preset, perform the following steps:

1. Continue with the previous exercise or open the *Presets2.max* file from the companion CD-ROM.

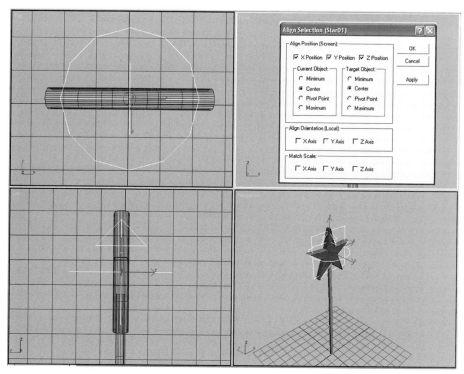

figure | 6-29 |

Use the Align Selection dialog box to align the center of the particle system to the center of the star.

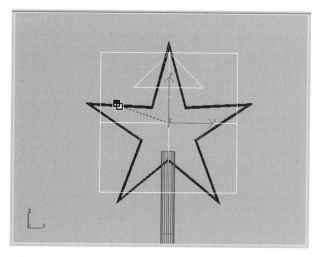

figure | 6-30 |

Linking the particle system to the star causes any of the stars movements or rotations to be inherited by it.

figure | 6-31 |

With the particle system selected, select the preset to load in the Load/Save Presets rollout.

figure | 6-32 |

The Trail preset emits a trail of particles behind the particle system wherever it moves.

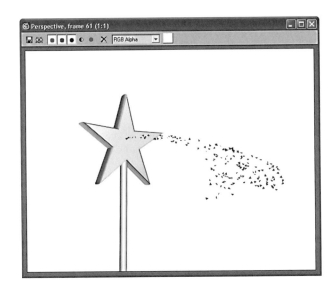

2. Select the particle system and then open the Modify panel.

3. In the Particle Generation rollout, increase the Life value to 25 to create longer trails. The other Particle Timing parameters would need to be changed if the animation length were set to any value greater than 100 frames.

4. Change the Size value to 1.5 and set Grow For to 10 so that the particles grow for the first 10 frames they are alive (see Figure 6-33).

5. Expand the Particle Type rollout. In the Standard Particles section, select SixPoint to cause the emitter to emit 2D six-pointed star-shaped particles (see Figure 6-34). Alternatively, you could also select Instanced Geometry (see Figure 6-35) as the particle type and the star as the instanced geometry. However, the Size value must be reduced significantly, to about 0.1.

6. Expand the Load/Save Presets rollout.

7. Enter a name for the new preset, consisting of the current particle system's parameters, in the Preset Name field and then click the Save button. The new preset is created and added to the Saved Presets list (see Figure 6-36).

figure | 6-33 |

Increase the particle Size and Life and add a Grow For factor.

figure | 6-34 |

Particle system
with the particle
type set to
Standard Particles
and SixPoint.

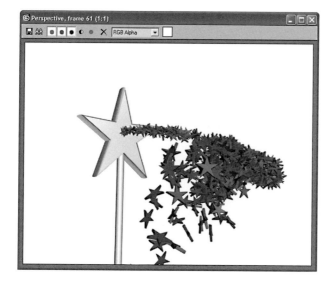

figure | 6-35 |

Particle system with
the particle type set
to Instanced
Geometry.

figure | 6-36 |

Name and add the preset in the Load/Save Presets rollout.

SUMMARY

In this chapter you learned about the various particle systems available in 3ds Max with a focus on the Super Spray particle system. You learned how to create particle systems and set their particle quantity, as well as the timing to which the particle emission will adhere. The different types of particles available in 3ds Max were also covered, including instanced geometry, and the methods for creating new particles once a particle impacts a deflector. Space warps and their effect on particles were addressed, and we covered the loading and saving of particle presets. Particle systems can add a great number of focused or apparently random objects to your scenes, which you can control at the system level without controlling each particle's parameters directly.

in review

1. What is the difference between an event-driven particle system and a non-event-driven particle system?

2. What is the difference between the Life and Display Until parameters?

3. What are the three major types of particles a Super Spray particle system can emit?

4. Name five space warps that can affect a particle system.

5. How is a space warp instructed to affect a particle system?

6. What is particle spawning?

7. What must you be cautious of when spawning particles?

8. What do particle presets do?

↗ EXPLORING ON YOUR OWN

1. Particles, like any other geometry in 3ds Max, can have a material applied to them. Apply a material to your particle system directly, and apply a material to geometry that is instanced by the particle system.

2. Rendering effects can be applied to particle systems. Apply a Lens Effects Glow effect to a particle system so that each particle glows as it is emitted.

3. Modifiers, such as Bend or Twist, do not affect the direction of any particles. Experiment with the Mesher compound object, which gives you the ability to create a mesh stand-in for a particle system.

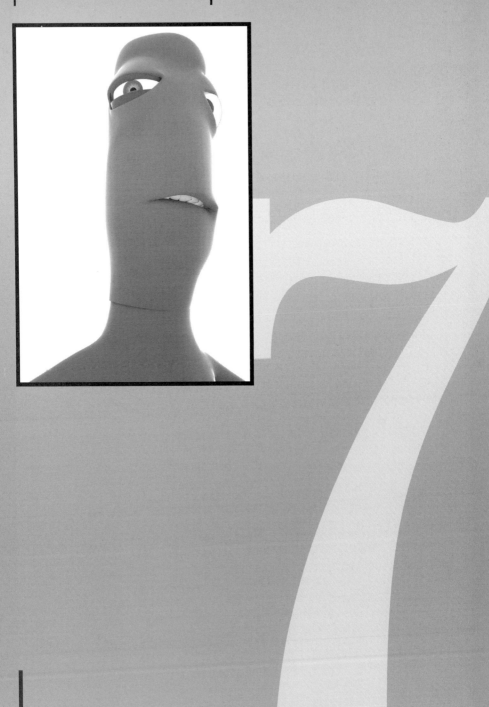

charting your course

Welcome to the last chapter of the book! With your acquired knowledge of animation you are now ready to begin applying the tools of the trade. In this chapter you have the opportunity to implement actual industry techniques for developing sophisticated animation. You will use 3ds Max's powerful animation tools and, via step-by step instructions, you will set up a project and implement the tools necessary to achieve great results.

This chapter incorporates three projects that cover a broad range of techniques used in the animation field. The first project uses a typical high-rise building to demonstrate camera and motion animation. In the second project, real-time motion and collision are reconstructed in Max's reactor utility. The last project uses Max's crowd simulation to animate complex behaviors of many entities simultaneously. Each of the three techniques covered constitute tools that can be applied to many types of challenges animators face each day.

 chapter objectives

- **Create industry-relevant animations utilizing new and previously learned techniques**
- **Manipulate animation using the Curve editor**
- **Effectively use Max's reactor to create an accident reconstruction**
- **Imitate a real-world condition using Max's crowd simulation program**

PROJECT 7–1: ARCHITECTURAL ANIMATION

Introduction

You have just finished an architectural model of a prominent sky-scraper in a major metropolitan city. Your client, Mr. Gunderson, calls to congratulate you on a job well done, and he requests an animation be created showing the new building in all its glory. He already has some pre-conceived ideas as to how to approach the animation.

Because the computer model of the building has all four sides com-pleted, you know you can animate most of the structure from any angle. However, the city block the building rises from was modeled with minimal detail except for one corner. Knowing the extent of your computer model and understanding the client's objectives are critical in reaching a solution for the animation. Hearing that the deadline for the project is reasonable, a rare occurrence, you cheer-fully commit to the endeavor.

Getting the Job

Because Mr. Gunderson, like many clients, does not know the details of computer animation, he does not necessarily have an understand-ing of how long such an animation should last or if it should be composed of many different camera angles or only one angle. What he does know is people and how to create a stimulating atmosphere. Mr. Gunderson explains that the animation will be used at a public showing used to generate excitement about the project.

Projection monitors will be used to display the animation on large 8-foot-by-10-foot screens placed throughout the auditorium. There will be other videos presented as well, and your animation will be just one part of the bigger show. He further explains that it is important to make the connection between the condominium units up in the sky and the bustling environment below: "The ten-ants in this building will have the luxury of having their privacy in the sky while having all of the amenities of big-city living within a short walking distance."

Now that you have listened to your client's needs, it is time for you to bridge the gap between your world of animation and your client's objectives and offer him solutions. You propose a single camera that starts high in the sky, looking up at the crown of the building. The camera then slowly moves down as it circles the building until it reaches street level. The camera continues to look up to the top of the building, but now you can also see the street, cars moving, and umbrellas for outside dining. You explain that a single camera can tell the entire story. Cameras from different perspectives could be animated as well, but you will need to model more of the surrounding area to accommodate these new views. Because of time constraints and financial considerations, Mr. Gunderson is quite happy with your single-camera approach.

Camera Placement

In the following exercise you will create a camera and animate its motion. Although the actual number of keyframes is minimal, developing a process that helps you find those important positions to place your camera is crucial. There are two sides to animation: implementing your ideas into the computer and observing your results.

Too often animators spend most of their time building and animating, and they fail to spend time simply watching their results. Always take time to observe your animations, even in Wireframe mode, and think about how others will interpret it. Does the camera move too fast or too slowly? Does the motion feel unnatural?

1. Go to File > Open and select *tower_start.max* from the *Chapter 7* folder of the companion CD-ROM. There should be one group within this file consisting of two car objects, two splines, and one building object. One note regarding the car objects: they are used as placeholders and could be replaced by higher-definition car models later. (To select these objects in this exercise, you will be using the Select Objects dialog box, shown in Figure 7-1.) Figure 7-2 shows all four viewports of the starting model. Note that Units in the Units Setup dialog box (see Figure 7-3) are set to Decimal Inches. There are several reasons for selecting a specific unit measure. In

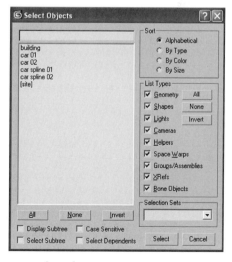

figure |7-1|

Select Objects dialog.

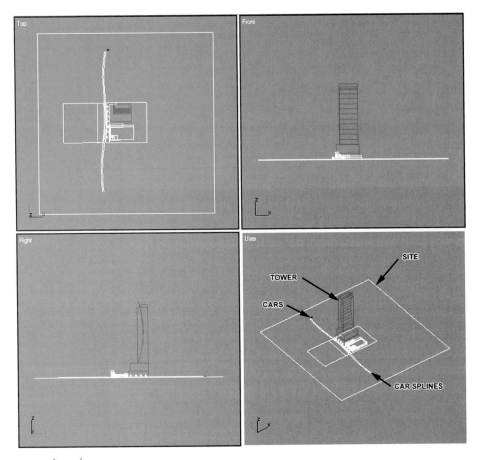

figure | 7-2 |

Four viewports showing the starting model in Wireframe mode.

architectural modeling, this is necessary in building objects to their proper dimensions. Having a specific scale you can relate to ensures that any objects you create are properly proportioned in relation to the model as a whole and relative to one another. Another reason is lighting. Sophisticated lighting techniques use your computer model's scale to properly cast and bounce light. Another convention we want to use in this project is that when looking in the Top viewport, North is up. Not all projects need to have North oriented upward; this is a convenience that helps people communicate where they are relative to objects in the scene.

2. By default, the Time slider in 3ds Max is set for 101 frames of animation (from zero to 100). Typical animations need 30 frames for 1 second of animation (for NTSC), so 100 frames provides a little more than 3 seconds. Although you do not yet know exactly how long your camera move will be, we will make an initial estimation for a 10-second animation (300 frames). Select the Time Configuration button (see Figure 7-4), and in the Time Configuration dialog box that appears (see Figure 7-5), change Length to *300*.

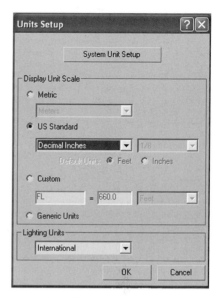

figure |7-3|

Units Setup dialog.

3. There are two types of cameras 3ds Max provides: Target and Free. We will use the Target camera. Although both types of cameras can technically mimic each other, each has its advantages based on what and how you need to animate. The Target camera allows us to animate the camera and its target independently. In architecture, it is important to understand what the camera is intended to focus on. The target of a camera gives you this visual cue and assists

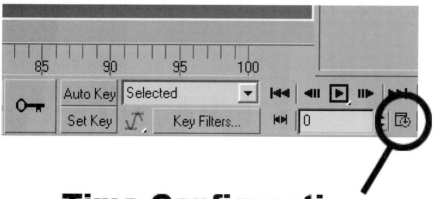

Time Configuration

figure |7-4|

Time Configuration button.

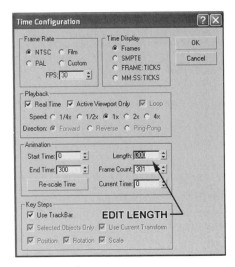

figure | 7-5 |

Time Configuration dialog set to 300 frames.

you in the creation of your animation. Go to the Top viewport (see Figure 7-6). Create a Target camera and place the camera in the lower portion of the screen and the target near the north side of the building.

4. Because we want to start high and move to the base of the building, we have a couple of choices as to how to do this. We could position the camera close to the top of the building and animate its position to be at the base at the end of the animation, or we could keep the camera at pedestrian level (about 5 feet 6 inches above the street plane) and animate the camera's lens. So which direction do we choose? Rather than arbitrarily picking a solution, it is always helpful to have a story or metaphor to help direct our efforts.

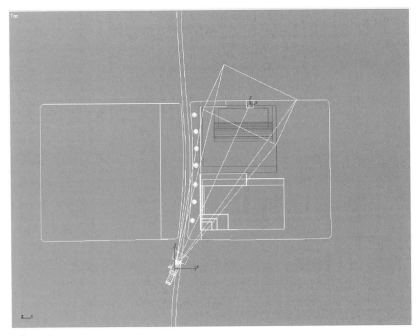

figure | 7-6 |

Top viewport showing placement of Target camera.

In this case, a person might be walking along the street and looking up at the building. The person then slowly looks down to the base of the building. This condition indicates that we want to animate the camera's lens length as opposed to animating its position. We could have just as easily constructed a story about a magical entity that wisps in from the clouds to visit the new building and lands at its base, but this would change the entire feel of the animation, and it might not be what the client wants. With the Move Transform Type-In tool (see Figure 7-7), set the position of the camera to *(0, 0, 66) Absolute: World*. An alternative way of inputting these numbers is to use the type-ins at the bottom of the user interface. After the Move tool has been activated, these three fields can be modified in a manner similar to using the Move Transform Type-In tool.

5. Adjust the camera's target. The target needs to be placed near the top of the building. A good way to adjust the general position of the target is to change the viewport to the camera's view and, with the camera's target selected, use the transform gizmo and move the target straight up in the Z axis until the top of the building is in the center of the screen. The precise position of the camera's target can be specified using the Move Transform Type-In tool (see Figure 7-8) to set the *Absolute: World* position to *(2523, 5282, 8026)*.

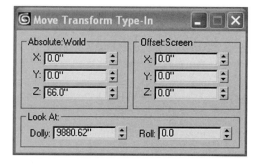

figure | 7-7 |

Move Transform Type-In using absolute values.

figure | 7-8 |

Move Transform Type-In tool for setting the camera's target.

figure |7-9|

Camera Lens setting of
135 mm at frame 0.

6. Next we will need to adjust the length of the camera's lens, so make sure to have one of your viewports be that of the camera's. Select the camera, and then select the Modify panel. Set Lens to *135 mm* (see Figure 7-9). Feel free to experiment and choose a different value depending on how close or far away from the crown of the building you want to be. Figure 7-10 shows the camera's view.

7. Animate the camera. Move the Time slider to frame 300. Turn on Auto Key mode by clicking the Auto Key button. The button will turn red, as will the Time slider bar and the outline around the active viewport. This color indicates that you are in Auto Key mode. Anything you move or any variable you change in this mode will become animated. Select the camera in the Top viewport and move it straight up (the positive Y direction) so that the camera moves beyond the building. If you use the Move Transform Type-In tool, set the new position to *(0, 5812, 66)*.

8. With the Auto Key button still active and the camera still selected, go to the Modify panel and change the length of the camera lens to *24 mm*. The camera lens sizes are shown in Figure 7-11.

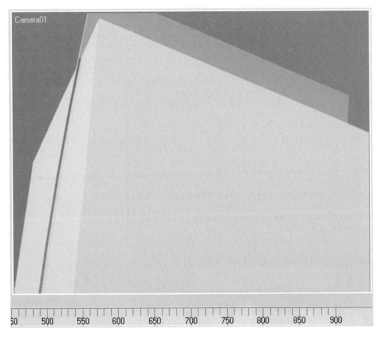

figure |7-10|

Viewport of camera after placement.

9. Making sure the Auto Key button is still active, select the camera's target and move it to the bottom of the building. If you want to use the Move Transform Type-In tool to specify the location precisely, change the location of the target to *(1900, 4213, 66)*.

10. Turn off Auto Key mode and view your progress in the camera viewport by playing the animation. Depending on how powerful your video card is, you may have to change the viewport to Wireframe mode rather than Smooth > Highlights so that you can see the motion of the camera in real time (or at least close to real time).

11. The first thing you may notice is that the animation plays fast. Knowing that the audience has never seen this project before helps make the decision to slow down the animation so that people have time to absorb the details. There are times when a client may want an animation that is fast-paced with many transitions, but this was not requested, nor does the time or budget permit it. Go back to the Time Configuration dialog box and change Length to *900* (see Figure 7-12). This should be

MODIFIED LENS SIZE

ANIMATION INDICATORS

figure | **7-11** |

Camera lens sizes.

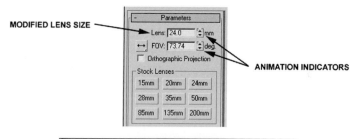

EDIT LENGTH

figure | **7-12** |

Time Configuration dialog with Length set to 900.

enough time to work with for now. Note that the trackbar in 3ds Max has stretched to include frames 0 through 900.

12. Select the camera. You should see two keyframes in the track-bar, which represent the two keys you created for the camera. 3ds Max will display in the trackbar the keyframes of the object you actively select. If no keys are in view, nothing is animated on that object. Using the mouse, select the keyframe located at frame 300 (see Figure 7-13). The keyframe becomes white, indicating it is selected. With the mouse, slide the key to frame 720. By adding more frames between the two keyframes you have increased the camera's motion from 10 seconds to 24 seconds along the Time slider (see Figure 7-14).

13. Test the animation by playing it and viewing it in the camera's viewport. This time the camera moves more slowly, allowing for more time to view the building.

14. When you create keyframes, 3ds Max automatically creates an ease-out and ease-in condition at each keyframe. How these conditions manifest themselves in your animation is that when you play your scene you will notice that the camera starts off slowly and accelerates slightly to reach a constant speed. As the camera approaches your last keyframe, you see the camera slow down before it comes to a complete stop. 3ds Max allows you to change these ease-out/ease-in settings. In our case, we want the camera to start off at full speed because we want the initial view of the tower to be immediately moving at constant

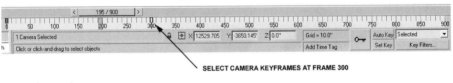

SELECT CAMERA KEYFRAMES AT FRAME 300

figure | 7-13 |

Selection of camera's keyframes at frame 300.

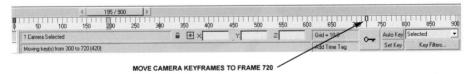

MOVE CAMERA KEYFRAMES TO FRAME 720

figure | 7-14 |

Movement of keyframes along Time slider.

speed. However, we want the camera to ease to a stop because we plan to continue with other effects in the animation after the camera stops, and an abrupt stop would feel unnatural and distracting.

15. Select the camera and the camera's target. Right-click in any viewport to reveal 3ds Max's Quad menu (see Figure 7-15). Select Curve Editor (see Figure 7-16). The Curve editor allows

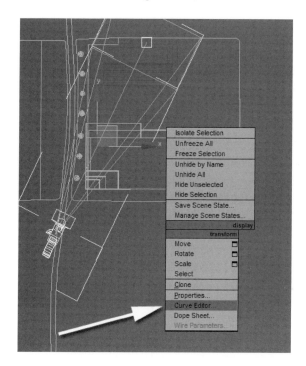

figure | 7-15 |

Quad menu.

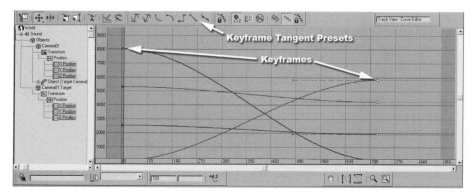

figure | 7-16 |

Curve editor.

for detailed interpolation between keyframes. Keyframes are denoted by small boxes, and the curves that connect them are known as function curves. Because the camera and its target are selected, by default the Track View > Curve Editor selection displays the attributes of the selected object. You should see all curves associated with the camera and camera's target with their keyframes. Looking more closely at the curves you should see that they slope away from the keyframes (see Figure 7-17). This sloping indicates the amount of easing in or out that occurs in the animated object associated with this curve. While in the Curve editor, use the mouse to select the keyframes at frame 0. The keyframes will turn white in the Key window, indicating that those keyframes are now selected. Select the Set Tangents to Linear button (see Figure 7-18) at the top of the window. You will see the curves straighten after the keyframe at frame 0, but the second keyframe's tangent retains its curve (see Figure 7-19). With experience you will quickly be able to identify how an object moves by simply looking at these curves. Adjusting your animation in the Track View > Curve Editor dialog box saves a lot of time.

figure | 7-17 |

Tangent detail of curve for camera.

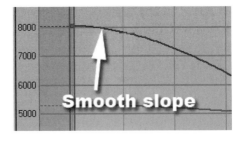

figure | 7-18 |

Tangent buttons in Curve Editor dialog.

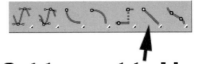

figure | 7-19 |

Slope of changed curves.

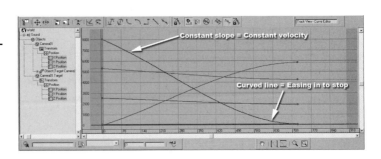

16. Test the animation. You should see that the camera is now doing what we set out to accomplish.

Car Placement

Now that the camera is placed, we will want to add moving cars on the street. We waited to add the cars until now because we wanted to lock down the camera's position so that we can time the cars to coincide with the camera. Although cars can be animated in the same way we animated the camera (by creating keyframes at strategic points along our intended path), we will employ the use of dummy objects and path constraints to simplify our efforts.

1. You will see that there are two splines along a curvy road. Two cars are located near the end of the two splines, as shown in Figure 7-20.

2. In the Top viewport, go to Create > Helpers > Standard > Dummy and create a dummy object anywhere in the scene (see Figure 7-21).

3. With the dummy object selected, select Animation > Constraints > Path Constraint from the Main menu (see Figure 7-22). 3ds Max then requires you to select a spline to which to link this dummy object. Select *car spline 01*. The dummy object and spline temporarily blink white, indicating that you have successfully constrained the dummy object along your path. The dummy object also repositions itself to one end

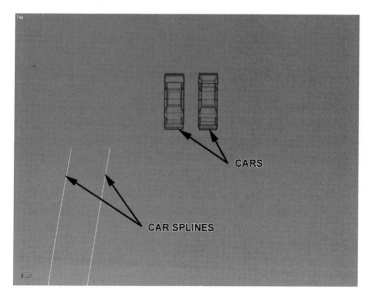

figure | 7-20 |

Pair of cars near end of splines.

figure | 7-21 |

Dummy object
near car.

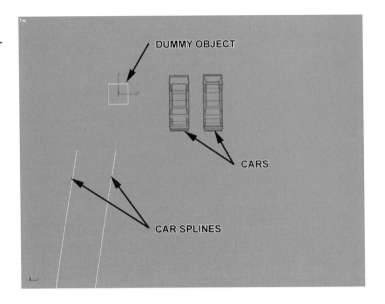

figure | 7-22 |

Selection menu for
path constraint.

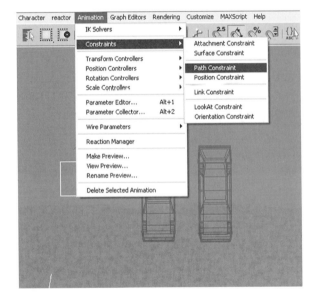

of the line. Once the dummy object has been constrained by
the path, go to the Motion panel under the Path Parameters
rollout and check the Follow option (see Figure 7-23). The
Follow option will align the object to the trajectory as it follows
the contour. The dummy object will position itself in reference
to the end of the trajectory line where the first vertex is located.
If you wanted the dummy object to be on the other end of the
trajectory line, you could simply select the line and change the
vertex on the other end to be the first vertex.

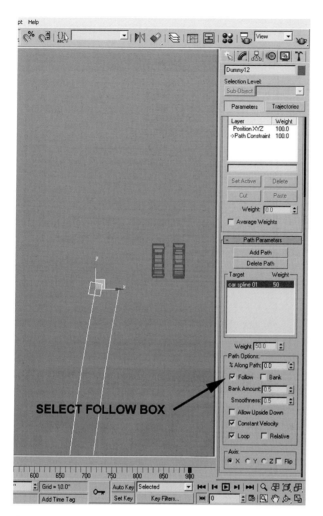

SELECT FOLLOW BOX

figure |7-23|

Follow option.

4. Play the animation and observe what happens from the Top viewport and the camera viewport. The dummy object moves from one end of the line to the other over the extent of your animation, which in this case is 900 frames. Note also that while the dummy object is selected you should have two keyframes in the trackbar: one at frame 0 and the other at frame 900.

5. We now need to find the correct position for the dummy object. Although the speed of the dummy object along the path is reasonable for vehicle speed, it does not make an appearance in our camera viewport. We would like the dummy object to move past the camera once the camera is at street level (about frame 700). Go to the Top viewport and enter *700* in the Current Frame field, located in the Animation Controls area of the interface. Select the camera so that you can see the camera's view range, indicated by

the light blue triangle emanating from the camera. We need to have the dummy object next to the camera at this point.

6. Adjust the dummy's position. Position the Top viewport so that you can see the dummy object and the camera. Select the dummy object and then select the Motion tab. Directly above the Follow check box is a spinner labeled % Along Path. This tells you the dummy object's position on the path. Adjusting this number changes the location of the dummy object (see Figure 7-24). Play the animation and observe the camera vantage point. Once the camera reaches street level, you will want the dummy object to come into view. At about frame 700 you will be at street level. Adjust % Along Path to *35%*.

7. Link one of the cars to the dummy object. Change the Current Frame field to 0. In the Top viewport, select one of the cars and

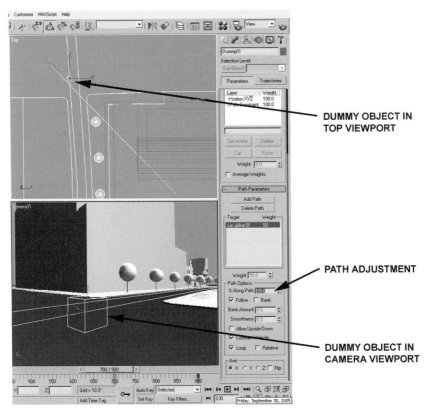

DUMMY OBJECT IN
TOP VIEWPORT

PATH ADJUSTMENT

DUMMY OBJECT IN
CAMERA VIEWPORT

figure | 7-24 |

Adjustment of dummy object along path.

align it to the dummy object using the Align tool. You will need to adjust the car's orientation to make sure the car wheels are resting directly on top of the road plane and that the car is rotated slightly to match the dummy object's orientation to the line. With the car is still selected, use the Select and Link tool to link the car to the dummy object, as shown in Figure 7-25.

8. Test and observe your animation by clicking the Play Animation button in the Animation Controls area. You should see your car move past the camera at frame 700 and drive down the street (see Figure 7-26).

9. Create another dummy object and use Animation > Constraints > Path Constraint to attach it to the same spline. This time, adjust the % Along Path of the dummy object to be directly behind (but not too close to) the previous dummy object. As before, position and link another car to this new dummy object.

10. Add more dummy objects to the remaining spline and link corresponding cars to each of them. Make sure to include cars linked to the other spline, which represents cars traveling in the opposite direction. Build as much traffic as suits your taste. Watch the movie files, showing two completed versions of this exercise: one with placeholder geometry and the other with final geometry. Open the completed 3ds Max file *ch7_tower_complete.max* from the companion CD-ROM to see the final results.

Rendering

What your client requests will dictate how you will render your final animation. If he or she requests NTSC, you need to render

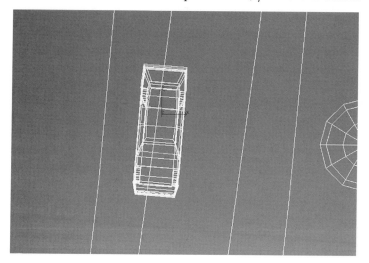

figure | 7-25 |

Linking the car to the dummy object.

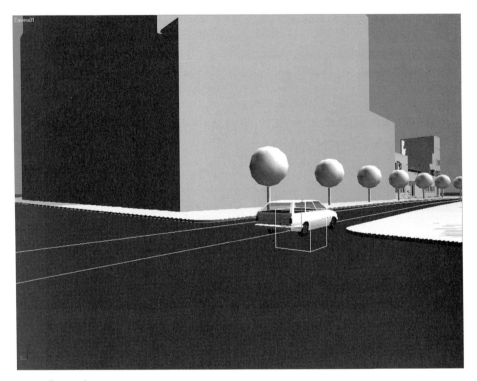

figure | 7-26 |

Camera viewport with dummy-linked car in view.

your animation using 720 × 486 pixels with a 0.9-pixel aspect ratio. But prior to rendering your final animation, you will render your animation several times to observe your tests.

These animations can be any size you want, but they are usually dictated by how long it will take to render or how much detail is necessary. Usually animators will render 320 × 240 animations so that they can quickly check their progress. Never wait until the end of your project to render it. Rarely is an animation accurately put together in one pass.

Summary

Architectural animation is more about composition and timing than about complex technical animation tricks. Knowing this, you need to be able to model your scenes quickly so that you can take the time to observe your preliminary animations.

PROJECT 7–2: REACTOR

Introduction

Unfortunately, car accidents happen every day. Often the accidents will result in entangled litigation and need to be resolved using a variety of methods. Arguments by attorneys play an important role in convincing and proving these cases. Computer animation is also used to demonstrate these arguments through reconstructive movies. The power of these types of animations lies in the fact that they can duplicate the condition of the accident and then provide visuals from virtually any vantage point, helping to corroborate testimony and clarify misconceptions.

Getting the Job

Before starting a project dealing with accident reconstruction, you need to gather all available information. In this particular case, you learn that the accident involves two passenger cars that collided at a city intersection. After the collision, one of the cars continued to slide into one of the buildings located at the intersection. This is the point of contention in this accident. The building management company is suing for damages against the driver's insurance company to pay for the cost of fixing the damage to the building. Several photographs of the scene have been provided. Police officers have provided further information. The direction of the cars was gathered by eye witnesses standing near the site. The speed of the cars at the time of impact was determined by skid analysis.

The client, an attorney, explains that this animation does not need to be photorealistic. There needs to be enough detail in the model to give people an understanding of the area, but budget is not available to create cinema-quality movies. The preliminary schedule is set to go to court in 10 days. This may change and be pushed further out, but there is no way to know at this time how backlogged the courts are, so you must budget your time and fee to accommodate this time span. Because 3ds Max incorporates the Reactor functionality, this type of accident reconstruction will be handled quite easily.

Scene Static Elements

Before getting to the animation of the cars, the initial scene needs to be modeled. Using the photographs and visiting the site (if it is located in your city) will provide enough information to build the mesh. Because this exercise is focusing on the Reactor portion of the project, this part of the project will be bypassed and the site will already be put together before you begin using Reactor.

1. Open scene *reactor_start.max*. You will see a scene that has a city block containing parked cars, a car waiting to cross a street, and another car approaching the intersection of the street (see Figure 7-27). We are going to set up a Reactor scene to crash these two cars together to formulate a simple simulation of a car crash.

figure | 7-27 |

Screen image of starting scene.

Create Rigid Body Collection

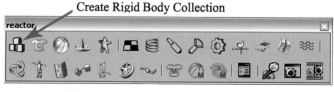

figure |7-28|

Reactor toolbar.

2. Reactor is a plug-in included in 3ds Max that calculates collisions between objects in an animated scene. For Reactor to
   work, the animator must gather the objects involved in the simulation into a grouping; these groupings are known as Reactor
   collections or simply collections. The collection type we will be
   using is the Rigid Body collection. Other types of collections
   Reactor uses are Rope and Cloth. This collection is like a toy box
   you fill up with what you would like Reactor to simulate for you.
   If it is not in the toy box, Reactor will not use it. The first thing to
   do, then, is to create our collection. Simply select the Create
   Rigid Body Collection button on the Reactor toolbar (see
   Figure 7-28). (If you do not see your Reactor toolbar, right-
   click in a blank area of the Main toolbar and then click
   Reactor.) Click somewhere in the scene and an icon for your
   collection will appear.

3. With your collection icon selected, go to the Modify panel
   and add the cars, buildings, streets, and curbs by clicking the
   Add button and selecting the items you wish to add from the
   RB Collection Properties rollout (see Figure 7-29). Click OK.
   Do not include the group named *DO_NOT_ADD roadlines*
   to this list. Reactor does not work well with this group.

4. In Reactor, you must set the mass for each object. Things
   you do not want to be affected by gravity or collisions
   remain at a mass of 0. Things you do want to be affected by
   gravity and collisions must have mass. For this scene, we
   want the cars in the scene to be affected. In the Reactor
   toolbar (see Figure 7-30), click Open Property Editor. This
   opens the Rigid Body Properties dialog box, as shown in
   Figure 7-31. The first parameter at the top is Mass. Select all
   of your cars, including Fast Car and Slow Car, and then
   enter a value of *1000* in the Mass parameter. All of your cars
   will now have a mass of 1,000.

figure |7-29|

RB Collection Properties
rollout.

Open Property Editor

figure | 7-30 |

Reactor toolbar.

figure | 7-31 |

Rigid Body Properties dialog.

5. Your scene can now be simulated with Reactor. Click the Analyze World button on the Reactor toolbar (see Figure 7-32) and you will notice that Reactor tests for any errors in the scene. If you have errors, read them and make the proper adjustments. Ignore the error message about your large geometry, because it is only a warning. If there are no errors, select Continue and then click the Preview Animation button on the Reactor toolbar. The Reactor Real-Time Preview window will appear with a preview of the scene, as shown in Figure 7-33. If you press the P key, you will begin the preview. For this exercise, we set the cars slightly higher off the ground so that you can see the cars fall to the street. Press P again to stop the render after your cars have settled on the pavement. To save these new car positions, pull down the MAX menu in the Reactor Real-Time Preview window and select Update MAX. Exit the Real-Time Preview window and you will notice that the cars have been positioned according to the Reactor simulation.

6. With the cars in position, it is time to animate the initial velocity of the cars so that they can crash (see Figure 7-34). Reactor calculates initial velocity according to the velocity set by the keyframes in 3ds Max. This means you need to use 3ds Max to move and animate the cars in such a way

Analyze World   Preview Animation

figure | 7-32 |

Reactor toolbar.

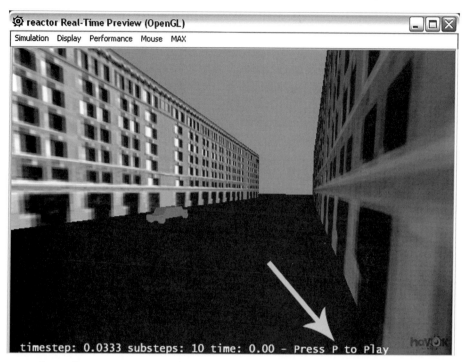

figure | 7-33 |

Reactor Real-Time Preview window.

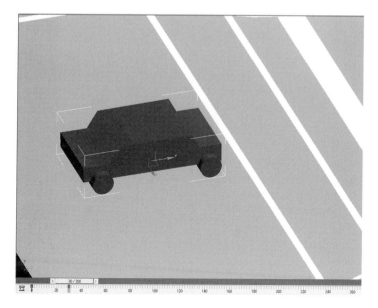

figure | 7-34 |

Animating the cars.

that when we begin our simulation the cars will have velocity stemming from the movement we keyframe in. Our first step is to select the Slow Car and set a movement key at frame 5 by right-clicking the Time slider and checking off the Rotation and Scale check boxes. Click OK. Activate Auto Key, move the Time slider to 30, and move Slow Car to the middle of the intersection. By scrubbing the Time slider, test your animation to make sure the car is slowly moving into the intersection.

7. Repeat step 6 for Fast Car. However, you are moving this car a lot farther in a much shorter period of time (see Figure 7-35). With Auto Key still activated, move Fast Car into the intersection at frame 30. Make sure the cars are very close to each other but not touching, and make sure Fast Car is to the side of Slow Car right before impact. Scrub the Time slider and check to see that you have an obvious movement.

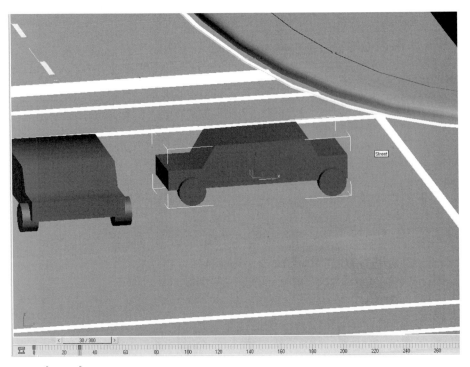

figure | 7-35 |

Animating the cars continued.

8. The Reactor simulation currently starts at frame 0 and runs through frame 100. At frame 0 we have no velocity from our two cars. For the initial velocity to work, we need to begin the simulation at a frame where our two cars are moving. Frame 15 should work fine. To change this, select the Utilities tab of the Command panels. At the bottom of the tab is the Reactor button. Click the button and the global options will appear (see Figure 7-36). Expand the Preview & Animation rollout and the first set of parameters you see are those of starting and ending the animation. Set Start Frame to 15 and End Frame to 300. Save a new iteration of the file.

9. You are now ready to test your simulation. Click Preview Animation once again from the Reactor toolbar. This will run the Analyze the World functionality. Press the P key and watch your cars crash. If you want to watch it more than once, click Simulation at the top and select Reset Animation. You can also use all of the viewport pan/zoom/rotate commands in the Reactor Real-Time Preview window (see Figure 7-37). When you are finished previewing, deactivate the Auto Key function.

10. If you are not happy with how your cars crash, move the keyframes to increase or decrease the velocity of the cars. You can also tinker with the mass of the cars to make the crash change. Keep previewing the animation until you are satisfied, and then click the last button on the Reactor toolbar, which is the Create Animation button (see Figure 7-38). Now Reactor will simulate 300 frames and add those keyframes to the cars. You will then have your finished simulation. Via the Unhide Objects dialog box (see Figure 7-39), unhide the two "nice" cars to use some better models for the cars. Then you can hide Slow Car and Fast Car. The final screen image is shown in Figure 7-40. (The "nice" cars are already linked to the low-poly cars. We did not simulate these cars because Reactor cannot use groups for simulations.)

figure | 7-36 |

Reactor utility rollouts.

Summary

To see the final results, open the 3ds Max file *reactor_final.max* from the companion CD-ROM and view the completed animation *reactor_animation.mov*.

figure | 7-37 |

Reactor Real-Time Preview window.

figure | 7-38 |

Reactor toolbar
showing Create
Animation button.

figure | 7-39 |

Unhide Objects
dialog.

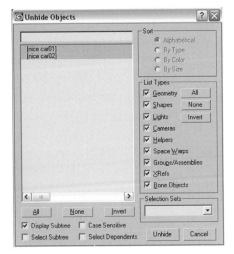

figure | 7-40 |

Final screen.

PROJECT 7–3: CROWD SIMULATION

Introduction

An advertising agency has just contacted you and would like to know if you can help it with a small animation that would simulate bees moving from a hive to flowers. Because this project is only being proposed, at this point the ad agency does not require a final polished product. However, it does need a preliminary animation it can splice into its proposal.

Projects often start this way. Before the main project is started, a smaller mini-project is developed to help art directors, writers, and managers get a clearer understanding of exactly what they need to focus on. Camera angles, scene timing, and object motion are focused on to give the development team something to react to. Without this, everyone will have his or her own image of what the project should look like, and there will be no way to develop or move forward with a single idea in consultation with the design team. Right or wrong, good or bad, the preliminary animation is an invaluable tool for moving the creative process forward.

Getting the Job

Even for animations modest in concept, you need to establish with your client what needs to be done. In this case, the ad agency does not have much figured out yet regarding the specific elements in the scene. They do not care what types of flowers are used, and they do not have a preference as to what the beehive should look like. All they want at this point is to see bees move from one location to another. This sounds like a perfect use of 3ds Max's crowd simulation functionality.

Applying Crowd Simulation

You explain that you will create a very generic scene that includes a beehive, a flowerpot the bees will fly to, two trees, and a yard. The bees will leave the hive, go to the flowers, and then return to the hive. The art director agrees to this and emphasizes the importance of establishing the nature of the bee movement.

1. Open the file *crowd_start.max* from the companion CD-ROM. In this file we have a yard with two trees, a honeybee, a beehive, and two potted flowers. Our goal is to make a swarm of bees fly from the hive to the flowers to collect nectar, and then return to the hive.

2. We will start by creating a Crowd object and a Delegate object. Select Create tab > Helpers > Standard. This opens the Standard Helper Object Type rollout, as shown in Figure 7-41. You should see buttons for creating a Crowd object and a Delegate object.

3. The Crowd object is the main controller for our crowd simulation. It lets you add and modify behaviors in your scene. Click the Crowd button and then click and drag in the Top viewport to create the Crowd object. It does not really matter where the Crowd object is placed. Place it where it will be conveniently clicked on, because it will need to be selected several times.

4. Now we need to create the Delegate object. Delegates are placeholders for the individual members of a crowd. In this case, they will represent the bees in the simulation. A Delegate object will appear as a small pyramid. Create the Delegate object in the Top viewport next to the

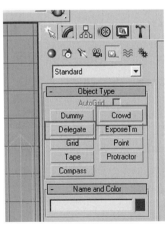

figure | 7-41 |

Standard Helper Object Type rollout.

beehive. Additional Delegate objects have been created and hidden. Unhide them by selecting Display tab > Hide rollout > Unhide All button. Now there are nine Delegate objects within the hive and the one you just created outside it, as shown in Figure 7-42.

5. Now that we have a Crowd object and some Delegate objects to work with, they need to have a behavior assigned to them. Currently they are just sitting there with nothing to do. Select the Crowd object and go to the Modify tab. Click the Behavior Assignments button to open the Behavior Assignments and Teams dialog box (see Figure 7-43).

6. In the Behavior Assignments and Teams dialog box you should see all the Delegate objects listed in the Assignment Design area. We could assign each of our Delegate objects its own behavior, but that would take some time. Instead, we will group the Delegate objects as a team and assign them all a behavior at once.

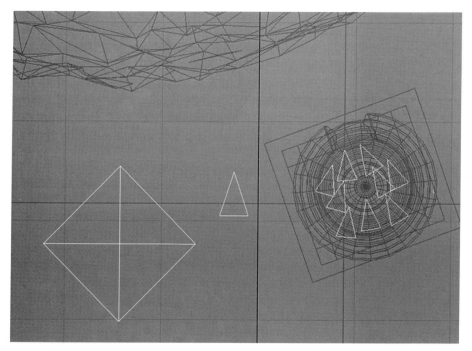

figure | 7-42 |

Crowd and Delegate object creation.

figure | 7-43 |

Crowd rollouts.

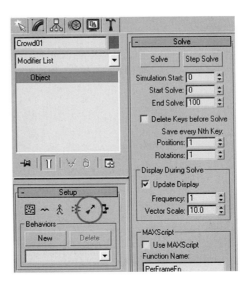

7. Click the New Team button. The Select Delegates dialog box appears with our Delegate objects listed. Click the All button to select all of the Delegate objects, and then click OK. In the Teams section at the top, we can see that the new team is named *Team 0*. Rename it *Swarm* by double-clicking the name and typing a new descriptor name.

8. Add a behavior to the list. Click the New Behavior button. You will see the Select Behavior Type dialog box with a list of behaviors. Select Wander Behavior from the list and then click OK (see Figure 7-44).

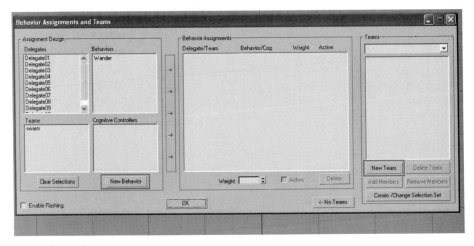

figure | 7-44 |

Behavior Assignments and Teams dialog.

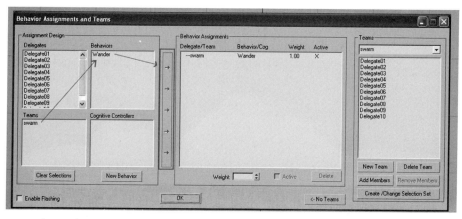

figure | 7-45 |

Assigning behaviors to teams.

9. Because 3ds Max crowd simulation allows for many teams and behaviors, we need to link our *Swarm* team to our Wander behavior. To do this, click Swarm, found on the lower left of the Teams list, click the Wander behavior, and then click the big vertical New Assignment button.

10. In the Behavior Assignments section (see Figure 7-45), you should see Swarm assigned to Wander Behavior, with a weight of 1.00 (weight refers to the amount of influence a behavior has in relation to other behaviors) and an X, indicating that the behavior is active.

11. Now that we have something for our Delegate objects to do, let's run a test and see what happens. Click OK to close the Behavior Assignments and Teams dialog box. In the Solve rollout, click the Solve button.

12. Once the computer has finished solving the crowd simulation, we can activate Play Animation to watch the animation. Notice any problems? Our delegates are moving pretty fast for bees, the animation stops far short of our 200-frame timeline, and our Delegate objects are ignoring everything and wandering blindly through the scene.

13. Change the End Solve value to 200 so that the simulation will run the length of our timeline (see Figure 7-46).

14. Slow down the Delegate objects so that they are not zipping about as much. We could edit each Delegate

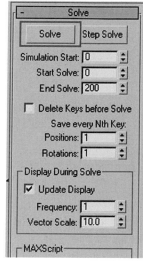

figure | 7-46 |

Crowd solutions.

object individually by clicking on each one to open its behaviors, but that would take a while, and it is much easier to edit them all at once. To do that, click the Multiple Delegate Editing button, which opens the Edit Multiple Delegates dialog box, as shown in Figure 7-47.

15. Now we can change how our Delegate objects will behave by adjusting them all at once. We can even set up random differences in the way our Delegate objects behave. The first thing you will

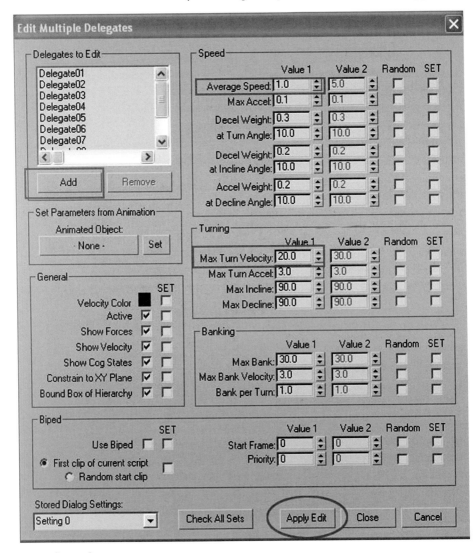

figure | 7-47 |

Edit Multiple Delegates dialog.

notice is that none of the objects are listed yet. Click the Add button to select all of the Delegate objects to add them to this edit list. Set Average Speed to *1.0*; this should give a more realistic speed for the bees. Set Max Turn Velocity at *20.0*; this will slow down the turns. Click the Apply Edit button to save the changes and exit.

NOTE: There are many parameters that can be adjusted in this panel. When you are finished with the exercise, feel free to experiment with different settings to create a variety of results.

16. We now need to give the Delegate objects some direction. This can be done by adding another behavior (see Figure 7-48). Open the Behavior Assignments panel by clicking the Behavior Assignments button. The bees need to seek out the flowers. Click New Behavior. From the resulting list, select Seek Behavior. Click OK. Just as before, link the Swarm team to the new Seek Behavior. Click OK.

17. The bees now have a new behavior, Seek, but they need to know what to seek. There is a drop-down menu under Behaviors in the Setup rollout. Select Seek from the list. The large button labeled *None* in the Seek Behavior rollout allows us to select the object in the scene to be used as a seek target. But first let's make the target.

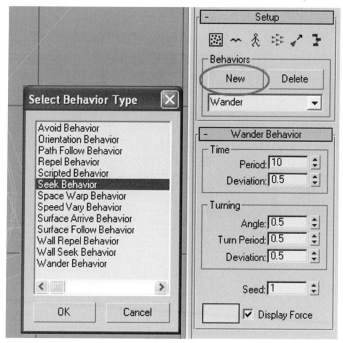

figure | 7-48 |

Adding behaviors

18. Create two dummy objects and place them over the flowers. These will serve as the scent the bees are attracted to (see Figure 7-49). Name these dummies *Flower_Seek01* and *Flower_Seek02*.

19. Select the Crowd object. Click the Multiple Selection button and select (highlight) the *Flower_Seek01* and *Flower_ Seek02* dummy objects (see Figure 7-50). In the Radius section, activate the Use

figure | 7-49 |

Seeking the flowers.

figure | 7-50 |

Selecting a target.

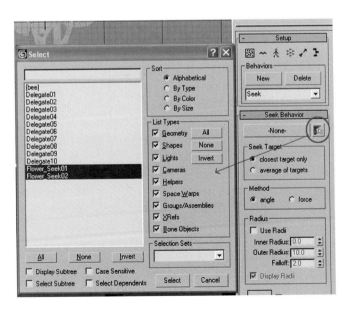

Radii check box and set Outer Radius to *250*. This will allow the bees to detect the flowers from the hive. Click the Solve button and see what happens.

20. Unfortunately, some of the bees are not getting to the flowers. To change this we will increase the weight of the Seek and Wander behaviors. Open the Behavior Assignments and Teams dialog box by clicking the Behavior Assignments button. Set the Seek behavior weight to *1.5* and reduce the weight of the Wander behavior to *0.5*. Now when the crowd solution is solved, the bees are heading straight toward the flowers.

21. You will notice that there are still a few issues. The bees are crowding one another and some of the bees are passing through tree trunks. To fix this we need to add yet another behavior. We can add behaviors by either opening the Behavior Assignments and Teams dialog box or by clicking the New button in the Behaviors area in the Setup rollout. For now, let's try clicking the New button to add an Avoid behavior.

22. Just like the Seek behavior, a dummy object needs to be created for the Avoid behavior. Create two dummy objects and place them over the tree trunks, as shown in Figure 7-51. Name the dummy objects *Tree Avoid01* and *Tree Avoid02*. Just as you did for the Seek behavior, assign these objects to the Avoid behavior.

23. Select Avoid from the drop-down list. Click the Multiple Selection button and select both dummy objects created in

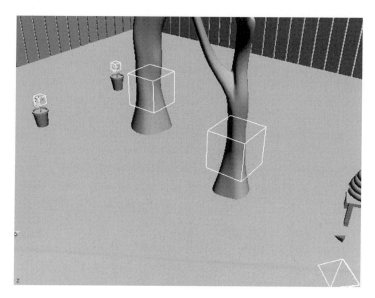

figure | 7-51 |

Creating things to avoid.

step 22. Select all Delegate objects so that they avoid one another in addition to avoiding the trees.

24. Now we need to assign this new Avoid behavior to our *Swarm* team. Open the Behavior Assignments and Teams dialog box by clicking the Behavior Assignments button. Assign our *Swarm* team to the new Avoid behavior. Click OK.

25. Solve the simulation. The bees avoid the trees and one another and seek out the flowers. Perfect, right? Well, why don't we have them head back to the hive after collecting the nectar. To do that, we must create a new Seek behavior for our swarm and a dummy object as a target for the behavior.

26. Set the weight of the new Seek behavior to *2.0*. Activate the Auto Key button and move the Time slider to frame 0. In the Behavior Assignments and Teams dialog box, select the Hive Seek behavior and then deactivate the Active check box. Drag the Time slider to frame 120, and then check the box to activate it. On this frame, we also want to deactivate the flower-seeking behavior. Highlight the behavior and then deactivate the Active check box. When you scrub the Time slider you should see the Active X in the Behavior Assignments area change from seeking one behavior to the other. Deactivate the Auto Key button and close the Behavior Assignments and Teams dialog box. Solve the simulation and watch what happens. The bees should avoid the trees and one another and seek out the flowers. At frame 120, they will turn around and head back to the hive.

27. We have one last thing to do. Our Delegate objects are still just little pyramids. We need to see our bees! Click the Scatter button. In the Scatter Objects dialog box (see Figure 7-52), click the Object to Clone button and select *[bee]*. There are ten Delegate objects, so we will need ten bees. Set the How Many parameter to *10*, click the Generate Clones button, and click OK.

28. Now we have ten clones of our original bee all sitting in the same spot. We need to attach these to our Delegate objects. To do that, click the Object/Delegate Associations button in the Setup rollout.

29. In the Object/Delegate Associations dialog box, shown in Figure 7-53, use the Add button in the Objects area to add the cloned bees. Do not include the original *[bee]* in this selection; just use the clones. You can hide the original *[bee]* when you are done with this part. Select the Add button in the Delegates

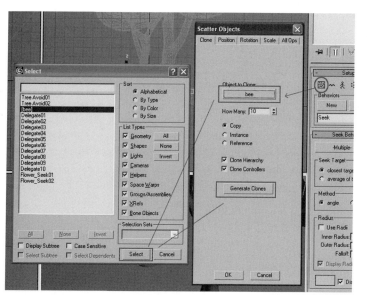

figure |7-52|

Scatter Objects
dialog.

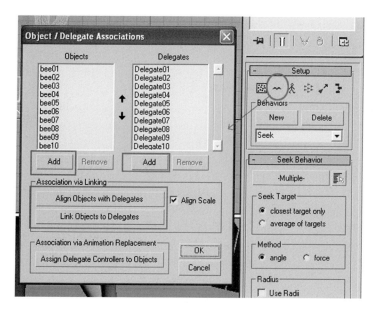

figure |7-53|

Object/Delegate
Associations dialog.

area and select all Delegate objects. Click the Align Objects
with Delegates button to move the bees to the Delegate objects.
Click the Link Objects to Delegates button to link each bee to
its respective Delegate object. Click OK.

Summary

Congratulations! You have completed the bee exercise. You can check the Helpers option in the Hide by Category rollout of the Display tab to hide the dummy boxes and Delegate objects. Scrub the Time slider to see the bees move around. The Crowd functionality incorporates many more advanced functions and behaviors, and even allows you to set up different animation clips for different behaviors. Spend some time experimenting, and you will be surprised by what you can create. Access the final 3ds Max file *crowd_final.max* from the companion CD-ROM and watch the animation file *crowd_animation.mov*.

SUMMARY

In this chapter you have explored a wide range of animation techniques used in the industry, such as architectural fly-bys, accident reconstruction for law firms, and motion simulation for ad agencies. These projects have utilized the techniques started in the previous chapter and have developed them into formidable tools you can apply to actual industry jobs.

Though many of the animations you see in movies and advertising look complex, they are essentially derived from very basic principles in animation. 3ds Max has an environment that provides ease of operation for the purpose of allowing you to spend more time designing and dreaming rather than struggling with complex rudimentary procedures. Learning powerful software takes discipline to overcome the initial learning curve, but through the techniques covered in this book you will be well equipped to move forward.

in review

1. What is the Curve editor?

2. What types of cameras does Max provide?

3. What is the importance of assigning mass in a Reactor solution?

4. What are the different types of collections in Reactor?

5. How do you add and modify behaviors?

6. What are delegates?

↗ EXPLORING ON YOUR OWN

1. Build a generic city block with boxes as buildings and move a car around the block with the camera following the car from behind. Experiment with additional city blocks (or use the previous city block and copy it multiple times) and develop a small matrix of roads, and animate the camera around the roadways. Try moving the camera around the roads at pedestrian level and alternatively place it above the buildings looking down.

2. Using Reactor, create a simple simulation of a box falling off a shelf onto a ground plane. Try adding multiple shelves and boxes for added interest and complexity of movement.

ADVENTURES IN DESIGN

SUBSTITUTE OBJECTS WITH PARTICLE FLOW

Particle Flow Basics

As discussed in Chapter 6, Particle Flow is an event-driven particle system. Rather than having an emitter that spews the particles, as well as parameters to control them, Particle Flow utilizes a flow chart analogy to define all aspects related to the particles—including quantity, appearance in renderings, display in viewports, speed, life, and many other factors. Particle Flow is an incredibly powerful set of tools that can help you achieve effects beautiful to look at and impossible to create with the other particle systems available in 3ds Max.

Options pertaining to the particles in a Particle Flow particle system are bundled into groups called *events*. Each item in an event is processed by 3ds Max in order, from top to bottom, with the result of one item being processed by the next. These options fall into two categories: *operators* and *tests*. Operators define the traits of the particles. For example, a Rotation operator defines the rotational aspect of the particles and a Force operator ties them to a space warp in the scene. Even the existence of particles is not inherent to Particle Flow (a Birth operator must be present to generate the particles).

Tests are features that determine whether the particles continue to the next item in the current event or are

passed on to another event in the system. When a particle meets the criteria set for the test, it is said to have tested "true" and is passed on to the event to which the test is wired. If you want the particles to perform a function at 30 frames and then leave the event, you place an Age test in the event with 30 set as the criterion for the test. Particles that do not test true continue to cycle through the event, so you must be vigilant and ensure that the fate of all particles is addressed. This is often solved by placing a Delete operator in an event to kill off any errant particles. The interface for Particle Flow is the Particle View dialog box, shown in Figure C-1, which is arranged in four uneven quadrants.

The *event display* area is where the events are created and arranged and where existing operators and tests are selected. New operators and tests are added to the system by dragging them from the *depot* in the bottom left-hand quadrant of the dialog window. Items dropped into an existing event are added to that event at the location they are dropped. Items dropped directly on an existing event entry replace that entry, and items dropped into an open area of the event display create new events. When an operator or test is selected in the depot, its description is displayed in the Description panel to the right of the depot. When an operator or

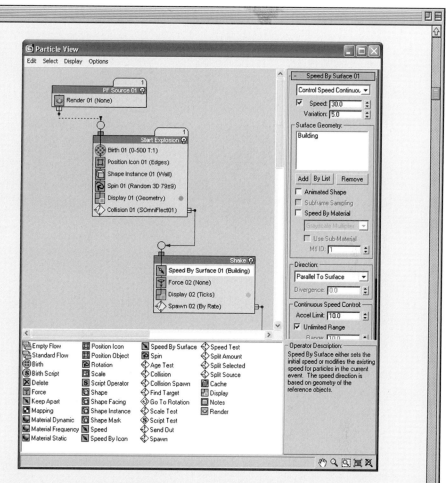

Figure C-1. The Particle View dialog is where Particle Flow particle systems are laid out.

test is selected in the event dialog box, its parameters display in the Parameters panel to the right of the event display.

This design exercise is going to explore the possibility of using Particle Flow to create the illusion of an object blowing up into thousands of pieces and then reassembling. 3ds Max is a surface modeling program, so there is no true mass for which to substitute. Thus, we will be placing our particles on the surface of one model and will have them quickly move away from those surfaces and then land on the surface of a similarly shaped model. In this case, Mr. Blue (the subject of several exercises in this book) will have his head, with a happy expression, blown up and then reassembled into a head with a slightly sick expression (as shown in Figure C-2). We will add Visibility tracks to each of the objects

Figure C-2. Mr. Blue as he will look before and after he explodes.

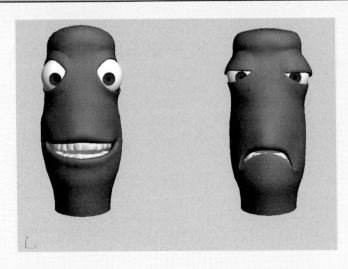

to control exactly when they will be visible during the animation.

1. Move the objects so that they occupy approximately the same location in the scene.

2. Open the Curve editor and add a Visibility track to each of the objects (see Figure C-3). Create two keys for each object's Visibility track at the points in time when you want the first one to fade out and the second to fade in. Short spans (two or three frames) between each key create a fast fade.

3. Open the Particle View dialog box by clicking Graph Editors > Particle View, or by pressing the 6 shortcut key.

4. Drag a Standard Flow particle flow system from the depot into the event display. This creates a small system (as shown in Figure C-4) with two events, the first of which is simply the Particle Flow icon.

▶ **NOTE:** A Visibility key value of 0.0 causes an object to be completely invisible, and value of 1.0 causes it to be completely visible (see Figure C-3). Values outside that range do not increase or decrease the visibility any more than is possible. The objects will not completely disappear in the viewports, for selection purposes, but entirely invisible objects will not render.

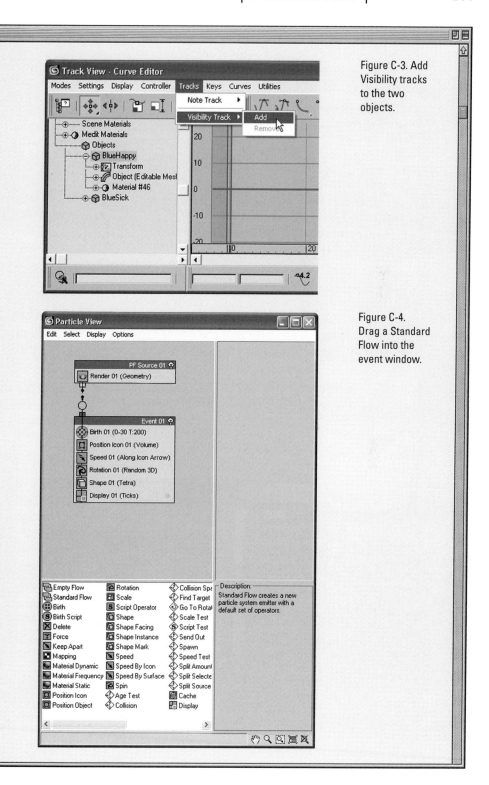

Figure C-3. Add
Visibility tracks
to the two
objects.

Figure C-4.
Drag a Standard
Flow into the
event window.

5. Select the Birth operator. In the Parameters panel, enter the value in the Emit Start and Emit Stop fields equal to the frame number at which the first object is set to disappear. This will cause all of the particles to be emitted at one time. Leave the Amount value at its default. This number is currently set low for an effective result and to allow for efficient viewport manipulation while building the particle system.

6. Drag a Position Object operator from the depot and drop it on top of the Position Icon operator to replace it. A red line will appear over the existing operator to indicate that it will be replaced.

7. Select the Position Object operator, and in the Parameters panel click Add and then select the object to be exploded. The object's name will appear in the Emitter Objects field. Your particle view should look similar to that shown in Figure C-5.

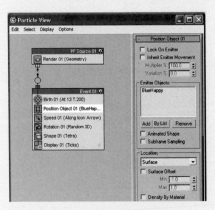

Figure C-5. The Particle View dialog is where Particle Flow particle systems are laid out.

The particles are placed on the surface of the object, but you may need to render the scene to see them.

8. Right-click the Speed operator and then choose Delete to remove it from the event. It is not required for this project.

9. Select the Shape operator and ensure that Tetra is selected as the Shape type. Decrease the Size value until the tetra shape is small enough, when rendered, to provide the best effect. See Figure C-6 for an example.

10. Add a Material Static operator to the event. Click None in the Parameters panel and then select the same material applied to the first object. This is the material the particles will be made of.

11. In the Command panel, select Create > Space Warps > Forces > Gravity and then create a Gravity space warp in the scene. Move the space warp so that it is centered within the objects. Switch to the Modify panel, select Spherical in the Force area, and then enter a negative Strength value. This will cause the particles to be pushed away from the Gravity icon.

12. Drag a Force operator to the event. In the Parameters panel, click the By List button. In the Select Force Space Warps dialog box, highlight the Gravity space warp and then click Select. The Gravity appears in the Force Space Warps field, as shown in Figure C-7, and the particles are now tied to the space warp.

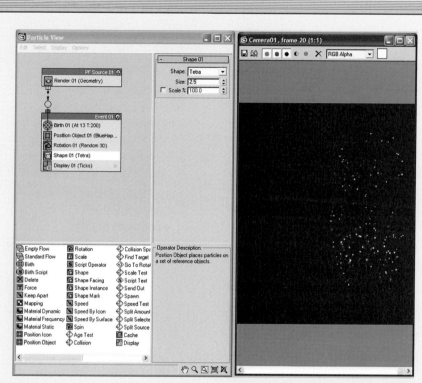

Figure C-6.
Drag the Time slider past the frame when the first object disappears and then render the scene.

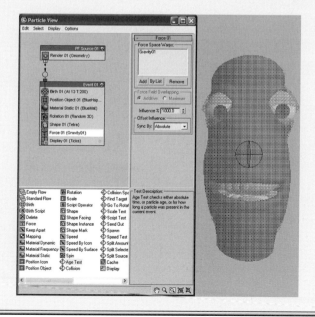

Figure C-7.
The Force operator links the particles to a space warp.

13. Add an Age test to the bottom of the event. This will be used to determine when the particles stop responding to the gravity and begin to seek the shape of the second object.

14. At the top of the Parameters panel, expand the drop-down list and select Event Age to synchronize the age test to the frame number, rather than the age of the particles (see Figure C-8). In the Test Value field, enter the frame number at which the particles will be passed onto the next event, which will bring the particles back toward the objects. Make sure there is a Variation value larger than zero so that the particles will respond less uniformly and more realistically.

15. Drag a Find Target test into the event display, but not into the current event. This will create a new event that only contains the Find Target test and a Display operator

that controls how the particles appear in the viewports.

16. Select the blue dot to the left of the Age test and drag to the circle at the top of the Find Target event. This will wire the age test to the next event so that any particles that test true for the age test are passed along to the next event (see Figure C-9).

17. The Find Target test designates an object for the particles to seek, and tests true when they collide with it. Select the Find Target test. At the top of the Parameters panel, expand the drop-down list and select Control By Speed. Expand the next drop-down list and select Target Point. In the Target section, click either Add or By List and select the object for the particles to assemble into. Finally, in the Docking Direction area, set Type to Icon Cylindrical or Icon Spherical, depending on the shape of your objects.

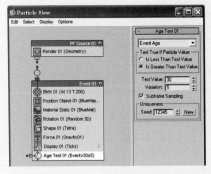

Figure C-8. The Age test determines when the particles move to the next event.

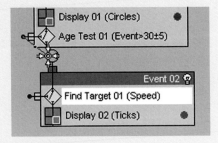

Figure C-9. Wire the Age test to the event with the Find Target test.

> **NOTE**: When you change frames, scrub the Time slider, or even change parameters you may notice 3ds Max's performance getting sluggish. This is caused by the number of particles in the scene and their display parameters. It is best to build the Particle Flow system with just enough particles to understand their actions without degrading your system's performance.

18. Add a Shape Mark operator to the event display as its own event, and then add an Age test to the same event. The Shape Mark operator leaves a color or material on the surface of an assigned object it collides with.

19. In the Parameters panel for the Shape Mark, set the object being assembled as the Contact Object. In the Size area, set the Length and Width values for the shape that will be applied to the surface of the Contact Object.

20. Select the Age Test and set Absolute Age at the top of the Age Test parameters. Set the Test Value to the frame at which the particles are to disappear, which would be the point in time where the second object is fading in. A small Variation value will ensure that all of the particles do not test true at the same time. Wire the Find Target test to the event with the Shape Mark operator (see Figure C-10).

21. Select the Material Static operator From Event 01, right-click, and then select Copy from the context

menu that appears. Right-click in the final event, and then select Paste Instanced to copy an instance

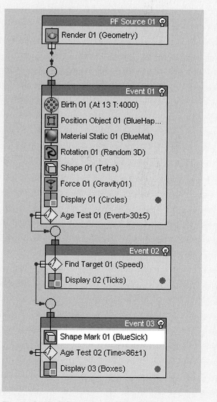

Figure C-10. Set up the Shape Mark operator and the new Age test and then wire the last two events together.

of the Material Static operator to that event and lock the materials together. Drag the new operator to the top of the event.

22. All that is left is to delete the particles. Drag a Delete operator into the event display to create a new event, making sure All Particles is selected in the Remove area of its parameters. Wire the last Age test you created to this new event. Any particle that tests true for the Age test, which tests for the particle's age, will be deleted.

23. Go back to the Birth operator and increase the Amount value until it is high enough to create the proper effect. Your Particle Flow setup should look similar to that shown in Figure C-11. Figure C-12 shows some of the possible progress shots.

As you can see, Particle Flow can provide you with finite control over your particles and how they act and look. The available operators and tests allow you to create effects that are not possible with the other particle systems in 3ds Max. Can this exercise be taken further? Absolutely.

For example, the first and second objects could be animated, as long as Animated Shape is selected in the Find Target test. Alternatively, Particle Age maps can be used in the objects' materials to control the particle color based on time. The Material Static operator could be used to alter the

materials based on any of the operator controls. Particle Flow is extremely powerful, and many 3ds Max artists are constantly pushing its limits to create fantastic artwork and effects.

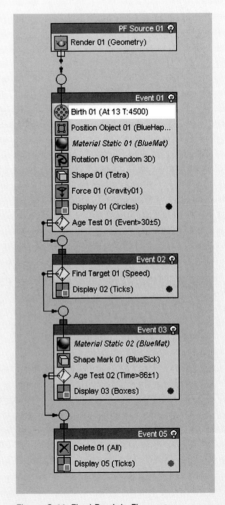

Figure C-11. Final Particle Flow setup.

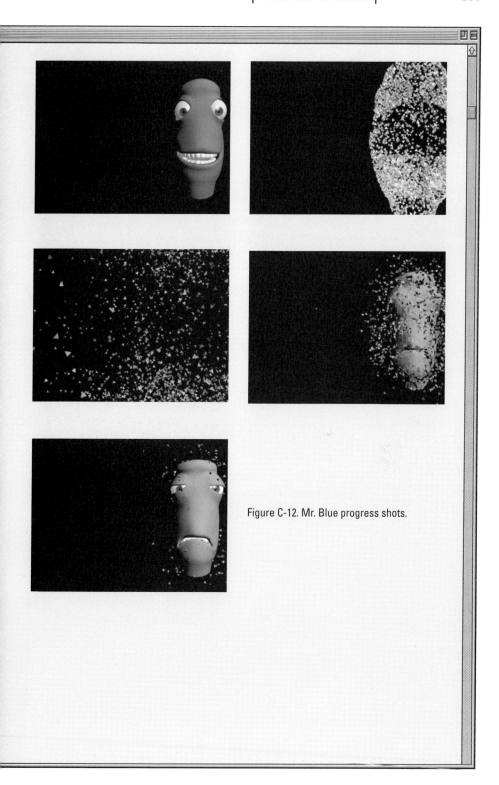

Figure C-12. Mr. Blue progress shots.

index